Signs
of the Times

Signs
of the Times

Reasons We Know the Rapture Is Near

by

Ed Rickard

 **The Moorings Press**

Some of the material in this book originally appeared on the author's website, *Bible Studies at the Moorings,* at themoorings.org. Printed copies can be obtained from Amazon.com. It is also available as a Kindle eBook.

All Scripture quotations, unless otherwise noted, are from the King James Bible (KJV).

Anthem

Rent by furious evil, all creation
Waits to see the nearing day
When stand revealed the sons of God,
In righteousness their white array.
Though bitter trial still befall us—
Sorrowing may not soon cease—
Yet someday our fal'tring steps
Will reach a lasting peace.

Every path that stretches into future
Scenes goes through a land of woe.
But graciously our Shepherd leads,
Now guarding us as on we go.
Though heavy night drapes all our vistas,
Whether to the left or right,
Sight bedimmed does not hold back
Those walking in His light.

Though it seems that hope is foolish comfort—
Swirling darkness fills the skies—
All men of God renounce despair,
They know that shadows tell us lies.
Though stiff-necked hatred still would thwart us—
Right is slow subduing wrong—
Let our blackest doubts be burned
In brightest fires of song.

– Ed Rickard –

Other Books by Ed Rickard from The Moorings Press

Daniel Explained/ A Commentary on the Book of Daniel

Primer of the Christian Life/ A Detailed Map of the Pilgrim's Road

James: Mirror for the Soul/ Lessons from the Epistle of James

In Perils Abounding/ A Commentary on the Book of Acts

Stepping-Stones: Christian Virtues/ Humility, Wisdom, Freedom from Covetousness, Thankfulness, and Joy in Tribulation

The Vegetable Soup Gang/ The Extraordinary Adventures of Some Ordinary Boys

Contact information@themoorings.org.

✛ ABOUT THE AUTHOR ✛

Ed Rickard (full name: Stanley Edgar Rickard, Jr.) received a B.S. with highest honors from Wheaton College in 1963, then a Ph.D. from Northwestern University in 1967. His undergraduate major was chemistry, and his graduate field was social psychology with emphasis on statistics and research methodology. His dissertation and two subsequent publications dealt with the causal analysis of correlations.

He began his career teaching at the undergraduate and graduate levels in the field of his doctorate. Later he taught Bible courses at a Christian college. His subjects included the Book of Daniel, Christian evidences, and graduate apologetics. More recently, he has served as principal of a Christian academy.

For a leading publisher of Christian school curricula, he wrote a high school physics text that has been widely used. His website, https://www.themoorings.org, has been a source of Bible studies since the early days of the web.

His wife and high school sweetheart, Julie, received a B.A. with high honors in French and English from Wheaton College and an M.A. in French from Northwestern University. When her video classes in high school French were available, they were used by many Christian schools and homeschools. In all of her husband's endeavors, she has been an indispensable adviser and helper.

Ed has two sons, seven grandchildren, and one great-grandchild. His older son is a pastor and his younger son is a minister of music. He counts all his family as a great blessing from God.

For the writer of this book, interest in prophecy is a family heritage. During many summer vacations when he was a young boy, his father took the family to a Bible conference at Gull Lake, Michigan, or Winona Lake, Indiana, where they heard leading Bible teachers of the day, and the subject was often prophecy. Then Ed's father went to work at Moody Bible Institute, which held a yearly Founder's Week Conference, and again prophecy was a frequent subject. Ed himself has studied prophecy in great depth. It is a major division of his website offering Bible studies, and he has written a commentary on Daniel based on extensive research.

✛ ABBREVIATIONS ✛

chap.	chapter	Mic.	Micah
Chron.	Chronicles	p.	page
Cor.	Corinthians	Pet.	Peter
Dan.	Daniel	pp.	pages
Eph.	Ephesians	Ps.	Psalm or Psalms
Gen.	Genesis	Rev.	Revelation
Heb.	Hebrews	Thess.	Thessalonians
Hos.	Hosea	Tim.	Timothy
Isa.	Isaiah	v.	verse
Jas.	James	vv.	verses
Matt.	Matthew	Zech.	Zechariah

+ SIGNS OF THE TIMES +

Contents

Chapter 1

✤ The Darkening Sky Ahead ✤

Over a century ago, the teachings of the psychotherapist Émile Coué gave rise to the popular saying, "Every day and in every way the world is getting better and better." People then were giddy with optimism that modern technology and government would soon erase the ills of mankind. They believed that progress was the normal flow of human history.

But as people today look about them, they see that the world is not getting better and better. It is getting worse and worse.

Mankind's predicament

Decline in economic security. Poverty is swallowing up new millions every year, especially in third-world countries.[1] Even in developed countries, prosperity is becoming more elusive, as young adults find it increasingly difficult to join the middle class. The percentage of people in their twenties who enjoy a middle-class income has declined in the last fifty years from 70% to 60%.[2] By far the greatest barrier confronting young people as they seek a comfortable place in society is the rising cost of higher education. This "has surged more than 538% since 1985. In comparison, . . . the consumer price index has jumped 121%."[3] To pay for college, many contract a huge debt that may drain income for a whole lifetime.

The percentage of the whole population belonging to the middle class is also falling.[4] And even for those with sufficient income to be considered members of this stratum of society, average income barely nudged upwards in the ten years preceding 2019, while many unavoidable costs rose sharply.[5] House prices doubled between 1995 and 2017.[6] One weight pulling down the middle class is the expense of healthcare. In the United States between 2008 and 2018, the portion of household income spent on health insurance premiums and deductibles climbed from 7.8% to 11.5%.[7]

The growing failure of modern economies to meet human needs is not limited to the downward slide of many individuals. Whole nations are moving along a road toward economic disaster. Irresponsible risk-taking by big corporations, their ability to shift resources and jobs across national boundaries, and deficit spending by governments are bringing the United States and other developed nations to the brink of financial collapse. The measure of national debt burdening the United States is in each new moment reaching a record high.[8] As of 11/22/19, it stood at well over twenty-three trillion dollars.[9] This amounts to more than $186,000 per taxpayer.[10]

Violence. And violence fills the earth. Whole societies, from Venezuela to Pakistan, are awash in blood. Parts of Africa are a battleground. Much of the Middle East is a war zone. Most alarming is the continuing existence of nuclear weapons in large stockpiles. The so-called nuclear club has for several decades been limited to nine members, but among them are the volatile nations of India, Pakistan, and North Korea.[11] Striving hard to join the club is war-prone Iran.

Even in developed nations standing aloof from war, the media are filled with reports of terrorism, social unrest, serial murder, sick crime, and suicide. The spotlight of news often returns to madmen gunning people down.

Back in the 1980s, the United States suffered about one mass shooting per year. Since then the frequency of such horrible moments has risen steadily until now it equals about ten per year. The number of fatalities between 2015 and 2019 approached four hundred.[12] Even sadder is the epidemic of suicide that has descended upon American young people. From 2007 to 2017, the suicide rate for persons aged ten to twenty-four soared 56%. The upsurge was especially pronounced in the youngest group, aged ten to fourteen. For them, the rate nearly tripled. Across this whole spectrum of ages, death by homicide was also becoming more common.[13]

We see similar trends in Europe. In late 2019, there were mass demonstrations in France to protest the recent outbreak of "femicide." In the previous year, a record number of women had been murdered by their current or former "life partner."[14]

Violence is also escalating in Latin America. In Mexico, for example, the number of homicides reached an all-time high in 2019.[15] The risk of being murdered was about six times higher than in the United States. Yet it was even more dangerous to live in Panama, where the same risk was ten times higher.[16]

Diseases. Many new diseases are emerging from nowhere. Fifty years ago the only sexually transmitted diseases (STDs) of significance were syphilis and gonorrhea. Both currently are more common than ever before,[17] but at the same time thirty-five new STDs have emerged to afflict millions.[18] Altogether, twenty million new cases appear each year just in the United States, victimizing about one fourth of the young people between ages fifteen and twenty-four.[19]

A growing threat to the human race in this age of massive global travel is pandemic diseases, each caused by a new infectious virus. The latest, spreading worldwide in 2020, is COVID-19. It is inflicting a death toll that may yet surpass two million.[20]

Besides the new diseases appearing on the scene, many age-old plagues that mankind has viewed as nearly eradicated are making a strong comeback. Several new strains of the bacteria responsible for tuberculosis have appeared, each more drug-resistant than the last.[21]   As a result, the disease is gaining ground even in the relatively advanced nation of China.[22]

Natural disasters.   Besides the disasters that man is inflicting upon himself, every kind of natural disaster besets the world. Storms and floods and wildfires and droughts are becoming more frequent and causing more death and destruction. Already in 1999, the Geoscience Research Group sponsored by Munich Re, world's largest reinsurer, reported that in the previous decade, the number of great natural catastrophes had increased by a factor of three since the 1960s.[23]   More recently, according to a report published in 2017 by the Food and Agriculture Organization of the United Nations, the incidence of natural disasters had increased fivefold since the 1970s.[24]

One recurring story in the news has drawn public attention to the disastrous wildfires raging every year in many places, especially Australia, California, and the Amazon region. In California, both the number of wildfires and the number of acres burned have been steadily increasing during the last forty years, reaching a climax in 2018 at the conflagration known as the Camp Fire,[25] which destroyed about 153,000 acres and 19,000 structures and left eighty-six people dead.[26] It was the worst fire in state history.[27]

Another kind of natural disaster that often inflicts enormous damage is hurricanes. One recent study has demonstrated that the biggest and strongest hurricanes are 3.3 times more frequent in our day than they were a century ago.[28]

Global perils.   Then there are the trends pointing to collapse of civilization. The amount of arable land on the planet will soon begin to shrink[29] while global population will continue to grow.[30]   The fossil fuels which serve as energy source for the greatest portion of human endeavors are, as generally agreed, about half gone. Present reserves will not last much longer if we measure time in decades, and nowhere do we see any prospect of an adequate and affordable replacement.[31]

Extinction of other species, including many that are beneficial in some respect, is proceeding rapidly. According to a report from the United Nations, "At least 680 species with backbones have already gone extinct since 1600. . . . More than 40% of the world's amphibian species, more than one-third of the marine mammals and nearly one-third of sharks and fish are threatened with extinction."[32] Even more alarming, the life forms that could soon disappear include more than 40% of the world's insect species, many performing a critical function in the maintenance of a local ecosystem.[33]   The beautiful monarch butterfly, a pollinator of many wildflowers,[34] is currently being considered for classification as an endangered species.[35] Also nearing extinction are several of the world's species of bumblebees that serve as important pollinators.[36] In the United States, even the population of honey bees is on a steep downward slope. A yearly decline evident since 2006 was greatest in 2018–2019, when the total managed population in commercial colonies dropped 40.7%.[37]

Perhaps the environmental crisis receiving greatest public attention is global warming. Whatever its cause, it is certainly a fact. The average surface temperature of Planet Earth during the decade 2009–2018 "was 0.93 ± 0.07 °C [about 1.7 °F] warmer than the pre-industrial baseline (1850–1900)."[38] One result is that the ice sheets and glaciers of the world are melting.[39] Although the Antarctic has so far gone opposite to the trend, the overall change in sea ice has averaged a loss of about thirteen thousand square miles per year since the late 1970s.[40] Yet another result that will become more evident soon in man's history is coastal flooding. In the twenty-one year span from 1993 to 2014, the global sea level rose 2.6 inches, and it is expected to continue rising at about one-eighth inch per year.[41]

God's book of answers

No wonder that people today are anxious about the future. To what bleak end are all these troubles leading us? What is the outlook for the human race? Can anyone tell us what is going to happen? No scholar or soothsayer can give us the answers. In all the world we find only one reliable source of information about things to come. That source is the Bible, the book which the Creator Himself gave to mankind so that they might understand His workings in history. Fully one fourth of this divinely inspired document is prophecy. So, to find out what lies ahead, we need only consult the Bible.

The man who was God

The main subject of the Bible is the man Jesus Christ. Who was He? He was a person of Jewish descent who lived two thousand years ago in the country of Palestine, then part of the Roman Empire. But He was no ordinary man. He was also God in the flesh. The Bible teaches that God is one Being in three persons named the Father, the Son, and the Holy Spirit.

The entire human race has estranged itself from God by choosing to live contrary to His will. Instead of fully obeying the moral laws inscribed on the human conscience and specified in the Bible, they all engage in sinful (that is, wicked) behavior, thus denying themselves the privilege of living with God after they die. Instead, they must go to hell, a place of punishment for sin. To remove sin's penalty from you and me and everyone else, the Father appointed the Son to be our Savior, a role He could fulfill only by entering this world as a man. The man He became was unique in being fully human as well as fully divine, unique also in being wholly without sin.

The story of His life appears in the four New Testament books called the Gospels: Matthew, Mark, Luke, and John. They tell us that His ministry as a prophet and teacher began when He was about thirty years old, and that for the next three and a half years, He walked throughout the land and challenged the people to seek the kingdom of God. Also, He presented Himself as the fulfillment of the Old Testament prophecies foreseeing that God would send into this world a sinless man—in Hebrew known as the Messiah, in Greek as the Christ—who would provide a full remedy for the sins of other men. In proof of His claims, Jesus performed many astounding miracles. On several occasions He raised the dead to life. Once, in the presence of thousands, He multiplied a few loaves and fishes into a meal sufficient for them all. Rather than deny His ability to perform wonders, His enemies accused Him of being a sorcerer (Matt. 12:24).

Yet the mobs who followed Him at the beginning of His ministry soon turned away when they discovered that His mission was essentially spiritual, not political. They wanted a deliverer from Roman oppression. The leaders of the Jewish nation likewise rejected Him. Regarding Him as a threat to their own power, they brought Him before the Roman governor, Pilate, and falsely accused Him of trying to make Himself king (Luke 23:2), a capital offense. Pilate bowed to their will and condemned Him to die by crucifixion, one of the cruelest ways of killing a man ever devised.

In His last hours, Jesus went through agony beyond our conception. As He hung upon the cross, He bore upon Himself all the sins of mankind (1 Pet. 2:21–24). Therefore, to the suffering of His body on the cross was added the suffering of His soul when God the Father turned away from the sin-bearer and suspended the infinite love that had bound them together throughout eternity past (Ps. 22:1; Mark 15:34). Altogether, Jesus' suffering amounted to full punishment for all the sins of all the people who will ever live on planet Earth. In other words, He endured a sum of pain equal to a just penalty for the entire mountain of human sin. Yet He made no attempt to escape, He uttered no complaint, and as He looked upon His crucifiers, He prayed, "Father, forgive them, for they know not what they do" (Luke 23:34).

We can be glad that the story of Jesus does not end at His death. During His ministry, He had taught that after lying in a tomb for three days, He would rise again. And the prophecy came true. Beginning on the third day after the Crucifixion, He was seen alive on numerous occasions, once by no less than five hundred people (Luke 24; John 20–21; 1 Cor. 15:4–8). After another forty days, He left this world and sat down at the Father's right hand in heaven. Many of His disciples witnessed His departure, known as the Ascension. As they stood amazed, He rose out of their sight into a cloud (Acts 1:4–11).

Then, according to Jesus' instructions, they returned to Jerusalem and waited to receive the Holy Spirit, for they could accomplish nothing without the Spirit's power. On the Jewish feast known as Pentecost, the Spirit descended with supernatural signs of His presence (Acts 2), and immediately the disciples began to preach the gospel—the message of salvation through Christ—with great success.

What did the gospel lay down as the requirement to be saved from sin's penalty? The requirement is very easy to understand and very easy to satisfy. It is only to be sorry for sin and to believe that Jesus is Savior and Lord. Following genuine belief, also known as faith, a person is indwelt by the Holy Spirit and enabled to change steadily into the likeness of the sinless Christ. The great benefit of faith is that it brings the privilege of living forever in a perfect world governed by an all-powerful, loving God (John 3:16).

The gospel quickly spread far and wide. Within the next generation, Christian preachers carried it throughout the Roman world and beyond. Wherever people responded with faith, the new believers met regularly for prayer, study of God's Word, and fellowship. The first local assembly of believers, the one in Jerusalem, was known from the beginning as a church, and the same term was used for the assemblies that sprang up in other cities. The entire body of believers everywhere was known as "the church" (Eph. 5:25).

The second coming of Christ

Yet despite God's gracious provision of salvation through Christ, the majority who have come under the preaching of the gospel in the last two thousand years have refused it. What then is man's future? Bible prophecy informs us that someday Christ will return to planet Earth and stop all the wickedness that is steadily worsening. Also, it gives us a detailed picture of the world at the time right before the coming of Christ. When we compare that picture with today's world, we find a perfect match. Everywhere we look, we see developments in line with prophecy. Each is a sign that our age, dominated by evil, is drawing to a close.

Footnotes

[1] See p. 103.

[2] "Governments Must Act to Help Struggling Middle Class," Organisation for Economic Co-operation and Development, 2019, Web (oecd.org/newsroom/governments-must-act-to-help-struggling-middle-class.htm), 11/22/19.

[3] "Understanding the Rising Costs of Higher Education," Best Value Schools, 2020, Web (bestvalueschools.com/understanding-the-rising-costs-of-higher-education/), 4/30/20.

[4] Greg Daugherty, "America's Slowly Disappearing Middle Class," Investopedia, 6/25/19, Web (investopedia.com/insights/americas-slowly-disappearing-middle-class/), 11/22/19.

[5] "Governments Must Act."

[6] Ibid.

[7] Erin Schumaker, "Middle-Class Americans Getting Crushed by Rising Health

Insurance Costs," ABC News, 11/21/19, Web (abcnews.go.com/Health/middle-class-americans-crushed-rising-health-insurance-costs/story?id=67131097), 11/25/19.

[8]Bill Chappell, "U.S. National Debt Hits Record $22 Trillion," NPR, 2/13/19, Web (npr.org/2019/02/13/694199256/u-s-national-debt-hits-22-trillion-a-new-record-thats-predicted-to-fall), 11/22/19.

[9]"U.S. National Debt Clock: Real Time," US Debt Clock.org, Web (usdebtclock.org), 11/22/19.

[10]Ibid.

[11]"List of States with Nuclear Weapons," Wikipedia, Web (en.wikipedia.org/wiki/List_of_states_with_nuclear_weapons), 11/21/19.

[12]Mark Follman, Gavin Aronsen, and Deanna Pan, "US Mass Shootings, 1982–2019: Data from Mother Jones' Investigation," Mother Jones, Web (motherjones.com/politics/2012/12/mass-shootings-mother-jones-full-data/), 11/13/19.

[13]Sally C. Curtin and Melonie Heron, "Death Rates Due to Suicide and Homicide among Persons Aged 10–24: United States, 2000–2017," NCHS Data Brief, No. 352 (Hyattsville, Md.: National Center for Health Statistics, 2019), 1–3, Web (stacks.cdc.gov/view/cdc/81944), 11/25/19.

[14]Angela Charlton and Thibault Camus, "Paris Protesters March against Deadly Domestic Violence towards Women," Time, 11/23/19, Web (time.com/5737967/paris-domestic-violence-protest/), 12/4/19.

[15]Travis Fedschun, "Mexican Gunbattle Near Texas Border between Suspected Cartel Members, Police Leaves at Least 21 Dead," Fox News, 12/1/19, Web (foxnews.com/world/mexico-cartel-member-gunbattle-police-texas-border), 12/3/19.

[16]"Crime in the United States," Wikipedia, Web (en.wikipedia.org/wiki/Crime_in_the_United_States), 12/3/19.

[17]See p. 107.

[18]See p. 106.

[19]See p. 107.

[20]"Covid-19 Coronavirus Pandemic," Worldometer, Web (worldometers.info/coronavirus/?utm_campaign=homeAdUOA?Si), 12/20/20.

[21]See pp. 108–109.

[22]See p. 109.

[23]Press Release by Geoscience Research Group of Munich Re, Web (munichre.com/ press_media/pm_artikel.php3?id=2&lang=eng), 7/13/00.

[24]"The Future of Food and Agriculture: Trends and Challenges," Food and Agriculture Organization of the United Nations (Rome, 2017), 5, Web (fao.org/3/a-i6583e.pdf), 9/10/19.

[25]Jessica Pettengill, "A History of California's Wildfires," ABC10, 11/18/18, Web (abc10.com/article/news/local/wildfires/a-history-of-californias-wildfires/103-615612991), 11/21/19.

[26]"Camp Fire Is Deadliest Wildfire in California History," ABC7 News, 8/14/19, Web (abc7news.com/the-deadliest-wildfires-in-california-history/4673982/), 11/21/19.

[27]Pettengill; "Camp Fire."

[28]Matt McGrath, "Climate Change: Bigger Hurricanes Are Now More Damaging," BBC News, 11/11/19, Web (bbc.com/news/science-environment-50380431), 11/21/19.

[29]See p. 104.

[30]See pp. 103–104.

[31]See pp. 104–105.

[32]Seth Borenstein, "UN Report: Humans Accelerating Extinction of Other Species," AP News, 5/6/19, Web (apnews.com/aaf1091c5aae40b0a110daaf04950672), 11/21/19.

[33]Francisco Sánchez-Bayo and Kris A. G. Wyckhuys, "Worldwide Decline of the Entomofauna: A Review of Its Drivers," Biological Conservation 232 (2019): 8–27, ScienceDirect, Web (sciencedirect.com/science/article/pii/S0006320718313636), 11/26/19.

[34]"Pollinators - Monarch Butterfly," National Park Service, Web (nps.gov/articles/monarch-butterfly.htm), 11/25/19.

[35] "Assessing the Status of the Monarch Butterfly," U.S. Fish & Wildlife Service, Web (fws.gov/savethemonarch/ssa.html), 11/25/19.

[36] "Why Are Bumblebees Going Extinct?" Genomics Research from Technology Networks, 8/24/18, Web (technologynetworks.com/genomics/news/why-are-bumblebees-going-extinct-308078), 11/25/19.

[37] Julia Jacobo, "Nearly 40% Decline in Honey Bee Population Last Winter 'Unsustainable,' Experts Say," ABC News, 7/9/19, Web (abcnews.go.com/US/40-decline-honey-bee-population-winter-unsustainable-experts/story?id=64191609), 11/25/19.

[38] "Global Warming," *Wikipedia,* Web (en.wikipedia.org/wiki/Global_warming), 11/25/19.

[39] Ibid.

[40] Bob Berwyn, "Why Is Antarctica's Sea Ice Growing While the Arctic Melts? Scientists Have an Answer," Insideclimate News, 5/31/16, Web (insideclimatenews .org/news/31052016/why-antarctica-sea-ice-level-growing-while-arctic-glaciers-melts-climate-change-global-warming?gclid=CjwKCAiAlO7uBRANEiwA_vXQ-_n_KVCwhtZLS-ECyRRmTQJsa1K3Ww1AjkaWWyKCXjO-X5AgY82u6xoCz3AQAvD_BwE), 11/21/19.

[41] "Is Sea Level Rising?" National Oceanic and Atmospheric Administration, Web (oceanservice.noaa.gov/facts/sealevel.html), 11/25/19.

Chapter 2

✢ The Urgent Need to Study Prophecy ✢

All true believers in Jesus Christ are constantly waiting with keen anticipation for Him to come back. Actually, He will return to our world twice. At His first coming, He will descend secretly and, in a single world-sweeping grab, snatch away all of His people to heaven. That exciting prospect for anyone who knows Christ is called the Rapture. At His second coming, He will descend in full glory, defeat His enemies with a few strokes of divine power, and make Himself king over all the earth. Between His two comings, the world will suffer divine judgment in the form of horrible catastrophes on a scale or of a kind never seen before. That period of nightmares worse than we can imagine is called the Tribulation.

Sadly, the Rapture will exclude many who regard themselves as Christians. A clear warning that even many churchgoers will not be taken appears in passage after passage of Bible prophecy. The purpose of this book is to give you all the information that you will need to escape the great sorrow and danger in being left behind. We will start by offering a Biblical perspective on our place in history.

Modern trends in the study of end-time prophecy

In the 1830s, a new interest in the prophetic Scriptures arose first among the Plymouth Brethren and then spread rapidly to other groups, so that by the 1870s, many Bible-believing Christians were studying things to come. Prophecy was a leading topic at the nineteenth-century Bible conferences that gave birth to the fundamentalist movement in America. This new interest, built on a growing sense that Christ's return was drawing near, did not soon fade, but increasingly preoccupied the body of Christ. The great wars and catastrophes that engulfed the world in the first half of the twentieth century seemed to confirm that we are living in the Last Days. After the founding of the state of Israel in 1948—a development viewed as a sure sign of the end times—the interest in prophecy rose to great excitement. Many preachers seldom let a month go by without devoting at least one sermon to God's prophetic timetable. Future events were often discussed on Christian radio programs, in Christian magazines, and at summer Bible conferences.

In recent years, however, the interest in prophecy has sharply declined. Many pastors have filed away their sermons on this subject, the result being a vacuum of good teaching that is being filled by twisted teaching. In the Christian media, prophecy has become the province of televangelists and online preachers who use sensational claims to reach the viewer's pocketbook. The books available in Christian bookstores and through Christian channels are a bizarre assortment, including some that deny the bodily return of Christ. Others, like the *Left Behind* series, which has grossed millions of dollars, are so full of nonsense that they have greatly discredited the study of prophecy.

Because of this decline in good teaching, the average man in the pew is now very confused about God's plan for the future. If you ask him the difference between a premillennialist and a pretribulationist, he will struggle to find the right answer. If you ask him to state his own position and defend it from the Scriptures, he will be speechless. He may not firmly grasp any prophetic idea except that Christ is coming again.

Yet his belief in the Second Coming may not be tied to any strong conviction that Christ will return soon. The teaching from many pulpits and lecterns in recent years has been that we cannot know whether Christ will come tomorrow or a thousand years from tomorrow. It is true, of course, that no one should try to predict the date of Christ's return. Yet there are many signs that His return is drawing near, very near. Anyone who ignores these signs places himself in dubious company—among the Pharisees and Sadducees whom Jesus rebuked when He said,

> 2 . . . When it is evening, ye say, *It will be* fair weather: for the sky is red.
> 3 And in the morning, *It will be* foul weather to day: for the sky is red and lowring. O *ye* hypocrites, ye can discern the face of the sky; but can ye not *discern* the signs of the times?
>
> – Matthew 16:2–3 –

Why we must know that we are living in the Last Days

The teaching that Christ may defer His coming until a time far in the future is doing grave harm to the church. One sad effect is that few Christians today are aware of their place in history. The church has forgotten the many voices that God raised to warn our fathers and grandfathers that the time of the end had arrived. William L. Pettingill, a leading Bible teacher in the period between the two World Wars, affirmed,

> The Book of Daniel . . . is no longer sealed, for The Time of the End is here and the words of our Lord Jesus come to us with great force: "Let him that readeth understand" (Matthew 24:15). He was speaking here of the prophecy of Daniel; and this is the only Book which our Lord has specifically commanded His disciples to understand. May He help us to obey His Word! Let us bring to the study of this Book willing minds and surrendered hearts, eager to know the truth and determined to obey it, in order that by means of our knowledge and obedience the name of our blessed Lord may be exalted.[1]

If history has already passed into the time of the end, the final con-summation cannot be far distant.

From the beginning of the Church Age until recently, the Lord left His people in the dark as to the time and season of His return (Acts 1:7; 1 Thess. 5:1), but He wants the present generation of believers to know that He is coming soon. Why must we know this? So that we will be alert to the special dangers besetting us.

Jesus Himself spoke of these dangers.

> 34 And take heed to yourselves, lest at any time your hearts be overcharged with surfeiting, and drunkenness, and cares of this life, and *so* that day come upon you unawares.
> 35 For as a snare shall it come on all them that dwell on the face of the whole earth.
> 36 Watch ye therefore, and pray always, that ye may be accounted worthy to escape all these things that shall come to pass, and to stand before the Son of man.
>
> - Luke 21:34–36 -

Escape what evil things? He is talking about the Tribulation. But when Jesus said that we should pray always, He did not mean that we should pray to escape the Tribulation, but rather that we will be accounted worthy of escape only if we are praying people. This is made clear in the context, where Jesus laments that saints with a habit of faith-based, persevering prayer will be rare at the time of His return (Luke 18:6-8). In light of these passages, we need to make prayer a high priority.

Paul also spoke of the dangers besetting us.

> 1 This know also, that in the last days perilous times shall come.
> 2 For men shall be lovers of their own selves, covetous, boasters, proud, blasphemers, disobedient to parents, unthankful, unholy,
> 3 Without natural affection, trucebreakers, false accusers, incontinent, fierce, despisers of those that are good,
> 4 Traitors, heady, highminded, lovers of pleasures more than lovers of God;
> 5 Having a form of godliness, but denying the power thereof: from such turn away.
>
> – 2 Timothy 3:1–5 –

Here we learn that many professing Christians in the Last Days will know nothing of godliness. They will be overgrown spoiled brats. Yes, they will go to church occasionally, but not because they want to find and follow God's will. They will see it as a good place to keep their children out of trouble or to enjoy entertaining meetings and meals and social gatherings, or perhaps even a good place to ease their conscience toward God, because a typical pastor in that time of history will tell them they're okay if they just come to church now and then. But what is the truth?

. . . Nevertheless when the Son of man cometh, shall he find faith on the earth?

- Luke 18:8 -

37 But as the days of Noe *were,* so shall also the coming of the Son of man be.
38 For as in the days that were before the flood they were eating and drinking, marrying and giving in marriage, until the day that Noe entered into the ark,
39 And knew not until the flood came, and took them all away; so shall also the coming of the Son of man be.
40 Then shall two be in the field; the one shall be taken, and the other left.
41 Two *women shall be* grinding at the mill; the one shall be taken, and the other left.

- Matthew 24:37-41 -

The truth conveyed by these and other texts we could cite was meant by God as a thunderbolt to shake the complacency of today's Christians. The truth is, very few will be taken at the Rapture. Jesus even compares the raptured saints to Noah and his family. They were just eight people out of perhaps the millions who were alive at the time of the Flood. We dare not manufacture self-serving exegetical schemes to rewrite and escape what Jesus is truly saying. He is telling you, make sure you are among the few.

If we recognize our place in history, we will be wary, vigilant, slow to mold ourselves after the example of others, quick to turn away from counterfeit godliness, and eager to heed those Scriptural admonitions written especially for our benefit, such as the following:

Not forsaking the assembling of ourselves together, as the manner of some *is;* but exhorting *one another:* and so much the more, as ye see the day approaching.

– Hebrews 10:25 –

Incidentally, this passage shows us that keeping up our church attendance must also be a priority. Don't slide. Except when you have been providentially hindered from coming, your excuse for staying away will not win a sympathetic hearing at heaven's throne.

One text clearly teaching that we stand near the end of the Church Age

What are the signs that Christ is coming soon? For starters, we will look at one especially helpful passage.

7 Be patient therefore, brethren, unto the coming of the Lord. Behold, the husbandman waiteth for the precious fruit of the earth, and hath long patience for it, until he receive the early and latter rain.
8 Be ye also patient; stablish your hearts: for the coming of the Lord draweth nigh.
9 Grudge not one against another, brethren, lest ye be condemned:

behold, the judge standeth before the door.

- James 5:7–9 -

The author's use of a developing crop to picture church history is reminiscent of Jesus' Kingdom Parables, especially the Parable of the Wheat and the Tares (Matt. 13:24–30, 36–43). Just because the patient husbandman is a poetic image, we should not, from an outlook that sees poetry as vague and imprecise, assume that his story is meaningless except as an illustration of patience. On the contrary, when we approach the compositions of great poets—the Miltons and Shakespeares of our world—we expect to find design in details. After all, depth and density of meaning are proofs of genius. Why should we expect anything less than genius in the Word of God? In every speck of matter that comes from the same creative source, we find design too intricate for human comprehension. It is therefore wise to assume that when James, the divinely inspired author whose work is infused with meaningful imagery, uses a farmer to represent Jesus waiting to return, he intended even the details of the image to be true prophecy.

When we view this text with eyes open to larger meaning, we find it highly significant for three reasons.

1. It agrees with several others that Jesus would return only after some delay. In the Parable of the Talents, where Jesus compares Himself to a man who returns home from a far country and rewards his servants according to their work while he was gone, He says that the man returns "after a long time" (Matt. 25:19). In a similar vein, Peter teaches that in the Last Days, men will arise who scoff at Jesus' promise to return. Why will they see it as a false promise? Because so much time has elapsed and still nothing has happened (2 Pet. 3:3–4). To correct their wrong perspective, Peter adds, "But, beloved, be not ignorant of this one thing, that one day *is* with the Lord as a thousand years, and a thousand years as one day" (2 Pet. 3:8). Who could fail to see his implication that the delay in Jesus' return might stretch to thousands of years? We find another warning of an extended Church Age in James's epistle. He compares Jesus to a husbandman who wants to harvest the fruit of his garden, but who chooses not to come for it immediately. Rather, he waits with long patience until the fruit is ready.

2. James says that the fruit will not be ready for His return until it has received both the early and the latter rains. Most commentators view the two rains as merely a way of describing a full growing season. But as we argued earlier, a better approach is to look for specific prophetic meaning. Rain is probably a metaphor referring to the Holy Spirit, whom Jesus likened to living water (John 7:37–39). Whatever the rain represents, its indisputable effect is to spur growth. So, James is clearly saying that the Church Age will continue until

there is a final period of growth to balance the growth at the beginning.

The prophecy has been fulfilled. Expansion in the church has been mainly confined to two historical periods. In its infancy the church spread like wildfire despite fierce opposition by the Roman government. Countless believers were martyred, yet the church thrived. This was the time of early rain. Vigorous growth of the church has also taken place during the modern era, since 1800. For the first time in history, the church has carried out Jesus' command to spread the gospel to the uttermost part of the earth. This has been the time of latter rain.

3. James tells us what will happen after the latter rain. The waiting will be over and the husbandman will come. Where do we stand in history? The latter rain has now fallen for generations, but it is subsiding. Missionary work is being scaled back. The churches in many countries are at some stage of drift into the waters of unbelief and corruption. Since Scripture foresees no more rain after the second outpouring, the apostasy we see all around us in our day must be the final apostasy foreseen in many prophecies (2 Thess. 2:1–3; 2 Tim. 3:1–5, 13; 4:3–4; Luke 18:8; etc.). Exactly how long this retreat from vital faith might continue, we have no idea. Nevertheless, we can be sure, as James says, that "the coming of the Lord draweth nigh."

A side benefit of our investigation of James's seemingly simple exhortation is the discovery of a double sign that the Lord's return is near: first, that the latter rain has fallen; second, that it is stopping.

Before closing his words of prophecy, James makes two key applications.

1. He stresses again that the imminent return of Christ makes it easier for us to endure the troubles of life in a wicked world (v. 7). The confidence that He is coming soon is the secret to waiting for Him with a patient heart. It removes the anxieties that would otherwise keep us unsettled and sad.

2. The imminent return of Christ is another incentive to guard our tongue (v. 9). James warns, "Grudge not one against another, brethren." "Grudge" renders a word suggesting complaints spoken with a sigh or groan. It could be translated "grumble." He evidently is not referring to passing frictions of a minor sort, soon forgiven and forgotten, because the consequence is severe—to be condemned at the Judgment Seat of Christ. There, although a believer will not have his salvation taken away, he may incur penalties. The kind of offense in James's mind is probably a chronic resentful attitude toward a brother, or a deliberate scheme to defame a brother for the sake of gaining some personal advantage, or a delight in gossiping about him because his failings, real or imagined, give the gossiper a sense of superiority—any of which may lead to the wars and fightings he discussed earlier (Jas. 4:1–2). The danger in holding on to such an

attitude is that our lives on earth might come to an end at any moment, perhaps through sudden death or even perhaps through the surprise return of Christ. In either event, there will be no chance to put away sin before we see our Judge. If we wish to protect ourselves from His displeasure, we must deal now with any wrong spirit that is poisoning our love for the brethren. Lest we balk at correcting ourselves, James reminds us that the Judge stands before the door. The image has two meanings. Christ is standing at the door of heaven, ready to pass through into our realm and steal away His people. He is also, figuratively speaking, standing at the door of the courtroom, ready to enter and conduct our trial. Let us therefore live as though we might at any moment receive a summons into His presence.

In describing this summons, Scripture compares the returning Christ to a thief who approaches secretly and strikes without warning.

> For yourselves know perfectly that the day of the Lord so cometh as a thief in the night.
>
> - 1 Thessalonians 5:2 -

The prize He will come to steal away is the church. He will instantly catch up living saints to His presence in the sky, and from there He will transport them to a heavenly refuge. When speaking of this approaching event, Christians call it the Rapture, a word with the basic meaning, "a lifting up and carrying away." All others alive on the earth when the church is removed will see nothing of the thief's work. They will know only that the saints have suddenly disappeared.

Soon after they go to heaven, the raptured saints will be judged.

> 10 For we must all appear before the judgment seat of Christ; that every one may receive the things *done* in *his* body, according to that he hath done, whether *it be* good or bad.
> 11 Knowing therefore the terror of the Lord, we persuade men; but we are made manifest unto God; and I trust also are made manifest in your consciences.
>
> – 2 Corinthians 5:10–11 –

Since the prospect put terror in Paul's heart, we may assume that whereas the good things will bring reward, the bad things will earn at least the Lord's frowning disapproval and perhaps even His hand of punishment (Luke 12:42–48). It is therefore obvious what lesson we should draw from the clear teaching of Scripture that Christ is coming soon. Our rapidly approaching trial before the Judgment Seat of Christ should motivate us to live, as Paul says, "soberly, righteously, and godly in this present world" (Titus 2:12).

After Christ comes for His church, the next event for the ungodly will also be judgment. The rapture of saints will usher in the period of world history known as the Tribulation. God will bring upon this world a rain of calamity unprecedented in the entire experience of mankind since the Flood. His purpose will be to try the hearts of men by giving them a clear choice between the rule of God and the rule of Satan. The calamity drowning the world will warn them that the certain consequence of preferring Satan will be their eternal destruction. The clear teaching of Scripture that Christ is coming soon has therefore a lesson for unbelievers as well as believers. The lesson is, if they wish to escape the Tribulation, they had better repent now, before it is too late.

Footnotes

[1]William L. Pettingill, *Simple Studies in Daniel,* 6th ed. (Findlay, Ohio: Fundamental Truth Publishers, [5th ed., ca. 1933]), 8.

Chapter 3

+ Seven Easy Signs +

What are the signs that Christ is coming soon? There are many, but in this chapter we will restrict our attention to seven of the easier signs.

First sign/ Christianity becoming the world's largest religion

The eight Parables of the Kingdom in Matthew 13 look ahead to the experience of the church. The third one, called the Parable of the Mustard Seed, uses gardening to illustrate spiritual truth (Matt. 13:31–32).

> 31 Another parable put he forth unto them, saying, The kingdom of heaven is like to a grain of mustard seed, which a man took, and sowed in his field:
> 32 Which indeed is the least of all seeds: but when it is grown, it is the greatest among herbs, and becometh a tree, so that the birds of the air come and lodge in the branches thereof.
>
> - Matthew 13:31–32 -

Jesus predicts that something exceedingly small, like a mustard seed, will grow to be exceedingly large, like a mustard plant towering above all the other plants of the garden.

What does this tremendous growth represent if not the growth of the church? The church indeed began exceedingly small, as only 120 people in the Upper Room (Acts 1:15). Yet the church—or, more precisely, nominal Christianity—has become the largest religion in the world. As recently as 2005, all the people throughout the world who called themselves Christians were far more numerous than the followers of any other religion. Although the organized church has split into many denominations, Christianity as a whole embraced about one third of the world's population. There were about as many Christians as Muslims and Hindus combined, these being the next two largest religious groups.[1]

So, the Parable of the Mustard Seed is a remarkable prophecy. Two thousand years ago, before the church even existed, Jesus knew that He was founding a religious movement that would continue and prosper until it overshadowed all rivals.

When did Christianity rise to dominance over other religions? Much evidence indicates that the church took its ascendant place in the world during the nineteenth century. Its tremendous growth then was the result of two major developments: (1) the colonial expansion of Christian nations, and (2) the development which we will now present as the second sign of the times. We will show later in this book that several prophecies mark the nineteenth century as the beginning of the Last Days.

Second sign/ the gospel reaching to the uttermost part of the earth

Elsewhere in His teaching, Jesus explained how the professing church would become so large. The dominance of Christianity over other religions would come about through worldwide evangelism. In Jesus' last instructions to the disciples, He viewed the bearing of gospel truth to men everywhere as a task that the church would actually accomplish.

> But ye shall receive power, after that the Holy Ghost is come upon you: and ye shall be witnesses unto me both in Jerusalem, and in all Judaea, and in Samaria, and unto the uttermost part of the earth.
>
> - Acts 1:8 -

In the words, "Ye shall be witnesses," He uses the future tense in what grammarians call "the indicative mood." That is, He is making a statement of fact. He is clearly saying that before He returns, Christian evangelists will actually reach the uttermost part of the earth.

The prophesy can be interpreted in two ways: either as a broad prediction that gospel witness will reach everywhere or as a narrow prediction that it will reach the one place furthest away. Where was Jesus when He made the prediction? He was on the Mount of Olives outside Jerusalem. In relation to that specific location, where is the uttermost part of the earth? It is the directly opposite point on the globe. That point lies in the South Pacific Ocean, and the closest inhabited island is Rapa-iti. Although small and remote, it was not overlooked in the early years of the modern missionary movement. The first preacher to land there was John Davies of the London Missionary Society. Soon after his arrival in 1826, all of the island's inhabitants adopted Christianity as their religion.[2]

Yet as we said, Jesus' instruction could be understood more generally as a prediction that the gospel would go everywhere in the world. This too has been fulfilled. The modern era since 1800 has been an age of great missionary enterprise, pushing the gospel to every nation under the sun. Statistics compiled in 2001 show that the church's goal of reaching the whole world has been substantially attained.

1. Radio with evangelical programming reaches 99% of the world's population in a language they can understand.

2. About 94% of the world's population lives in a culture with an indigenous witnessing church, and another 4% has a resident witness provided by outsiders.

3. In the 1990s, a broad-based initiative by American evangelicals to reach groups who had not yet heard the gospel was dramatically successful. This initiative, called The Joshua Project I, put church-planting teams in a thousand unreached cultures, about two thirds of those identified, and started churches of at least one hundred members in about half of the cultures where the teams had penetrated.[3]

We should not overstate the progress, however. Although the gospel is available to nearly everyone in the world today, personal evangelism has confronted only a small minority, and still a large percentage of the world's population has never actually heard the gospel. Yet what has been accomplished so far seems in itself a fulfillment of Jesus' prophecy that the gospel would go to the uttermost part before He returned. Within my lifetime, virtually all the last places deprived of the gospel have finally heard it. Today's global culture held together by mass communications has spread so aggressively that it has probably reached or will soon reach any remote tribes overlooked by missionaries. Thus, no uncompleted task prevents Christ from returning now.

The church's embrace of the whole modern world is a major sign that the end is near.

Third sign/ reemergence of Israel

In AD 70 the Romans demolished the city of Jerusalem and either killed or scattered most of the Jews living in Palestine. This catastrophe is clearly predicted in the Book of Daniel.

> 25 Know therefore and understand, *that* from the going forth of the commandment to restore and to build Jerusalem unto the Messiah the Prince *shall be* seven weeks, and threescore and two weeks: the street shall be built again, and the wall, even in troublous times.
> 26 And after threescore and two weeks shall Messiah be cut off, but not for himself: and the people of the prince that shall come shall destroy the city and the sanctuary; and the end thereof *shall be* with a flood, and unto the end of the war desolations are determined.
>
> - Daniel 9:25–26 -

Here is a brief but wonderfully rich prophecy that tells exactly when the Messiah would come. Then it reveals that after His death, the city and the Temple of Jerusalem would be destroyed.

The holocaust in AD 70 is predicted in the New Testament as well. On several occasions Jesus warned of the disaster about to fall on His nation.

> 20 And when ye shall see Jerusalem compassed with armies, then know that the desolation thereof is nigh.
> 21 Then let them which are in Judaea flee to the mountains; and let them which are in the midst of it depart out; and let not them that are in the countries enter thereinto.

22 For these be the days of vengeance, that all things which are written may be fulfilled.

23 But woe unto them that are with child, and to them that give suck, in those days! for there shall be great distress in the land, and wrath upon this people.

24 And they shall fall by the edge of the sword, and shall be led away captive into all nations: and Jerusalem shall be trodden down of the Gentiles, until the times of the Gentiles be fulfilled.

- Luke 21:20-24 -

Notice that Jesus not only foresaw the destruction of the city, but also the scattering of Jewish people to all nations. History soon confirmed the prophecy. After the holocaust in AD 70, the Jewish people never in ancient times succeeded in reorganizing and rebuilding their nation. A hundred years later, very few sons and daughters of Israel remained in Palestine.

Yet unlike so many other ethnic groups throughout history, the Jews never disappeared from the world stage. Their perseverance as a people is according to prophecy. The Old Testament clearly expects them to be occupying their homeland when the Messiah comes to set up His kingdom over the earth.

15 In those days, and at that time, will I cause the Branch of righteousness to grow up unto David; and he shall execute judgment and righteousness in the land.

16 In those days shall Judah be saved, and Jerusalem shall dwell safely: and this *is the name* wherewith she shall be called, The LORD our righteousness.

- Jeremiah 33:15-16 -

The New Testament gives us even clearer information. It says that during the Tribulation, not only will Israel be living in their homeland, but also they will have a Temple in Jerusalem; specifically, that a future world ruler will make their Temple the center of a new religion featuring himself as god. In Scripture, this evil figure in the end times is given various names, including the man of sin (below) and the Antichrist (1 John 2:18).

3 Let no man deceive you by any means: for *that day shall not come,* except there come a falling away first, and that man of sin be revealed, the son of perdition;

4 Who opposeth and exalteth himself above all that is called God, or that is worshipped; so that he as God sitteth in the temple of God, shewing himself that he is God.

- 2 Thessalonians 2:3-4 -

All the Biblical prophecies of a future Jewish presence in Palestine were obviously doomed to prove false unless at some point in history the Jews regathered in the land. Among these prophecies are some which specifically inform us that the Jews will occupy Palestine during the end times as the result of a prior return from exile. Of particular interest is a prophecy of Jeremiah.

> 3 For, lo, the days come, saith the Lord, that I will bring again the captivity of my people Israel and Judah, saith the Lord: and I will cause them to return to the land that I gave to their fathers, and they shall possess it. . . .
> 5 For thus saith the Lord; We have heard a voice of trembling, of fear, and not of peace.
> 6 Ask ye now, and see whether a man doth travail with child? wherefore do I see every man with his hands on his loins, as a woman in travail, and all faces are turned into paleness?
> 7 Alas! for that day *is* great, so that none *is* like it: it *is* even the time of Jacob's trouble; but he shall be saved out of it.
> 8 For it shall come to pass in that day, saith the Lord of hosts, *that* I will break his yoke from off thy neck, and will burst thy bonds, and strangers shall no more serve themselves of him:
> 9 But they shall serve the Lord their God, and David their king, whom I will raise up unto them.
>
> - Jeremiah 30:3, 5–9 -

Jeremiah affirms that before the time of Jacob's trouble, many Jews will return to the land of their fathers. In the last two centuries, many prominent teachers of prophecy have equated the time of Jacob's trouble with the Tribulation, the intensely troubled time that will precede the coming of Christ to set up His kingdom. A strong basis for their reasoning is the close parallel between Jeremiah 30:7 and another text addressed to the Jewish nation:

> 21 For then shall be great tribulation, such as was not since the beginning of the world to this time, no, nor ever shall be.
> 22 And except those days should be shortened, there should no flesh be saved: but for the elect's sake those days shall be shortened.
>
> - Matthew 24:21–22 -

Here we find Jesus' description of the Tribulation during its last phase. Since the Tribulation still lies in the future, the regathering that Jeremiah foresees cannot be the return of Jews from captivity in Babylon. Why? Because their reoccupation of the land at that time failed to be permanent. Centuries later, in AD 70, they were again dispossessed and scattered. The regathering that Jeremiah foresees must therefore be the flow of Jews in multiplied thousands back to Palestine in modern times. The culmination was the founding of modern Israel in 1948.

I am old enough to remember the impact that the refounding of Israel had upon the church. Bible-believing Christians everywhere were excited to see this fulfillment of prophecy. They viewed it as a sure sign that the Lord's return was drawing near. The event was amazing however you look at it. Somehow a dispersed and downtrodden people had managed to preserve their cultural and religious identity for almost two thousand years. And then somehow they managed to establish a new nation on the same territory occupied by their ancient forefathers. The history of man had never before seen anything remotely similar.

Fourth sign/ Jewish reoccupation of Jerusalem

In Jesus' warnings of the holocaust in AD 70, He did not view the coming Jewish dispersion as the end of the story. Look again at Luke 21:20–24 on pages 19 and 20. Rather, He stated that control of Jerusalem would remain in gentile hands only until "the times of the Gentiles" had been fulfilled. He was clearly implying that the Jews would then regain control. What did He mean by the expression "times of the Gentiles," which occurs nowhere else in Scripture? It must denote the historical period since Pentecost—the period when the church has been carrying the gospel of salvation to the whole world, gentiles as well as Jews. We conclude that in Jesus' reference to the times of the gentiles, He intended the whole Church Age.

So, His teaching that Jerusalem would be a gentile city until the end of the Church Age gives us a strong light on our place in history. We learn from it that the recent departure of gentile power from the city is a sure sign that Christ is about to return.

Gentile control of the city has been waning now for almost two centuries. Jewish reoccupation of Jerusalem began with an influx of Jewish settlers in the nineteenth century. Then its Jewish population grew steadily until Israel attained statehood in 1948. Soon afterward, the new nation absorbed the western sector of the city into its territory. During the 1967 war, the Israelis also added the eastern sector, establishing sovereignty over the whole city.[4] Although they have allowed Muslims to retain their shrine on Temple Mount, this site is not outside Jewish control. Thus, it can no longer be said that the city is trodden down by gentiles. The city is not only a solid component of the nation of Israel; it is also teeming with Jews and flourishing with Jewish life and culture.

Yet Jesus said that Jerusalem would not escape gentile domination until the times of the gentiles—that is, the Church Age—had been fulfilled. The Jewish reoccupation of Jerusalem is therefore a specific and compelling sign that the Church Age is drawing to a close. Thus, as we examine our place in history, we must attach special importance to Israel's conquest of Jerusalem in 1967.

Fifth sign/ world government

We read in the Book of Daniel about a dream that God sent to Nebuchadnezzar, the Babylonian king. In this dream, the king saw a great image of a man, and the portions of his body were made of different metals. None of the king's counselors could interpret the dream except the young Jewish captive Daniel, who declared that the image represented a series of kingdoms.

31 Thou, O king, sawest, and behold a great image. This great image, whose brightness *was* excellent, stood before thee; and the form thereof *was* terrible.
32 This image's head *was* of fine gold, his breast and his arms of silver,

> his belly and his thighs of brass,
>
> 33 His legs of iron, his feet part of iron and part of clay.
>
> 34 Thou sawest till that a stone was cut out without hands, which smote the image upon his feet *that were* of iron and clay, and brake them to pieces.
>
> 35 Then was the iron, the clay, the brass, the silver, and the gold, broken to pieces together, and became like the chaff of the summer threshingfloors; and the wind carried them away, that no place was found for them: and the stone that smote the image became a great mountain, and filled the whole earth.
>
> 36 This *is* the dream; and we will tell the interpretation thereof before the king.
>
> 37 Thou, O king, *art* a king of kings: for the God of heaven hath given thee a kingdom, power, and strength, and glory.
>
> 38 And wheresoever the children of men dwell, the beasts of the field and the fowls of the heaven hath he given into thine hand, and hath made thee ruler over them all. Thou *art* this head of gold.
>
> 39 And after thee shall arise another kingdom inferior to thee, and another third kingdom of brass, which shall bear rule over all the earth.
>
> 40 And the fourth kingdom shall be strong as iron: forasmuch as iron breaketh in pieces and subdueth all *things:* and as iron that breaketh all these, shall it break in pieces and bruise.
>
> 41 And whereas thou sawest the feet and toes, part of potters' clay, and part of iron, the kingdom shall be divided; but there shall be in it of the strength of the iron, forasmuch as thou sawest the iron mixed with miry clay. . . .
>
> 44 And in the days of these kings shall the God of heaven set up a kingdom, which shall never be destroyed: and the kingdom shall not be left to other people, *but* it shall break in pieces and consume all these kingdoms, and it shall stand for ever.
>
> - Daniel 2:31–41, 44 -

Here is a difficult prophecy, but not all things worth knowing, nor all things God expects us to know, are simple.

From the head to the legs, Daniel counted four kingdoms beginning with the head of gold, which he identified as Babylon. Elsewhere the Book of Daniel helps us name the next two kingdoms. The arms and chest of silver are Medo-Persia, and the belly and thighs of bronze are Greece (Dan. 8:20–21).[5] Next came the legs of iron. The church from earliest times has identified these as Rome.[6] Then Daniel said, "And whereas thou sawest the feet and toes, part of potters' clay, and part of iron, the kingdom shall be divided" (v. 41). It is evident, therefore, that the feet and toes together represent a single kingdom, coming fifth and last in the whole series.

For two reasons, the fifth kingdom cannot be an ancient one like the preceding four.

1. Neither Rome nor any other kingdom of the past was ever divided into ten parts. Yet such a division must exist during the period of history symbolized by the toes.

2. As the king watched the dream, a great stone fell on the feet and crushed the whole image (v. 34). Daniel revealed that the stone represents the everlasting kingdom of God (v. 44). So, the falling of the stone pictures the future moment in history when God will violently

intervene to set up His kingdom in place of the degenerate kingdoms of the earth. That will happen at the Second Coming of Christ. We conclude that the fifth kingdom, the kingdom corresponding to the feet of the image, will exist at Christ's return.

The Book of Revelation reveals that the last ruler of the fifth kingdom will be the sinister figure known as the Antichrist, also known as the Beast. How extensive will be his kingdom? Many teachers of prophecy have believed that he will rule over a confederation of ten European nations. They have argued that these must be ten in number since the last kingdom is likened to feet with ten toes. Indeed, the Book of Revelation foresees ten kingdoms at the end of the present age.

> 12 And the ten horns which thou sawest are ten kings, which have received no kingdom as yet; but receive power as kings one hour with the beast.
> 13 These have one mind, and shall give their power and strength unto the beast.
>
> - Revelation 17:12–13 -

But for a proper interpretation, we must read the preceding passage in conjunction with another.

> And it was given unto him [the beast] to make war with the saints, and to overcome them: and power was given him over all kindreds, and tongues, and nations.
>
> - Revelation 13:7 -

Taken together, these two passages seem to say that the ten will give the Beast power that is worldwide in extent. So, we do not gain the impression that these ten are a group of small nations in Europe. Rather, they appear to be kingdoms spanning the whole earth. In other words, a world government will be in place before the Beast arises.

We conclude that the fifth kingdom destined to suffer the tyranny of the Beast must be a world government. Will that government arise in the future, or does it already exist? The previous four kingdoms— Babylon, Medo-Persia, Greece, and Rome—all exercised authority over the Jews when they were living in their own land. So, it is reasonable to suppose that the fifth kingdom represents another kingdom with authority over an existing Jewish nation.

The kingdom governing the Jewish nation before it was dissolved in AD 70 was Rome, the fourth division of the image. The fifth division, the feet and toes, must therefore represent whatever kingdom has governed the Jewish nation since it reemerged in 1948. That kingdom can be none other than the United Nations, which came into being just a few years earlier, in 1945. The UN played an instrumental role in creating the state of Israel, and ever since it has sought to oversee Israel's relations with hostile neighbors. And, as prophecy foresees, the UN is indeed a government spanning the whole world.

In my commentary on Daniel, I show that the UN perfectly matches Daniel's description of the fifth kingdom. I show also that the ten toes represent ten regional associations that will eventually embrace all nations.[7]

Sixth sign/ apostasy in the church

In his second epistle to the Thessalonians, Paul takes up the subject of final things.

> 1 Now we beseech you, brethren, by the coming of our Lord Jesus Christ, and *by* our gathering together unto him,
> 2 That ye be not soon shaken in mind, or be troubled, neither by spirit, nor by word, nor by letter as from us, as that the day of Christ is at hand.
>
> - 2 Thessalonians 2:1–2 -

He is seeking to counter a false teaching circulating among the Thessalonians that "the day of Christ is at hand." The words " is at hand" are better translated "has come."[8]

The effect of this teaching was to arouse anxiety and dread. Why? Because these Thessalonians understood from Old Testament prophecy and from Paul's teaching that the Day of Christ—that is, the Day of the Lord—would bring great trouble. Divine wrath in full measure would visit the earth. The prospect of living through such a time caused them to be "shaken in mind."

Paul allays their fears. When he says, "We beseech you, brethren, by the coming of our Lord Jesus Christ, and by our gathering together unto him, that ye be not soon shaken in mind, . . . , as that the day of Christ is at hand," he means that they need not worry about living through the time of great trouble, for when Christ comes at the dawning of His day, the first task on His program will be to gather the church unto Himself. He will remove His saints from the world before horror and havoc descend upon it.

How will He remove them? At the time of their departure, He will not show Himself to the whole world. Rather, as we noted in chapter 2, He will come secretly like a thief in the night and steal them away.

> 42 Watch therefore: for ye know not what hour your Lord doth come.
> 43 But know this, that if the goodman of the house had known in what watch the thief would come, he would have watched, and would not have suffered his house to be broken up.
> 44 Therefore be ye also ready: for in such an hour as ye think not the Son of man cometh.
>
> - Matthew 24:42–44 -

> For yourselves know perfectly that the day of the Lord so cometh as a thief in the night.
>
> - 1 Thessalonians 5:2 -

> But the day of the Lord will come as a thief in the night; in the which the heavens shall pass away with a great noise, and the elements shall melt with fervent heat, the earth also and the works that are therein shall be burned up.
>
> - 2 Peter 3:10 -

At the event known as the Rapture, all true believers in Christ will suddenly disappear and rise into His presence. Immediately afterward, history will enter its tragic climax, the period known as the Tribulation. The world will descend into unspeakable turmoil and suffer devastating plagues. Then Christ will come a second time. At the end of all the woe and misery, Christ will descend in glory, overthrow His enemies, and establish His kingdom on the earth.

Immediately following the text we quoted earlier from Second Thessalonians, Paul identifies one development preceding the Rapture.

> Let no man deceive you by any means: for *that day shall not come,* except there come a falling away first, and that man of sin be revealed, the son of perdition; . . .
>
> - 2 Thessalonians 2:3 -

The "day of Christ" (2 Thess. 2:2 on p. 25) will not come until there is a falling away. "Falling away" is *apostasia,*[9] root of our word "apostasy." The Greek word refers to a departure from true religion. Paul says that the falling away will come "first"—that is, before the day of Christ. Therefore, it must also precede the Rapture, which will initiate the day of Christ and the Tribulation.

As a side note, Paul informs readers of another proof that the day of Christ has not yet arrived. It is that the man of sin—the same person as the Antichrist—has not come onto the world scene. He seems to be implying that the Antichrist will be a recognizable figure quite early during the Tribulation.

Has the prophecy of end-time apostasy been fulfilled? Yes, at the dawn of the twenty-first century, the church of Jesus Christ is sick with apostasy. The disease that now fills the whole church germinated about 1800. At that time, doubt in the supernatural and in Biblical history began to infect organized Christianity. The Unitarians, prominent in New England, went so far as to reject the deity of Christ. After the publication in the 1860s of Darwin's *On the Origin of the Species*, many churches accepted his ideas and abandoned belief in the literal truth of the Scriptures. Since then, apostasy has steadily grown and spread. Today, few churches and church bodies remain committed to Biblical faith and practice. Western society as a whole, once composed of nations that prided themselves on being Christian, has become thoroughly secularized. We once called ourselves a Christian nation. Now that concept is generally seen as backward and degrading.

In other chapters we show that the apostasy of modern Christianity is a dominant theme of prophecy concerning the end times.

Seventh sign/ global telecommunications

Prophecy contains many hints of modern technology. One prime example is in the Book of Revelation. Before we examine it, however, we need to provide some background, starting with some key information about the Antichrist.

> 5 And there was given unto him a mouth speaking great things and blasphemies; and power was given unto him to continue forty *and* two months.
> 6 And he opened his mouth in blasphemy against God, to blaspheme his name, and his tabernacle, and them that dwell in heaven.
>
> - Revelation 13:5–6 -

Here we learn that before Christ descends to set up His kingdom on the earth, the Antichrist will reign for forty-two months. Near the beginning of this period, he will "blaspheme his [God's] name, and his tabernacle, and them that dwell in heaven." Paul foresaw the setting and occasion. After identifying the Antichrist as the "man of sin" (2 Thess. 2:3 on p. 26), he says,

> Who opposeth and exalteth himself above all that is called God, or that is worshipped; so that he as God sitteth in the temple of God, shewing himself that he is God.
>
> - 2 Thessalonians 2:4 -

The blasphemy will consist of both deeds and words. He will enter the Temple of God and make it the center of a cult devoted to worshiping his own person. Not content to be received as a god equal to other gods, he will claim to be the highest god of all, the god nonpareil.

In His Olivet Discourse, Jesus warned all Jews in Israel during the Tribulation to expect severe persecution after the Antichrist takes control of the Temple. His exact wording is critically important.

> 15 When ye therefore shall see the abomination of desolation, spoken of by Daniel the prophet, stand in the holy place, (whoso readeth, let him understand:)
> 16 Then let them which be in Judaea flee into the mountains:
> 17 Let him which is on the housetop not come down to take any thing out of his house:
> 18 Neither let him which is in the field return back to take his clothes.
> 19 And woe unto them that are with child, and to them that give suck in those days!
> 20 But pray ye that your flight be not in the winter, neither on the sabbath day:
> 21 For then shall be great tribulation, such as was not since the beginning of the world to this time, no, nor ever shall be.
>
> - Matthew 24:15–21 -

In other words, as soon as the Antichrist sets foot in the sanctuary, he will almost immediately begin his intense persecution of all Jews still faithful to the true God. Thus, his violation of the Temple will be the signal to believing Jews that they must, with all possible haste, flee to the wilderness.

Jesus' warning to anyone on his roof or in his field that he will not be able to afford even an extra five minutes to visit the house carries the implication that escape will be possible if they obey Him, but impossible if they do not. Yet if news of the event will come by word of mouth, there will be wide variation in the time of delay. Some will not hear it until hours later than others. To save five minutes by heeding what Jesus said will therefore be critical only for a few. It is far more reasonable and more respectful of His words to infer from them that all Jews will learn of the event at about the same time.

How will that be possible? Jesus provides the answer. He anticipates that those in the fields and on the housetops of Judea will be able to "see" the Antichrist as he enters the Temple. His wording strongly implies modern means of communication. By looking at screens fed by electronic networks, not only the people in Judea but also the whole world will witness the event as it happens.

It is interesting that another prophecy, speaking of an event at a slightly earlier point in history, also foresees video technology. This prophecy concerns the two witnesses who will first appear about seven years before the end of the Tribulation.

> 3 And I will give *power* unto my two witnesses, and they shall prophesy a thousand two hundred *and* threescore days, clothed in sackcloth.
> 4 These are the two olive trees, and the two candlesticks standing before the God of the earth.
> 5 And if any man will hurt them, fire proceedeth out of their mouth, and devoureth their enemies: and if any man will hurt them, he must in this manner be killed.
> 6 These have power to shut heaven, that it rain not in the days of their prophecy: and have power over waters to turn them to blood, and to smite the earth with all plagues, as often as they will.
> 7 And when they shall have finished their testimony, the beast that ascendeth out of the bottomless pit shall make war against them, and shall overcome them, and kill them.
> 8 And their dead bodies *shall lie* in the street of the great city, which spiritually is called Sodom and Egypt, where also our Lord was crucified.
> 9 And they of the people and kindreds and tongues and nations shall see their dead bodies three days and an half, and shall not suffer their dead bodies to be put in graves.
> 10 And they that dwell upon the earth shall rejoice over them, and make merry, and shall send gifts one to another; because these two prophets tormented them that dwelt on the earth.
> 11 And after three days and an half the Spirit of life from God entered into them, and they stood upon their feet; and great fear fell upon them which saw them.
> 12 And they heard a great voice from heaven saying unto them, Come up hither. And they ascended up to heaven in a cloud; and their enemies beheld them.
> 13 And the same hour was there a great earthquake, and the tenth part of the city fell, and in the earthquake were slain of men seven thousand: and the remnant were affrighted, and gave glory to the God of heaven.

- Revelation 11:3–13 -

Most Christians today believe, and correctly so, that these witnesses are figures from the past who will reappear suddenly on the earth. They are generally identified as either Enoch and Elijah or Moses and Elijah. My own position is that they are Moses and Elijah.

At the end of their ministry lasting 1260 days, they will be killed by the Beast—that is, by the Antichrist—and their dead bodies will lie unburied in Jerusalem for 3½ days. During this period, all the wicked of the world will rejoice at the Beast's victory over them. But then they will see the witnesses rise from the dead, and the raucous celebration of their deaths will instantly cease. Revelry will turn to fear. But notice the words of verse 9. It says plainly that for three and a half days the whole world will with morbid joy gaze at their dead bodies lying in Jerusalem. How can the whole world look together at a scene normally visible only if the viewer is standing no more than a few hundred yards away? The answer has become obvious only since the advent of global telecommunications. For 3½ days the people of the world will stare at electronic screens fixed hypnotically upon one picture: the bodies of the slain witnesses. The wicked will be unwilling to turn away from a sight that seems to vindicate their wickedness. Rather than risk public outrage over removal of the bodies, political leaders will allow them to lie where they fell.

Global telecommunications developed shortly after World War II. It is interesting that their coming onto the world stage roughly coincided with the refounding of Israel and certain other key signs of the times.

Footnotes

[1] "Worldwide Adherents of All Religions, Mid-2005," *Encyclopaedia Britannica Online,* Web (britannica.com/eb/article9432620/Worldwide-Adherents-of-All-Religions-Mid-2005), 2005.

[2] Rhys Richards, "The Earliest Foreign Visitors and Their Massive Depopulation of Rapa-iti from 1824 to 1830," *Journal de la Société des Océanistes,* 118, année 2004–1.

[3] Patrick Johnstone and Jason Mandryk, *Operation World: 21st Century Edition* (Bulstrode, Gerrards Cross, UK: WEC International, n.d.), 7.

[4] "Restoration and Freedom," Jerusalem Institute of Justice, Web (jij.org/news/restoration-and-freedom/), 9/10/19.

[5] Ed Rickard, *Daniel Explained,* 4th ed. (N.p.: The Moorings Press, 2020), 166–167, 199–200.

[6] Ibid., 59.

[7] Ibid., 69–79.

[8] William F. Arndt and F. Wilbur Gingrich, eds., *A Greek-English Lexicon of the New Testament and Other Early Christian Literature* (Chicago: University of Chicago Press, 1957), 266.

[9] George Ricker Berry, *Interlinear Greek-English New Testament* (N.p., 1897; repr., Grand Rapids, Mich.: Baker Book House, 1981), 731.

Chapter 4

✛ Three More Easy Signs ✛

Eighth sign/ The pope's emergence as a promoter of world government

Scripture clearly teaches that the Antichrist will be the last Roman ruler. His connection with Rome is manifest in many prophecies, which we will briefly consider here.

1. One source of helpful information is Daniel's vision of four monstrous beasts arising from the sea.

> 1 In the first year of Belshazzar king of Babylon Daniel had a dream and visions of his head upon his bed: then he wrote the dream, *and* told the sum of the matters.
> 2 Daniel spake and said, I saw in my vision by night, and, behold, the four winds of the heaven strove upon the great sea.
> 3 And four great beasts came up from the sea, diverse one from another.
> 4 The first *was* like a lion, and had eagle's wings: I beheld till the wings thereof were plucked, and it was lifted up from the earth, and made stand upon the feet as a man, and a man's heart was given to it.
> 5 And behold another beast, a second, like to a bear, and it raised up itself on one side, and *it had* three ribs in the mouth of it between the teeth of it: and they said thus unto it, Arise, devour much flesh.
> 6 After this I beheld, and lo another, like a leopard, which had upon the back of it four wings of a fowl; the beast had also four heads; and dominion was given to it.
> 7 After this I saw in the night visions, and behold a fourth beast, dreadful and terrible, and strong exceedingly; and it had great iron teeth: it devoured and brake in pieces, and stamped the residue with the feet of it: and it *was* diverse from all the beasts that *were* before it; and it had ten horns.
> 8 I considered the horns, and, behold, there came up among them another little horn, before whom there were three of the first horns plucked up by the roots: and, behold, in this horn *were* eyes like the eyes of man, and a mouth speaking great things.
> 9 I beheld till the thrones were cast down, and the Ancient of days did sit, whose garment *was* white as snow, and the hair of his head like the pure wool: his throne *was like* the fiery flame, *and* his wheels *as* burning fire.
> 10 A fiery stream issued and came forth from before him: thousand thousands ministered unto him, and ten thousand times ten thousand stood before him: the judgment was set, and the books were opened.
> 11 I beheld then because of the voice of the great words which the horn spake: I beheld *even* till the beast was slain, and his body destroyed, and given to the burning flame.
> 12 As concerning the rest of the beasts, they had their dominion taken away: yet their lives were prolonged for a season and time.
> 13 I saw in the night visions, and, behold, *one* like the Son of man came

> with the clouds of heaven, and came to the Ancient of days, and they brought him near before him.
>
> 14 And there was given him dominion, and glory, and a kingdom, that all people, nations, and languages, should serve him: his dominion *is* an everlasting dominion, which shall not pass away, and his kingdom *that* which shall not be destroyed.
>
> - Daniel 7:1-14 -

Here we find another view of the same kingdoms that appear in Daniel 2 (partially quoted on pp. 22–23). The change in imagery corresponds to a change in perspective. From Nebuchadnezzar's perspective, expressed in his dream, earthly kingdoms are a magnificent and awe-inspiring monument to man. But from God's perspective, revealed in the vision of Daniel 7, the same kingdoms are no better than vicious beasts. Babylon is a lion with eagles' wings. Medo-Persia is the bear raised on one side. Greece is the leopard with four wings. The dreadful and terrible beast is Rome.

The fifth kingdom appears abruptly in the simple statement, "And it had ten horns." Then in verse 8 we learn of another horn that appears after the ten. A full study of chapter 7 discovers that this eleventh horn is a person, the same evil person who appears in other visions of Daniel, each disclosing new information about him. He is none other than the monstrous ruler who will emerge before Christ returns; namely, the Antichrist.[1] In chapter 7, he emerges as an eleventh horn in the midst of ten horns. This prediction could hardly make it plainer that he will emerge during the period of the ten toes. Since Daniel's prophecy describes him as a horn on the fourth beast, the beast representing Rome, a reasonable conclusion is that the Antichrist will be the ruler of a revived Roman Empire.

2. When the Book of Daniel prophesies that Jerusalem would be destroyed after the Messiah is cut off, it then proceeds to look even farther into the future.

> 25 Know therefore and understand, *that* from the going forth of the commandment to restore and to build Jerusalem unto the Messiah the Prince *shall be* seven weeks, and threescore and two weeks: the street shall be built again, and the wall, even in troublous times.
>
> 26 And after threescore and two weeks shall Messiah be cut off, but not for himself: and the people of the prince that shall come shall destroy the city and the sanctuary; and the end thereof *shall be* with a flood, and unto the end of the war desolations are determined.
>
> - Daniel 9:25–26 -

We learn that after Christ's death, Jerusalem would be destroyed by the people of the "coming prince." We show in our commentary on Daniel that the term refers to the Antichrist.[2] Jerusalem was destroyed in AD 70 by the Romans. It follows that the Antichrist will be a Roman ruler.

3. The Book of Revelation places the Antichrist in the succession of ancient Roman emperors.

7 And the angel said unto me, Wherefore didst thou marvel? I will tell thee the mystery of the woman, and of the beast that carrieth her, which hath the seven heads and ten horns.
8 The beast that thou sawest was, and is not; and shall ascend out of the bottomless pit, and go into perdition: and they that dwell on the earth shall wonder, whose names were not written in the book of life from the foundation of the world, when they behold the beast that was, and is not, and yet is.
9 And here *is* the mind which hath wisdom. The seven heads are seven mountains, on which the woman sitteth.
10 And there are seven kings: five are fallen, and one is, *and* the other is not yet come; and when he cometh, he must continue a short space.
11 And the beast that was, and is not, even he is the eighth, and is of the seven, and goeth into perdition.
12 And the ten horns which thou sawest are ten kings, which have received no kingdom as yet; but receive power as kings one hour with the beast.
13 These have one mind, and shall give their power and strength unto the beast.
14 These shall make war with the Lamb, and the Lamb shall overcome them: for he is Lord of lords, and King of kings: and they that are with him *are* called, and chosen, and faithful.
15 And he saith unto me, The waters which thou sawest, where the whore sitteth, are peoples, and multitudes, and nations, and tongues.
. . .
18 And the woman which thou sawest is that great city, which reigneth over the kings of the earth.

- Revelation 17:7–15, 18 -

Six have reigned until the moment John is writing, and the Antichrist will be another in the future (v. 10). Moreover, the beast representing the Antichrist carries the woman called "that great city, which [presently, in John's day] reigneth over the kings of the earth" (v. 18). Lest we fail to recognize Rome in this description, prophecy adds that she sits on seven mountains, or seven hills (v. 9). The city that has long been known as the city of seven hills is, of course, Rome.

How can we reconcile all these insights from prophecy with our position that the fifth kingdom is the UN? The answer is that prophecy also reveals that the Antichrist will be a world ruler (Rev. 13:7 on p. 24). Thus, it appears that the revived Roman empire under his dominion will not be confined to the territories of its ancient predecessor, but will embrace all the states and megastates on the earth. Its ten divisions will span the globe. In its extent, the fifth kingdom will equal the UN. In fact, as we have argued, the UN is the fifth kingdom.

If the UN is indeed equivalent to the fifth kingdom that will become a revived Roman Empire under the Antichrist, we infer that this organization will someday transfer its headquarters from New York City to Rome. The most likely reason is that New York will fall under divine judgment, making it unfit to carry on world government. We know that fairly early in the Tribulation, the world will become uncomfortably hot. In reference to all the martyrs who will arrive in heaven during the early portion of the Tribulation, a heavenly saint with the office of elder said to John, writer of the Book of Revelation,

> They shall hunger no more, neither thirst any more; neither shall the sun light on them, nor any heat.
>
> - Revelation 7:16 -

A really hot world will cause melting of ice sheets and extensive coastal flooding, making places like New York uninhabitable.

The beast who is the Antichrist will share power with two other beasts, both introduced in Revelation 13. The first is the dragon.

> 1 And I stood upon the sand of the sea, and saw a beast rise up out of the sea, having seven heads and ten horns, and upon his horns ten crowns, and upon his heads the name of blasphemy.
> 2 And the beast which I saw was like unto a leopard, and his feet were as the feet of a bear, and his mouth as the mouth of a lion: and the dragon gave him his power, and his seat, and great authority.
>
> - Revelation 13:1–2 -

The dragon is, of course, Satan (Rev. 20:2). The second is the beast with two horns like a lamb.

> And I beheld another beast coming up out of the earth; and he had two horns like a lamb, and he spake as a dragon.
>
> - Revelation 13:11 -

In other words, he will in some fashion resemble Christ, who bears the name Lamb twenty-seven times in Revelation. Another name for the second beast is "the false prophet."

> And I saw three unclean spirits like frogs come out of the mouth of the dragon, and out of the mouth of the beast, and out of the mouth of the false prophet.
>
> - Revelation 16:13 -

(See also Revelation 19:20; 20:10.) His lamblike horns are therefore a symbol of his pretense to stand in Christ's place as His authorized representative and spokesman. The false prophet will evidently be a conspicuous Christian leader. The most conspicuous is, of course, the pope. Although the false prophet will at first be a leader of organized Christianity, he will later forsake Christianity in any historic sense and encourage his followers to worship the Beast.

For confirmation that the false prophet is the pope, we will return to Revelation 17.

> 1 And there came one of the seven angels which had the seven vials, and talked with me, saying unto me, Come hither; I will shew unto thee the judgment of the great whore that sitteth upon many waters:
> 2 With whom the kings of the earth have committed fornication, and the inhabitants of the earth have been made drunk with the wine of her fornication.

> 3 So he carried me away in the spirit into the wilderness: and I saw a
> woman sit upon a scarlet coloured beast, full of names of blasphemy,
> having seven heads and ten horns.
> 4 And the woman was arrayed in purple and scarlet colour, and decked
> with gold and precious stones and pearls, having a golden cup in her
> hand full of abominations and filthiness of her fornication:
> 5 And upon her forehead *was* a name written, MYSTERY, BABYLON
> THE GREAT, THE MOTHER OF HARLOTS AND ABOMINATIONS OF
> THE EARTH.
> 6 And I saw the woman drunken with the blood of the saints, and with
> the blood of the martyrs of Jesus: and when I saw her, I wondered
> with great admiration.
>
> - Revelation 17:1–6 -

The wicked whore we find in this text (incidentally, the same as
Jezebel in Rev. 2:20–23) is one of three women that the Book of
Revelation uses to symbolize a religious body. The woman who gives
birth to the Messiah is Israel.

> 1 And there appeared a great wonder in heaven; a woman clothed with
> the sun, and the moon under her feet, and upon her head a crown of
> twelve stars:
> 2 And she being with child cried, travailing in birth, and pained to be
> delivered.
> 3 And there appeared another wonder in heaven; and behold a great
> red dragon, having seven heads and ten horns, and seven crowns
> upon his heads.
> 4 And his tail drew the third part of the stars of heaven, and did cast
> them to the earth: and the dragon stood before the woman which was
> ready to be delivered, for to devour her child as soon as it was born.
> 5 And she brought forth a man child, who was to rule all nations with a
> rod of iron: and her child was caught up unto God, and *to* his throne.
>
> - Revelation 12:1-5 -

The woman adorned as a bride for her husband is the church.

> 1 And I saw a new heaven and a new earth: for the first heaven and the
> first earth were passed away; and there was no more sea.
> 2 And I John saw the holy city, new Jerusalem, coming down from God
> out of heaven, prepared as a bride adorned for her husband.
>
> - Revelation 21:1-2 -

The woman in Revelation 17 who gains control over masses of people
by pursuing illicit relations with the godless rulers of this world and
by persecuting true men of God must therefore represent a false religion. These relations are pictured as illicit because they make her
faithless to the One who is supposedly her true husband. We conclude that the religion she symbolizes must be a counterfeit
Christianity.

As we observed before, prophecy identifies the woman as the city
that rules the world (Rev. 17:18) and sits on seven hills (Rev. 17:9).
Therefore, she is Rome. Now we discover that she is also a deviant
church body. If centered in Rome, she must be the Roman Catholic
Church. But how can she be both a city and a religion? The likely

answer is that God views essentially all Roman citizens as participants in the evil work done by the women. After all, the whole city has for many, many centuries revered the pope, supported all of the observances and policies of the Roman church, and prospered greatly from the wealth poured into Rome by masses of faithful Catholics.

Who then is the false prophet? Since the woman representing both the city and the church of Rome is pictured riding on the Antichrist (Rev. 17:3, 7 on pp. 32, 34), we conclude that they will be closely allied. It therefore seems likely that the false prophet is none other than the head of the Roman church; namely, the pope. Many leading teachers of prophecy in days past reached the same conclusion.

Satan, the Antichrist, and the false prophet will make up a counterfeit trinity that may appropriately be dubbed the infernal trio. They will not constitute an actual trinity (tri-unity), for they will not share the same essence. Though they achieve equal wickedness, they will remain three distinct beings. Satan will emulate God the Father; the Antichrist, God the Son; and the false prophet, God the Holy Spirit.

The Father gives all authority to the Son.

> 26 For as the Father hath life in himself; so hath he given to the Son to have life in himself;
> 27 And hath given him authority to execute judgment also, because he is the Son of man.
>
> - John 5:26–27 -

(See also Matt. 28:18; Ps. 2; Ps. 110.) In like manner, Satan will give "his power, and his seat, and great authority" to the Antichrist (Rev. 13:2 on p. 33).

The Holy Spirit directs worship to the Son.

> But when the Comforter is come, whom I will send unto you from the Father, *even* the Spirit of truth, which proceedeth from the Father, he shall testify of me:
>
> - John 15:26 -

(See also John 16:13–14.) In like manner, the false prophet will exalt the Antichrist.

> 11 And I beheld another beast coming up out of the earth; and he had two horns like a lamb, and he spake as a dragon.
> 12 And he exerciseth all the power of the first beast before him, and causeth the earth and them which dwell therein to worship the first beast, whose deadly wound was healed.
> 13 And he doeth great wonders, so that he maketh fire come down from heaven on the earth in the sight of men,
> 14 And deceiveth them that dwell on the earth by *the means of* those miracles which he had power to do in the sight of the beast; saying to them that dwell on the earth, that they should make an image to the beast, which had the wound by a sword, and did live.
>
> - Revelation 13:11–14 -

To promote worship of the Beast, the false prophet will even perform miracles.

In light of our discussion so far, certain recent developments take on huge significance. On July 7, 2009, the last pope, Pope Benedict XVI, issued an encyclical entitled "Charity in Truth" defining the church's outlook on global economic problems. Lamenting the growing divide between rich and poor, it advocated a "true world political authority" to assure that private businesses would serve the common good rather than the exclusive goal of making money.[3] Still during his tenure as pope, the Vatican's Justice and Peace Department, on October 24, 2011, circulated a document calling for "a supranational authority" with "universal jurisdiction" to guide economic policies and decisions. At first associated with the United Nations, it should later become an independent body with power to govern the world economy.[4] The new pope, Pope Francis, has reinforced his predecessor's proposals and carried them even further. In an encyclical issued on June 19, 2015, entitled "Care for Our Common Home," he raises the alarm that short of decisive action on a global scale, mankind is headed for environmental disaster. The solution? He says it is "to manage the global economy; to revive economies hit by the crisis; to avoid any deterioration of the present crisis and the greater imbalances that would result; to bring about integral and timely disarmament, food security and peace; to guarantee the protection of the environment and to regulate migration: for all this, there is urgent need of a true world political authority."[5]

As a result of positioning himself as a strong voice for world government, Pope Francis became the darling of the world's elite. His stature has declined recently because of the scandals infesting the Catholic church. Yet his successor, or perhaps Francis himself, may well succeed in recapturing the world's favor if he leads the church in the direction of conforming to politically correct views on sexuality. Once this happens, we can be sure that the papacy will indeed serve as the religious arm of the last world ruler, the Antichrist.

Ninth sign/ The emergence of political alignments in the Middle East corresponding to what prophecy portrays during the early Tribulation.

What will be the Antichrist's place of origin? When predicting where the Antichrist will first appear, Bible prophecy takes us down five tracks converging on the same conclusion.

1. As all scholars recognize, verses 3 through 35 of Daniel 11 summarize the coming experience of Israel during the 150 years between Alexander the Great's conquest of the Middle East and Israel's achievement of national independence in about 166 BC. The main figures throughout this lengthy passage are the rulers of two powerful dynasties that were remnants of Alexander's Greek Empire. One,

the Ptolemaic dynasty, controlled Egypt. The other, the Seleucid dynasty, held sway over a vast territory including not only modern Syria but also modern Iraq and adjoining regions. In the years just before 166, Israel was subject to a ruthless Seleucid monarch named Antiochus Epiphanes, who mercilessly persecuted the Jews. Only with miraculous divine help did they succeed in throwing off his tyrannical rule. Daniel 11, beginning in verse 21 and continuing through verse 35, provides a detailed account of his career.

21 And in his estate shall stand up a vile person, to whom they shall not give the honour of the kingdom: but he shall come in peaceably, and obtain the kingdom by flatteries.

22 And with the arms of a flood shall they be overflown from before him, and shall be broken; yea, also the prince of the covenant.

23 And after the league *made* with him he shall work deceitfully: for he shall come up, and shall become strong with a small people.

24 He shall enter peaceably even upon the fattest places of the province; and he shall do *that* which his fathers have not done, nor his fathers' fathers; he shall scatter among them the prey, and spoil, and riches: *yea,* and he shall forecast his devices against the strong holds, even for a time.

25 And he shall stir up his power and his courage against the king of the south with a great army; and the king of the south shall be stirred up to battle with a very great and mighty army; but he shall not stand: for they shall forecast devices against him.

26 Yea, they that feed of the portion of his meat shall destroy him, and his army shall overflow: and many shall fall down slain.

27 And both these kings' hearts *shall be* to do mischief, and they shall speak lies at one table; but it shall not prosper: for yet the end *shall be* at the time appointed.

28 Then shall he return into his land with great riches; and his heart *shall be* against the holy covenant; and he shall do *exploits,* and return to his own land.

29 At the time appointed he shall return, and come toward the south; but it shall not be as the former, or as the latter.

30 For the ships of Chittim shall come against him: therefore he shall be grieved, and return, and have indignation against the holy covenant: so shall he do; he shall even return, and have intelligence with them that forsake the holy covenant.

31 And arms shall stand on his part, and they shall pollute the sanctuary of strength, and shall take away the daily *sacrifice,* and they shall place the abomination that maketh desolate.

32 And such as do wickedly against the covenant shall he corrupt by flatteries: but the people that do know their God shall be strong, and do *exploits.*

33 And they that understand among the people shall instruct many: yet they shall fall by the sword, and by flame, by captivity, and by spoil, *many* days.

34 Now when they shall fall, they shall be holpen with a little help: but many shall cleave to them with flatteries.

35 And *some* of them of understanding shall fall, to try them, and to purge, and to make *them* white, *even* to the time of the end: because *it is* yet for a time appointed.

- Daniel 11:21-35 -

The close correspondence between these verses and actual events during his reign has left no doubt in the minds of scholars that the person they foresee is Antiochus. But notice in verse 35 a leap to events in the future; specifically, to the period called "the time of the end." The events prophesied in verse 36 (see below) and subsequent verses do not match anything in recorded history. They are a vision of what will happen during the Tribulation. The mighty king who is their main subject is the Antichrist. Scripture identifies him right at the outset as the future ruler who will presume to be superior to all the gods that mankind has worshiped in the past.

> 36 And the king shall do according to his will; and he shall exalt himself, and magnify himself above every god, and shall speak marvellous things against the God of gods, and shall prosper till the indignation be accomplished: for that that is determined shall be done.
> 37 Neither shall he regard the God of his fathers, nor the desire of women, nor regard any god: for he shall magnify himself above all.
>
> - Daniel 11:36–37 -

But notice that it introduces him simply as "the king," creating in the reader's mind a linkage with the king who until now has been the main subject. The clear intent is to mark a basic resemblance between the two kings—indeed, to reveal Antiochus as a type of the Antichrist. He is also presented as a type of the Antichrist in another of Daniel's visions, the one recorded in Daniel 8. Therefore, since Antiochus was a ruler of lands belonging to the Seleucid Empire, our presumption is that the domain of the Antichrist will be geographically similar; specifically, that its boundaries will include all or portions of Syria and Iraq.

2. A few verses later, in Daniel 11:40, the Antichrist is called "king of the north."

> And at the time of the end shall the king of the south push at him: and the king of the north shall come against him like a whirlwind, with chariots, and with horsemen, and with many ships; and he shall enter into the countries, and shall overflow and pass over.
>
> - Daniel 11:40 -

The same title has been used frequently throughout the preceding chapter. Whereas the Ptolemaic ruler is always called the king of the south, the Seleucid ruler is always called the king of the north.[6] Thus, many Bible students, both ancient and modern, have recognized that if the future Antichrist is a king of the north, his seat must be somewhere in Syria or Iraq.[7]

3. Isaiah repeatedly (Isa. 14:24–27; 30:31-33; 31:4–9) and Micah once (Mic. 5:2–8) refer to the Antichrist as the Assyrian.

In Isaiah 31, we learn how God will defeat the Antichrist.

> 4 For thus hath the Lord spoken unto me, Like as the lion and the young lion roaring on his prey, when a multitude of shepherds is called forth against him, *he* will not be afraid of their voice, nor abase himself for the noise of them: so shall the Lord of hosts come down to

fight for mount Zion, and for the hill thereof.

5 As birds flying, so will the Lord of hosts defend Jerusalem; defending also he will deliver *it; and* passing over he will preserve it.

6 Turn ye unto *him from* whom the children of Israel have deeply revolted.

7 For in that day every man shall cast away his idols of silver, and his idols of gold, which your own hands have made unto you *for* a sin.

8 Then shall the Assyrian fall with the sword, not of a mighty man; and the sword, not of a mean man, shall devour him: but he shall flee from the sword, and his young men shall be discomfited.

9 And he shall pass over to his strong hold for fear, and his princes shall be afraid of the ensign, saith the Lord, whose fire is in Zion, and his furnace in Jerusalem.

- Isaiah 31:4–9 -

God will descend to the mountain of Jerusalem to fight for Israel against the Assyrian (v. 4) and the Assyrian will fall when slain by a sword that is not human but divine (v. 8). Other prophecies of the Last Battle give us the same picture, for they see Christ descending upon the Mount of Olives to consume the forces that the Antichrist has brought against Jerusalem (Zech. 14:1–4, 9; Rev. 19:11–19), and they confirm that He will slay them all with the sword from His mouth (2 Thess. 2:8; Rev. 19:20–21).

In Isaiah 30, we learn the ultimate fate of the Antichrist.

For Tophet is ordained of old; yea, for the king it is prepared; he hath made it deep and large: the pile thereof is fire and much wood; the breath of the Lord, like a stream of brimstone, doth kindle it.

- Isaiah 30:33 -

The Assyrian will be cast into the hell called Tophet. The hell currently occupied by the damned is Hades. Tophet is the eternal lake of fire, which Scripture also calls Gehenna. In Revelation, we learn that the first occupants of the lake of fire will in fact be the Antichrist and the false prophet.

And the beast was taken, and with him the false prophet that wrought miracles before him, with which he deceived them that had received the mark of the beast, and them that worshipped his image. These both were cast alive into a lake of fire burning with brimstone.

- Revelation 19:20 -

When Scripture names the Antichrist as the Assyrian, it is presumably informing us that his homeland will be the region of ancient Assyria; that is, northern Iraq.

4. The Book of Revelation teaches that the Antichrist will be a king of Babylon.

10 And the fifth angel poured out his vial upon the seat of the beast; and his kingdom was full of darkness; and they gnawed their tongues for pain,

11 And blasphemed the God of heaven because of their pains and their sores, and repented not of their deeds.

> 12 And the sixth angel poured out his vial upon the great river Euphra-
> tes; and the water thereof was dried up, that the way of the kings of
> the east might be prepared. . . .
> 18 And there were voices, and thunders, and lightnings; and there was a
> great earthquake, such as was not since men were upon the earth, so
> mighty an earthquake, *and* so great.
> 19 And the great city was divided into three parts, and the cities of the
> nations fell: and great Babylon came in remembrance before God, to
> give unto her the cup of the wine of the fierceness of his wrath.
>
> - Revelation 16:10–12, 18–19 -

Now we have come to an especially dense riddle. Most students of
prophecy have equated Babylon in these verses with Rome, for in the
next chapter, the whore who undeniably symbolizes Rome is called
"Mystery, Babylon the Great" (Rev. 17:5 on p. 34). But she is not
Babylon in a literal sense, but rather "Mystery, Babylon." In other
words, while declining to tell us her actual identity, Scripture is revealing that she will be fundamentally the same as Babylon. How
will she be the same? At the beginning of the Tribulation, she will
host world government. Rome then will be the capital of the world,
just as Babylon will be its capital when Christ returns. How do we
know that global political authority will shift from one city to the
other? Here is the decisive text.

> 15 And he saith unto me, The waters which thou sawest, where the
> whore sitteth, are peoples, and multitudes, and nations, and tongues.
> 16 And the ten horns which thou sawest upon the beast, these shall
> hate the whore, and shall make her desolate and naked, and shall eat
> her flesh, and burn her with fire.
> 17 For God hath put in their hearts to fulfil his will, and to agree, and
> give their kingdom unto the beast, until the words of God shall be
> fulfilled.
>
> - Revelation 17:15–17 -

At some point during the Tribulation, the nations of the world under
the leadership of the Antichrist will burn Rome to the ground. Upon
his return from the dead, described in Revelation 13 (Rev. 13:1–5 on
p. 166), the Antichrist will command destruction of Rome as part of
his program to erase all vestiges of Christianity. At the same time he
will transfer his capital to the site of ancient Babylon.

Why there? First and foremost, because it is where Satan scored
a huge victory over mankind by seducing men soon after the Flood
into building the tower of Babel. It is likely where he introduced
them to idol worship and perhaps even to worship of himself. Yet
also the Antichrist will choose Babylon because it lies within his own
homeland.

5. Some popular writers on prophecy have claimed that the Antichrist will emerge from Europe. But prophecy itself, in agreement
with its clear signals that he will come from Seleucid territory,
strongly suggests that he will be a Muslim when he appears on the
world scene. The relevant text is Daniel 11:36–37 (quoted on p. 38).

Although the KJV is a wonderful translation, it is not divinely inspired, and sometimes it makes mistakes. Here we have an example of an especially unfortunate mistake. This text says that the Antichrist will blaspheme the God of gods, an obvious reference to the real God of heaven. Yet he will spurn other gods as well. One in particular will be the "God of his fathers." Another will be "the desire of women." And besides these, he will refuse to "regard any god: for he shall magnify himself above all." In the phrase, "God of his fathers," *God* should not be capitalized, because the writer includes him among the false gods distinct from the real God. The wording sets aside any possibility that the Antichrist will come from a European country where the ancestral deity is the God of Christianity. But it certainly fits the clear warnings in prophecy that he will be a king of the "north," a term pointing to modern Syro-Iraq, where the ancestral deity is not the real Jehovah, but Allah, a false god.

When Satan grooms a Muslim for the role of Antichrist, he will be pursuing a smart strategy. He wants to put his own puppet in the place of world ruler, yet he faces many obstacles to achieving this goal. Chief among them is probably the Muslim world. Muslims are the most factious group in the world today—the group most resistant to leadership foreign to their own culture and religion. Therefore, the easiest way to achieve world government embracing even the Middle East may be to raise a professing Muslim to supreme authority.

Still more information about the political world of the Antichrist emerges from prophecy. During the opening phases of the Tribulation, the dominant events on the world stage will be wars between the king of the north and the king of the south–that is, Egypt.

> 40 And at the time of the end shall the king of the south push at him: and the king of the north shall come against him like a whirlwind, with chariots, and with horsemen, and with many ships; and he shall enter into the countries, and shall overflow and pass over.
> 41 He shall enter also into the glorious land, and many *countries* shall be overthrown: but these shall escape out of his hand, *even* Edom, and Moab, and the chief of the children of Ammon.
> 42 He shall stretch forth his hand also upon the countries: and the land of Egypt shall not escape.
> 43 But he shall have power over the treasures of gold and of silver, and over all the precious things of Egypt: and the Libyans and the Ethiopians *shall be* at his steps.
> 44 But tidings out of the east and out of the north shall trouble him: therefore he shall go forth with great fury to destroy, and utterly to make away many.
> 45 And he shall plant the tabernacles of his palace between the seas in the glorious holy mountain; yet he shall come to his end, and none shall help him.
>
> - Daniel 11:40–45 -

Although its people are followers of Mohammed, Egypt will initially oppose the Antichrist. Likewise among his enemies, the Antichrist will count Muslim nations to the north (presumably, Turkey) and to the east (presumably, Iran) (v. 44). Yet needless to say, the foremost enemy of the Antichrist will be the non-Muslim nation of Israel. After conquering it (v. 41), he will even presume to build his palace on Temple Mount (v. 45).

Yet we argued earlier that when the Antichrist rules the world, his capital will be Rome. How will he transfer his seat of power from the Middle East to Europe? The answer requires a fuller picture of events soon after the Rapture. The world then will be engulfed by wars on a scale mankind has never seen before. The Antichrist's elevation to global authority will doubtless come about as one provision of a final peace settlement.[8]

Never in history did the political landscape foreseen in prophecy become a reality until recently. Who was the first to fulfill the Bible's description of the Antichrist? Saddam Hussein, leader of Iraq, met nearly all the requirements. He fell short mainly because he did not control Syria, and he lacked the personal genius and charisma that the Antichrist will doubtless display to his followers. We might call him a proto-Antichrist. In fact, there have been proto-Antichrists throughout history.

> Little children, it is the last time: and as ye have heard that anti-christ shall come, even now are there many antichrists; whereby we know that it is the last time.
>
> - 1 John 2:18 -

Among them we might name Napoleon and Hitler. Napoleon was such a clear foretaste of the Antichrist that he awakened in many Christians a new interest in prophecy.[9] As we survey world history during the Church Age, it almost seems as if each new proto-Antichrist who appears on the world stage is a closer match to the final Antichrist who will become ascendant in the end times.

Hussein was put out of the way by a coalition of nations under the leadership of the United States. But after his death, yet another proto-Antichrist appeared. It was Abu Bakr al baghdadi, leader of ISIS. After this terrorist group began conquering land in 2014, the former nation of Iraq split apart, with much of the Sunni region in the west coming under the control of ISIS while all the Shiite region in the east remained loyal to the government in Baghdad. For the first time since Israel regained nationhood, a sovereign Muslim state came on the scene with territorial boundaries drawing together parts of Iraq and Syria and with ambition to bring all former Seleucid domains under its control. Moreover, the caliphate governed by Abu Bakr exhibited the other traits that will be seen in the kingdom of the Antichrist. Although Egypt is also Muslim, it has always opposed ISIS. Its leaders have never been friendly to radical Islam of the sort that breeds terrorism. Also, neither Iran nor Turkey welcomed any alliance with the caliphate. And, of course, Abu Bakr and his followers were deeply hateful toward Israel.

At the present time, it appears that ISIS has been driven out of power. For several years under President Obama, the United States did not take decisive military action against Abu Bakr, but after President Trump assumed office, our nation did initiate a strong offensive that succeeded in taking away all of the caliphate's territory. Then, on 10/26/19, American forces succeeded in eliminating Abu Bakr himself. Therefore, history has proved him to be another proto-Antichrist. Yet political dynamics in the Middle East are always poised to create a successor in the same mold. Should American influence and power wane in the region, Satan could easily raise up another charismatic leader to rekindle radical Islam and create another regime with control first over portions of Syria and Iraq and then over a wider region equivalent to the initial kingdom of the Antichrist.

Tenth sign/ The victory of gay rights

To understand the significance of recent court rulings favoring so-called gay rights, we must look at Luke 17:22-37.

> 22 And he said unto the disciples, The days will come, when ye shall desire to see one of the days of the Son of man, and ye shall not see *it*.
> 23 And they shall say to you, See here; or, see there: go not after *them*, nor follow *them*.
> 24 For as the lightning, that lighteneth out of the one *part* under heaven, shineth unto the other *part* under heaven; so shall also the Son of man be in his day.
> 25 But first must he suffer many things, and be rejected of this generation.
> 26 And as it was in the days of Noe, so shall it be also in the days of the Son of man.
> 27 They did eat, they drank, they married wives, they were given in marriage, until the day that Noe entered into the ark, and the flood came, and destroyed them all.
> 28 Likewise also as it was in the days of Lot; they did eat, they drank, they bought, they sold, they planted, they builded;
> 29 But the same day that Lot went out of Sodom it rained fire and brimstone from heaven, and destroyed *them* all.
> 30 Even thus shall it be in the day when the Son of man is revealed.
> . . . .
> 34 I tell you, in that night there shall be two *men* in one bed; the one shall be taken, and the other shall be left.
> 35 Two *women* shall be grinding together; the one shall be taken, and the other left.
> 36 Two *men* shall be in the field; the one shall be taken, and the other left.
> 37 And they answered and said unto him, Where, Lord? And he said unto them, Wheresoever the body *is*, thither will the eagles be gathered together.
>
> - Luke 17:22–30, 34–37 -

As we will demonstrate in the next chapter, a careful examination of verses 34 to 37 leaves no doubt that Jesus is foreseeing the Rapture. In language that is both poetic and dramatic, Jesus describes the event as a sudden disappearance of people here and there followed by eagles coming together at a body. What He surely means is that the people taken from the earth will ascend and gather where the body of Christ is waiting in the sky. The body of Christ is the church (Eph. 1:22–23). But notice where He places the Rapture in history. The days preceding it will resemble the days of Noah (vv. 22-27) and also the days of Lot (vv. 28-33). The saints will escape from this depraved world just as Lot escaped from the depraved city of Sodom.

What was the characteristic and pervasive vice of Sodom? Homosexuality, known throughout history as sodomy. Jesus seems to be giving us a strong hint that the Rapture will remove saints from this world after it has become infected with this particular vice, which Scripture describes as the final tendency of human lawlessness.

> 18 For the wrath of God is revealed from heaven against all ungodliness and unrighteousness of men, who hold the truth in unrighteousness;
> . . . .
> 22 Professing themselves to be wise, they became fools,
> 23 And changed the glory of the uncorruptible God into an image made like to corruptible man, and to birds, and fourfooted beasts, and creeping things.
> 24 Wherefore God also gave them up to uncleanness through the lusts of their own hearts, to dishonour their own bodies between themselves:
> 25 Who changed the truth of God into a lie, and worshipped and served the creature more than the Creator, who is blessed for ever. Amen.
> 26 For this cause God gave them up unto vile affections: for even their women did change the natural use into that which is against nature:
> 27 And likewise also the men, leaving the natural use of the woman, burned in their lust one toward another; men with men working that which is unseemly, and receiving in themselves that recompence of their error which was meet.
>
> - Romans 1:18, 22–27 -

The decision of the Supreme Court on June 26, 2015, to follow the lead of most European countries in legalizing "gay marriage" therefore seems like the fateful rebirth of a world once destroyed, the world of Sodom and Gomorrah. Doubtless we should mark the date as a point of no return to a world still open to the work of God. From now on, the Lord could come at any time to spare our families from ruin by further exposure to a culture degenerate beyond repair.

The ruins of Sodom are likely covered by the waters known as the Dead Sea, which is the lowest point on the face of the planet. It is impossible not to recognize these facts as God's comment on sodomy. Yet we must remember Jesus' grim warning to Jews who rejected Him after seeing His miracles and hearing His teaching.

> 23 And thou, Capernaum, which art exalted unto heaven, shalt be brought down to hell: for if the mighty works, which have been done in thee, had been done in Sodom, it would have remained until this day.
> 24 But I say unto you, That it shall be more tolerable for the land of Sodom in the day of judgment, than for thee.
>
> - Matthew 11:23–24 -

The only unforgivable sin is rejection of Christ.

Application

In the last two chapters of this book we have looked at ten signs of the times—ten developments in the world that have already fulfilled Bible prophecies concerning the Last Days. What do the signs of the times indicate? That Christ is coming soon.

In order to make the proper application to our daily lives, we must recognize that the purpose in studying Bible prophecy is not to tease idle curiosity or provide sensational entertainment. Rather, it is to provoke godly living so that we will be ready to meet Christ.

> 12 Teaching us that, denying ungodliness and worldly lusts, we should live soberly, righteously, and godly, in this present world;
> 13 Looking for that blessed hope, and the glorious appearing of the great God and our Saviour Jesus Christ;
> 14 Who gave himself for us, that he might redeem us from all iniquity, and purify unto himself a peculiar people, zealous of good works.
>
> - Titus 2:12-14 -

Are you ready to meet Him? If you are not saved, He will not take you at His coming. You will be among the masses who are left behind. That is a frightening prospect, for you will be doomed to endure the Tribulation. The world has never gone through anything so terrible. The judgments that will fall from the hand of God defy description. It will be a time of wholesale devastation. The world will collapse into ruins. One of the calamities that will strike the earth will annihilate fully one third of the world's population (Rev. 9:18). No person in his right mind would want to live through that evil hour. It will be a traumatic nightmare in all respects except that it will be real.

How can you escape the Tribulation? Be sure you know Christ. If you do not know Him, you will remain here when all true Christians depart, and you will partake of God's wrath. What does it mean to be a Christian? It does not mean that you go to church. It does not mean that you have been baptized. It does not mean that you have a high opinion of Jesus. No, it means that you have a relationship with Him.

How do you establish such a relationship? By receiving Him as your Lord and Savior.

> . . . Believe on the Lord Jesus Christ, and thou shalt be saved . . . .
>
> - Acts 16:31 -

Jesus is the Lord God who created you, so you have an obligation to serve Him. He is also your Savior. Although He existed forever as God the Son, He forsook heaven with all its privileges and became a man in this world. He lowered Himself by taking on human flesh. Why? So that He might die a horrible death on a cross. In that way He paid the penalty for your sin.

Do you understand that you are a sinner? You break God's law every day, whether by lying or stealing or lusting or hating or denying God His due.

> For all have sinned, and come short of the glory of God;
>
> - Romans 3:23 -

Because of your sin, God cannot take you into His presence when you die, nor can He take you into His presence at the Rapture. You do not deserve to be rewarded with life in a sinless world.

But God does not desire to reject you. He does not desire to punish you by putting you in hell forever. So, He has furnished an alternative, a way of escape. As we said before, all that is required of you is simply to receive Jesus Christ as your Lord and Savior. Accept the salvation that He provided by taking upon Himself the total punishment for your sin. Believe on Him.

Forming the right relationship with Christ is not your whole obligation. It is just the first step in a long journey. As a Christian you will be expected to serve Christ. But if you have truly received Him, you will be willing to go down the road of faithful service.

Footnotes

[1]Rickard, *Daniel*, 167–187.

[2]Ibid., 280–286.

[3]Pope Benedict XVI, *Caritas in Veritate* (n.p.: Libreria Editrice Vaticana, 2009), 5.67.

[4]Pontifical Council for Justice and Peace, "Towards Reforming the International Financial and Monetary Systems in the Context of Global Public Authority" (N.p., 2011), Web (vatican.va/roman_curia/pontifical_councils/justpeace/documents/rc_pc _justpeace_doc_20111024_nota_en.html), 7/17/19.

[5]Pope Francis, *On Care for Our Common Home* (n.p.: Libreria Editrice Vaticana, [2015]), 5.175.

[6]Rickard, *Daniel*, 322–337.

[7]Ibid., 210, 221.

[8]Rickard, *Daniel*, 170, 350–351, 365–371.

[9]Walter K. Price, *The Coming Antichrist,* 2nd ed. (Neptune, N.J.: Loizeaux Brothers, 1985), 37–38.

Chapter 5

✛ Basic Doctrine on Christ's Return ✛

Before we embark on further discussion of signs, we need to present the basic doctrine that serves as foundation for our interpretation of prophecy. This doctrine encompasses eight truths.

1/ The return of Christ is now imminent, just as it has been imminent ever since Christ ascended into heaven.

The so-called doctrine of imminence ("imminent" means soon) is the belief of Christians that Christ will soon return to this world. The Bible texts teaching imminence are too many to be listed here. A few will suffice to show that this doctrine is a major theme of the New Testament.

> For yet a little while, and he that shall come will come, and will not tarry.
>
> - Hebrews 10:37 -

> 7 Be patient therefore, brethren, unto the coming of the Lord. Behold, the husbandman waiteth for the precious fruit of the earth, and hath long patience for it, until he receive the early and latter rain.
> 8 Be ye also patient; stablish your hearts: for the coming of the Lord draweth nigh.
> 9 Grudge not one against another, brethren, lest ye be condemned: behold, the judge standeth before the door.
>
> - James 5:7–9 -

The imminent return of Christ has been a core belief of the church ever since it was founded. Modern skeptics, however, view this belief with scorn. They agree that the New Testament views Christ's return as an event in the near future. But they point out that He has not come back in the nearly two thousand years since the New Testament was written. So, they say, the New Testament is obviously dead wrong—that early Christians were deluded in expecting a quick return of Christ. The teaching of imminence was for them a false promise.

Yet Peter anticipated this attack on the truthfulness of the Bible.

> 3 Knowing this first, that there shall come in the last days scoffers, walking after their own lusts,
> 4 And saying, Where is the promise of his coming? for since the fathers fell asleep, all things continue as *they were* from the beginning of the creation.
> 5 For this they willingly are ignorant of, that by the word of God the

heavens were of old, and the earth standing out of the water and in the water:

6 Whereby the world that then was, being overflowed with water, perished:

7 But the heavens and the earth, which are now, by the same word are kept in store, reserved unto fire against the day of judgment and perdition of ungodly men.

8 But, beloved, be not ignorant of this one thing, that one day is with the Lord as a thousand years, and a thousand years as one day.

9 The Lord is not slack concerning his promise, as some men count slackness; but is longsuffering to us-ward, not willing that any should perish, but that all should come to repentance.

10 But the day of the Lord will come as a thief in the night; in the which the heavens shall pass away with a great noise, and the elements shall melt with fervent heat, the earth also and the works that are therein shall be burned up.

- 2 Peter 3:3–10 -

Peter said that the promise of Christ's return "soon" reflects God's view of time. God reckons a thousand years as no more than a day. Hence, the whole Church Age, from Pentecost until now, has lasted barely two days. From this compressed perspective, the Second Coming will fall within the near future of any moment since the church began.

2/ The right attitude is to remain watchful.

Although God has always known that Christ's return would be delayed thousands of years, He has commanded every believer in every age to watch for it. And as he watches, he should never grow too sleepy to keep looking upward. Rather, he should keep an attitude of expectancy, as if Christ's coming could happen at any moment.

That is our obligation as well. The command to watch for Christ's return is a major feature of the New Testament. Twelve times, in stating our duty as we wait for Him, it uses the word "watch."

Watch therefore: for ye know not what hour your Lord doth come.

- Matthew 24:42 -

Remember, Christ will come more than once. The first time, He will come as a thief and steal away His church. Believers will be caught up at the event known as the Rapture. So, the Rapture is the event that will enable eagerly watching believers to see Christ.

3/ Signs have appeared throughout Church history, and especially recently, that encourage us to hope that the Lord's return is drawing near.

Many modern teachers of Bible prophecy have gone astray in their teaching. They rephrase the doctrine of imminence, making it say not that Christ is coming soon, but that He could come at any time in the future, just as He could have come at any time in the past.

This new teaching is not only erroneous, but dangerous. Its teachers argue that if Christ's return at the Rapture has been possible ever since the Church Age began, then prophecy must be silent about any events preceding the Rapture. In other words, we should not think that the Rapture will follow certain signs marking the approach of the end. The same teachers insist that if there were signs, then the only believers entitled to view Jesus' return as imminent would be those alive after the last sign had come to pass. All believers living earlier in history, before the last sign, would know that it was not yet time for Jesus to come.

How do these teachers explain Peter's warning of scoffers in the Last Days (2 Pet. 3:3 on p. 47) and Paul's warning of perilous times in the Last Days?

> This know also, that in the last days perilous times shall come.
>
> - 2 Timothy 3:1 -

Since both warnings seem addressed to believers living in history's climactic period, neither can accomplish its purpose unless believers then are able to recognize their place in history. To escape from this difficulty, many modern teachers of prophecy argue that such texts describe the whole Church Age—that there have always been scoffers like Peter describes and wicked men like Paul describes. The Last Days, they say, began at Pentecost. The scoffers and wicked men we see in our day merely confirm that we live in the Church Age. They are not a specific sign that the Church Age is drawing to a close.

The claim that there are no signs of Christ's coming has come onto the scene fairly recently. It is a new twist in Bible interpretation. My father's generation as well as earlier generations of fundamentalists firmly believed both in the imminence of Christ's return and in the anticipation of His return by a series of specific signs, and they saw no contradiction between these two beliefs. Which view is correct—the older or the newer? For three reasons I side with my forefathers.

1. The Bible teaches that we will be able to see Christ's return drawing near.

> Not forsaking the assembling of ourselves together, as the manner of some *is;* but exhorting *one another:* and so much the more, as ye see the day approaching.
>
> - Hebrews 10:25 -

> 2 For yourselves know perfectly that the day of the Lord so cometh as a thief in the night.
> 3 For when they shall say, Peace and safety; then sudden destruction cometh upon them, as travail upon a woman with child; and they shall not escape.

> 4 But ye, brethren, are not in darkness, that that day should overtake
> you as a thief.
> 5 Ye are all the children of light, and the children of the day: we are not
> of the night, nor of darkness.
> 6 Therefore let us not sleep, as *do* others; but let us watch and be sober.
>
> - 1 Thessalonians 5:2–6 -

The Lord rebuked the church of Sardis because they did not anticipate the hour of His coming.

> Remember therefore how thou hast received and heard, and hold
> fast, and repent. If therefore thou shalt not watch, I will come on thee as
> a thief, and thou shalt not know what hour I will come upon thee.
>
> - Revelation 3:3 -

In any journey, how do you know that you are getting close to the
end? You rely on signs along the way, each one announcing that you
have come closer to the goal. Likewise, as we go through history, we
see events along the way that mark our progress and assure us that
the end is approaching.

2. There were signs of the times before the first coming of Christ.

> 1 The Pharisees also with the Sadducees came, and tempting desired
> him that he would shew them a sign from heaven.
> 2 He answered and said unto them, When it is evening, ye say, *It will be*
> fair weather: for the sky is red.
> 3 And in the morning, *It will be* foul weather to day: for the sky is red
> and lowring. O *ye* hypocrites, ye can discern the face of the sky; but
> can ye not *discern* the signs of the times?
>
> - Matthew 16:1–3 -

For example, the time of His coming was set by Daniel's prophesy of
sixty-nine weeks.

> Know therefore and understand, *that* from the going forth of the
> commandment to restore and to build Jerusalem unto the Messiah the
> Prince *shall be* seven weeks, and threescore and two weeks: . . . .
>
> - Daniel 9:25 -

And these sixty-nine weeks were nearing completion when Jesus rebuked the religious leaders.[1] If there were signs of His first coming,
should we not expect signs of His second coming? If we ignore them,
we are as blind as the Pharisees and Sadducees.

3. There have already been many signs during the Church Age.
Each has been a fulfilled prophecy showing God's people that the
return of Christ was getting closer. But now, incredibly, the dominant view is that the Bible reveals nothing about the details of history
between Pentecost and the Rapture. This view is convincing only to
the ignorant. Here we will provide just one counterexample. As we
showed on pp. 19–20 and 31, the Old Testament clearly predicts that
Jerusalem would be destroyed soon after the death of the Messiah.
Christ foresaw the same disaster.

41 And when he was come near, he beheld the city, and wept over it,

42 Saying, If thou hadst known, even thou, at least in this thy day, the things *which belong* unto thy peace! but now they are hid from thine eyes.

43 For the days shall come upon thee, that thine enemies shall cast a trench about thee, and compass thee round, and keep thee in on every side,

44 And shall lay thee even with the ground, and thy children within thee; and they shall not leave in thee one stone upon another; because thou knewest not the time of thy visitation.

- Luke 19:41–44 -

(See also Luke 21:20–24 on pp. 19–20.) The city was in fact leveled to the ground in AD 70. The Christians alive in those days could rightly see the event as a sign that history was advancing toward its conclusion.

On my website I show that the early church witnessed other signs as well.[2] In chapters 2 and 3 of this book, I present no less than ten major signs that have appeared in recent history, and in the other chapters I present many more. All these signs have taken the form of datable or roughly datable events. None is a general condition prevailing throughout the Church Age. Hence, the often heard claim that there are no signs of Christ's coming is incorrect.

We still must deal with this question: If the Bible prophesies a long series of events before Jesus' coming, how has the church from earliest times managed to keep an expectant attitude? How has it been able to obey the command to remain watchful, as if Jesus might return at any time? Most Bible teachers today answer the question by denying that the Bible provides signs of Christ's return. But this modern outlook is simplistic and rests on a humanistic assumption— the assumption that we in ourselves can figure out what the Bible teaches. In fact, we cannot figure it out except by the help of the Holy Spirit. Perhaps with the exception of a few godly men, He generally has not allowed the church to predict signs before they occur. Rather, He has brought them to the attention of the church only after they have gone by.

For example, the reemergence of Israel is surely a sign of the approaching end. But before the Jews began returning to Palestine in the nineteenth century, the church did not foresee them regathering there, or imagine that such a regathering must precede Christ's coming. The church did not look for the sign before it appeared.

4/ We now live in the Last Days.

Scripture never provides the exact date of the Second Coming. It tells us only that the event will happen soon. Yet Scripture also suggests that Christ's return will not happen immediately. Rather, there will be some delay. We find this suggestion in many texts, but we will focus on one in particular (2 Pet. 3:3–10 on pp. 47–48). Here, Peter leaves two strong clues that the Second Coming will be postponed a long while.

1. What is Peter's purpose in telling us that God sees a thousand years as a mere passing day? Is he not hinting that the delay before Christ's return might stretch out to thousands of years?

2. He says that before Christ returns, scoffers would aggressively challenge the teachings of the Bible. The day of doubt would arrive long after "the fathers" had died. Who are these fathers? The scoffers who speak of them cannot be referring to their own fathers, because they are treating the time lapse since they died as very long. The scoffers are referring to the fathers of the church, especially the prophets and apostles who were the source of these teachings. In other words, the fathers belong to Peter's generation. So, it is evident that the scoffers would not appear until a time in the distant future.

Notice that the scoffers would regard the founders of the church as their own spiritual fathers. It is evident that in the Last Days a profound disbelief in the Bible would prevail even among those who consider themselves Christian. Although belonging to organized Christianity, they would reject much of what the Bible says. We see, therefore, that Peter agrees with many other prophecies that the church would eventually sink into apostasy.

Peter identifies the period of final apostasy as the Last Days. Like Paul, Peter sets the Last Days in the future. Paul says, "This know also, that in the last days perilous times shall come [future tense[3]]" (2 Tim. 3:1). Likewise, Peter says, "There shall come [future tense[4]] in the last days scoffers" (2 Pet. 3:3). It is therefore evident that the period they intend by the term "Last Days" does not take in the whole Church Age. Rather, they are looking well beyond their own time, when Christianity was still in its infancy, to a distant time when Christianity has gone past its peak into a period of steep decline.

Peter's discussion of the Last Days is the most helpful we have for dating when they began. He says that the most popular teachers in the church of the Last Days would tell fables rather than the truth, and he warns what these fables would be.

He says first that the scoffers of the Last Days would question the Second Coming. The Second Coming is a central teaching of the New Testament. It gives hope to a suffering church that evil in the world will someday be overthrown. Yet Peter makes the shocking prediction that the day would come when many in the church would regard the promise of Christ's coming as no more than an ancient superstition. If we search church history, we find that such skepticism hardly existed before the nineteenth century. Only after the rise of modern liberalism and modern skepticism did multitudes in the church begin to doubt core doctrines of the Bible. We conclude, then, that Peter is looking ahead to the sort of apostasy that has appeared only in modern times. The times in which we live must, therefore, be equivalent to what he calls "the last days."

He says also that in the last days people would question the Genesis accounts of early history. In his outline of the world view that these scoffers would adopt instead, we find three beliefs prevalent today.

1. They would believe in a beginning (v. 4). Indeed, the Second Law of Thermodynamics compels modern science to admit that the universe must have started at a definite time. Modern science tells the following story: "All the matter of the universe was originally squeezed into a huge, superdense fireball. Being supremely unstable, this fireball exploded within a moment after coming into existence, and from the Big Bang, as it is called, all matter and energy raced outward into the vast reaches of space. Today, every celestial body is still moving rapidly away from every other celestial body." This picture of origins is, of course, merely false speculation.

2. They would believe that the history of the earth has never been interrupted by unusual events like the Flood (vv. 5–6). The prophecy has come true. The dominant view of modern science is that all past changes in the earth have been like the gradual changes we see today—that the present condition of the earth owes nothing to great catastrophes, but rather is the end product of a uniform development. The doctrine that the past is like the present is known as uniformitarianism.

3. They would believe in something called "creation" (v. 4). The word can refer to either a creative process or a created thing. In the Greek text, the word is not preceded by a definite article.[5] Verse 4 says only "the beginning of creation." Therefore, the word likely denotes a creative process. What the scoffers would acknowledge is that everything did not suddenly appear in its present form. While rejecting special creation by God, they would believe that a creative process has been at work since the beginning to bring the universe from a state of primordial chaos to the elegant complexity we see today. The doctrine that the universe has undergone such a development is known as evolution. Together, the doctrines of uniformitarianism and evolution imply that the universe is very old.

It is evident that the scoffers who would someday appear within the church and challenge the teachings of the Bible are men of the modern era, living within the last two hundred years. When Peter speaks of the Last Days, he is pointing to the very time in which we live. The view of origins that he describes is the same view promoted by modern science. Paul, looking into the distant future at the science of the Last Days, describes it as fables.

3 For the time will come when they will not endure sound doctrine; but after their own lusts shall they heap to themselves teachers, having itching ears;

4 And they shall turn away *their* ears from the truth, and shall be
turned unto fables.

- 2 Timothy 4:3–4 -

The many warnings in the New Testament that the final state of
the church would be inglorious, as it sank ever deeper into corruption, are intended to strengthen the few believers who would remain
in the Last Days. An understanding of their discouraging circumstances eases their sense of isolation. It assures them that God's
program for the Church Age has not collapsed in failure, but has
unfolded exactly as He said it would. It helps them to guard their
own integrity against the many threats which have overthrown the
integrity of others. And, finally, it encourages them to rejoice that the
Church Age will soon be over, when Christ comes to assert Himself
as King of the world.

In summary, then, to what does the term "last days" refer? As
used by Peter in the passage we have just studied in detail, the term
refers to the time when mankind would adopt a world view that we
recognize as modern skepticism and modern science. It therefore
refers to the whole modern era, beginning about 1800. The rise of a
world view in perfect agreement with Peter's picture of what men
would believe in the Last Days is another major sign that we are approaching the end.

5/ All the developments that Jesus set before the Tribulation have come to pass.

The Olivet Discourse, recorded in Matthew 24 and 25, is Jesus'
extended sermon on prophecy. It was given in response to questions
that certain disciples brought Him concerning the future. They
asked Jesus for "the sign of thy coming, and of the end of the world"
(Matt. 24:3). In reply, Jesus gave a lengthy preview of events preceding His coming in glory.

He divided the Tribulation into two distinct periods, the first
called "the beginning of sorrows" (Matt. 24:8), the second called
"great tribulation, such as was not since the beginning of the world to
this time, no, nor ever shall be" (Matt. 24:21). Yet He not only sur-
veyed chief developments during these periods of earth history after
the church was removed; He also told what would happen during the
period immediately before the Tribulation.

4 . . . Take heed that no man deceive you.
5 For many shall come in my name, saying, I am Christ; and shall deceive many.
6 And ye shall hear of wars and rumours of wars: see that ye be not
troubled: for all *these things* must come to pass, but the end is not
yet.

- Matthew 24:4–6 -

Jesus informed His disciples that the world before the Rapture would have two dominant characteristics: (1) it would be full of religious deceivers (v. 5); (2) its people would hear of wars and rumors of wars (v. 6). We will demonstrate that both prophecies were uniquely fulfilled in the twentieth century, especially after 1948, when the nation of Israel was reestablished and history entered its final hour.

The religious deceivers. Jesus said that they would be recognized by their possession of three attributes.

1. They would "come in my name" (v. 5). That is, they would not be Hindus, theosophists, New Age gurus, or even cult leaders like Sun Myung Moon. Rather, they would claim to be Christians and would be so regarded by the generality of mankind.

2. They would be "many" in number and would "deceive many" (v. 5). Jesus was evidently not talking about madmen or cult leaders. People like Charles Manson and David Koresh are always few in number, and they have limited influence. Rather, Jesus was foreseeing developments in regular organized Christianity.

3. They would say, "I am Christ" (v. 5).

Two movements in the modern church fit these predictions.

1. Since 1900, mainline Protestantism and even segments of Catholicism have been dominated by a theology known as Modernism. The basic tenet of Modernism is that the historical Jesus was no more than a man. From the belief that all humanity shares the essential nature of Christ has followed the presumption that everyone has Christ-potential—that everyone can, by following His example, become His moral and spiritual equal. In whom do the leaders of Modernism believe that Christ-potential is more fully realized than in themselves? Indeed, many among them pose as the very likeness of Christ. Yet though they heap upon themselves and their followers the flattery that they were imitating Christ, knowing Christ, and becoming Christ, they are in fact walking in obedience to their father, the devil.

2. Also after 1900 but even more prominently after 1948, a new brand of deviant Christianity succeeded in gaining millions of adherents. This is the modern tongues-speaking movement, embracing all churches that call themselves Pentecostal or charismatic. Many leaders of this movement pretend that by a mere exhalation of their lips or wave of their hand or chanting of their voice they can communicate the Spirit to others. In effect, they put themselves in Christ's place and virtually say, "I am Christ," for the Spirit proceeds from Him alone (John 15:26; 16:7). The apostles were able to furnish the Spirit to the newly converted Samaritans, but only by prayer exalting Christ as the true giver (Acts 8:15–17), whereas Pentecostal televangelists and their ilk put the camera on themselves, creating the impression that the Spirit moves in obedience to their will. Moreover, as proof of their power, faith healers claim to perform miraculous healings, although these can never be verified, and other preachers

in the same camp point to the bizarre behavior that they can induce in their followers by supposedly giving them the Spirit—behavior interpreted as a sign of the Spirit's presence. The usual sign is the mouthing of meaningless sounds, which is mistaken for speaking in tongues. Other signs are violent agitation of the body, swooning, falling down, or even hysterical laughter. This travesty of true worship hinders any real working of the Spirit to build faith and godliness.

Wars and rumors of wars. Although the prophecy, "And ye shall hear of wars and rumors of wars" (Matt. 24:6), generally describes the whole twentieth century, developments since 1948 furnish a precise fulfillment. The prophecy has three components, each of which has been verified through the unfolding of history.

1. Jesus was evidently foreseeing a time beset by many wars. The year at the outset, 1948, was preceded in the twentieth century by two world wars, the widest and most destructive conflicts the world has ever seen. The second, ending right before 1948, ushered mankind into the era of atomic weapons. Efforts after World War II to build a lasting peace were stymied by nationalistic aspirations in the third world and by unyielding antagonism between the democratic West and the Communist East. Since 1948, wave after wave of strife has erupted upon the sea of nations: the Indian partition, the Chinese Revolution, the Korean War, several Arab-Israeli wars, the civil war in Indonesia, the Vietnam War, the war in Afghanistan, the war in Bosnia, the Gulf War, wars in Africa, wars in Latin America, wars everywhere except in the richest nations. It is obvious that although wars and rumors of wars have been incessant throughout history, bloodshed mounted to a climax in the twentieth century. It has been estimated that in all the wars of human history before 1900, about forty million combatants died. Yet in wars from 1900 to 1987, the comparable tally was about thirty-eight and a half million.[6] By the end of 1999, wars in the twentieth century were more deadly than in all previous centuries combined.

2. Jesus' specific prediction was not that there would be wars, but that mankind would hear about them. In Jesus' day, people in one region of the world had little knowledge of events in regions far away. But today, as a result of modern communications, every war, no matter how remote, reaches the attention of the media and becomes world news. In the last two centuries, and particularly in the last century since the advent of radio, daily reportage has been obsessed with war violence and with diplomatic maneuverings either to avert or resolve it. An important milestone along the way was 1948, because in that year consumer demand for television, invented about twenty years earlier, began to surge. Television added to war news a vividness and immediacy that greatly magnified war's place in public consciousness. Never before had men heard so much about war. Never before had war been such a continuing preoccupation.

3. Not only did Jesus say that there would be wars and that men

would hear about them; He said also that they would hear about rumors of wars. In what other period of history was man as obsessed with the mere possibility of war as he was after atomic bombs fell on Hiroshima and Nagasaki? Throughout the Cold War, fears of a nuclear holocaust haunted mankind. I remember going through civil defense drills as a school child in the early '50s. The purpose was to ready us for nuclear attack. I remember the disbelief and disquiet that followed Sputnik, launched by Russia in the late '50s. I remember also the grim apprehension that gripped America during the Cuban missile crisis in the early '60s. Nuclear war was never more than a rumor, but no other rumor of war has so transfixed the minds of men and so shaped a whole period of history. The easing of tensions between East and West did not, however, bring mankind to a tranquil assurance of future peace. A new worry has emerged to unsettle the minds of people everywhere. After violent Muslim extremism spread to a worldwide theater of operations in the '90s, and especially after 9/11, people in the Western world have been unable to escape from the daily possibility of a terrorist strike close to home. Terrorism has therefore become another menace generating endless rumors of war such as Jesus envisioned in the end time.

From our examination of the Olivet Discourse, we have learned that today's world exactly conforms to the world that Jesus pictures as immediately preceding the Tribulation. Indeed, prophecy gives no hint of anything more that must happen before history enters its next phase, the time of sorrows. The next event on the prophetic calendar is the Rapture.

6/ Although we know generally that we live near the end of the Church Age, we cannot set a date for Christ's return.

Signs are not intended to help us predict when Christ will come. When the nation of Israel was founded in 1948, people in the churches were excited. They felt that Christ might return any day. Yet they were no more able to set the date of His coming than they were before. We will never be able to set the date. Why?

> But of that day and hour knoweth no *man*, no, not the angels of heaven, but my Father only.
>
> - Matthew 24:36 -

The answer is simple. The date is a closely guarded state secret. Anyone who tries to tell us when Christ will come brands himself as a deceiver and a false prophet. There is a compelling reason why God denies us such information.

> But know this, that if the goodman of the house had known in what watch the thief would come, he would have watched, and would not have

suffered his house to be broken up.

- Matthew 24:43 -

"Good man" is old King James wording with no basis in the Greek. The translation renders a single Greek word that does not characterize the man as good or bad. It merely signifies a householder or master of a house.[7] Who is the master of this world? Consider what Jesus said at the Last Supper.

Hereafter I will not talk much with you: for the prince of this world cometh, and hath nothing in me.

- John 14:30 -

Jesus was referring to Satan. Indeed, Satan now sits on the throne of this world, although he is only a usurper who will someday be supplanted by the rightful king, who is Christ. Jesus says the secrecy of His return is a ploy to hamper Satanic opposition. It reflects high strategy in God's war against Satan. We do not know what forces or tactics Satan could employ against the removal of the church from this world, but he will not be able to offer resistance of any kind. Christ will strike as a thief in the night (1 Thess. 5:2 on p. 49). Like a thief, He will take something from another's house—the church out of Satan's kingdom.

7/ At Christ's return, all saints on the earth will suddenly disappear.

The similarity of the returning Christ to a thief in the night yields valuable information.

1. Christ will come by surprise, at a moment no one anticipated.

2. His coming will be without noise or visible display. The saints He removes will just suddenly disappear. No one who scorns the Bible will understand why they disappeared. Immediately the devil will likely come forward with explanations that will satisfy many of the ungodly.

3. He will come at night—that is, when the world is asleep. To be asleep means to be mindless of spiritual things. The Rapture will occur and judgment will commence at a moment when the world as a whole has forgotten God, dismissed His Word as mere fairy tales, and abandoned itself to the worship of self and sin.

37 But as the days of Noe *were*, so shall also the coming of the Son of man be.
38 For as in the days that were before the flood they were eating and drinking, marrying and giving in marriage, until the day that Noe entered into the ark,
39 And knew not until the flood came, and took them all away; so shall also the coming of the Son of man be.

- Matthew 24:37–39 -

For an even fuller picture of the Rapture, we must look again at Luke 17:34-37.

> 34 I tell you, in that night there shall be two *men* in one bed; the one shall be taken, and the other shall be left.
> 35 Two *women* shall be grinding together; the one shall be taken, and the other left.
> 36 Two *men* shall be in the field; the one shall be taken, and the other left.
> 37 And they answered and said unto him, Where, Lord? And he said unto them, Wheresoever the body *is*, thither will the eagles be gathered together.
>
> - Luke 17:34–37 -

Words in italics, such as "women" in verse 35 and "men" in verses 34 and 36, are not in the original. The original speaks only of two in a bed, two grinding together, and two in the field. What do you think these verses are talking about? The great majority of Bible-believing Christians in the modern age have believed that they are speaking of the Rapture.

Proof of this interpretation lies in a careful examination of the Greek original. The word "taken" in verses 34, 35, and 36 is *paralambano*,[8] which means "to take with" or "along."[9] Jesus used the same word on another occasion also. At the Last Supper, He said,

> 2 In my Father's house are many mansions: if *it were* not *so*, I would have told you. I go to prepare a place for you.
> 3 And if I go and prepare a place for you, I will come again, and receive you unto myself; that where I am, *there* ye may be also.
>
> - John 14:2–3 -

The word "receive" is again *paralambano*.[10] The middle clause could be rendered, "I will come again, and take you alongside myself." When will He bring living saints alongside Himself? He will do so when He raptures them. So, if *paralambano* in John 14:3 refers to a rapture, it is reasonable to suppose that the same word in the prophecy, "The one shall be taken," also refers to a rapture.

Three times in Luke 17, Jesus says that "the one shall be taken, and the other left." (vv. 34, 35, 36). The repetition of these solemn words alerted His disciples to their importance. But they could not determine what He meant. It seemed to them that He had omitted some crucial information. So, they asked, "Where, Lord?" (v. 37). They wanted to know where the one will be taken. Jesus obliged them with an answer that must have left them even more perplexed. He said, "Wheresoever the body is, thither will the eagles be gathered together" (v. 37).

All this is rather mysterious because the meaning is hidden behind symbols. What is the body? The body is the body of Christ. What are the eagles? These are saints in their immortal state. Jesus is predicting the great gathering of saints that will take place at the time of Christ's return.

15 For this we say unto you by the word of the Lord, that we which are
alive *and* remain unto the coming of the Lord shall not prevent them
which are asleep.
16 For the Lord himself shall descend from heaven with a shout, with
the voice of the archangel, and with the trump of God: and the dead
in Christ shall rise first:
17 Then we which are alive *and* remain shall be caught up together with
them in the clouds, to meet the Lord in the air: and so shall we ever
be with the Lord.

- 1 Thessalonians 4:15–17 -

The gathering will be "in the air," even "in the clouds" (v. 17). Living
saints will participate in this gathering as a result of being raptured. Thus, Jesus' answer to the question, "Where will the one be
taken?" is not so difficult after all. He says simply that the one will
be taken up into the sky to join all the other saints assembling before
Christ at His return—Christ and all His saints together comprising
His body.

Notice that the eagle is a fitting symbol of what every saint will
become, for in our immortal state we will be able to fly unfettered by
gravity. Moreover, like the eagle, we will have a distinctly noble
bearing and will dwell in the highest places. And just as the eagle
has a remarkable keenness of vision, so we will have access to all
treasures of wisdom and knowledge. Several texts underscore the
resemblance between the eagle and the perfected saint. When
speaking of God as a source of blessing, the psalmist says,

Who satisfieth thy mouth with good *things;* so *that* thy youth is re-
newed like the eagle's.

- Psalm 103:5 -

This promise is best understood as a promise of immortality. Just as
an eagle retains the vigor of youth, so the saints of God will stay
youthful forever. We find a similar promise in the Book of Isaiah.

But they that wait upon the LORD shall renew *their* strength; they
shall mount up with wings as eagles; they shall run, and not be weary;
and they shall walk, and not faint.

- Isaiah 40:31 -

Not only will the saints be able by self-renewal to overcome every
manner of weakness; they will "mount up with wings as eagles." In
other words, they will be able to ascend the sky, as they will do at the
time of the Rapture.

Some Bible students treat Luke 17:37 as parallel in meaning to
the passage where Jesus describes His glorious descent at the end of
the Tribulation.

27 For as the lightning cometh out of the east, and shineth even unto
the west; so shall also the coming of the Son of man be.
28 For wheresoever the carcase is, there will the eagles be gathered together.

- Matthew 24:27–28 -

But the texts in Matthew and Luke are contrastive rather than parallel. In Luke, Jesus says that eagles will be gathered at the "body" (soma,[11] which refers to a living body[12]). In Matthew, Jesus says that eagles will be gathered at the "carcase" (ptoma,[13] which refers to a dead body, a corpse[14]). The latter prediction will be fulfilled when Christ overpowers His enemies at Armageddon. Who will follow Christ as He descends at His second coming? The army of heaven, consisting of all the saints.

> 11 And I saw heaven opened, and behold a white horse; and he that sat upon him *was* called Faithful and True, and in righteousness he doth judge and make war.
> 12 His eyes *were* as a flame of fire, and on his head *were* many crowns; and he had a name written, that no man knew, but he himself.
> 13 And he *was* clothed with a vesture dipped in blood: and his name is called The Word of God.
> 14 And the armies *which were* in heaven followed him upon white horses, clothed in fine linen, white and clean.
> 15 And out of his mouth goeth a sharp sword, that with it he should smite the nations: and he shall rule them with a rod of iron: and he treadeth the winepress of the fierceness and wrath of Almighty God.
> 16 And he hath on *his* vesture and on his thigh a name written, KING OF KINGS, AND LORD OF LORDS.
>
> Revelation 19:11–16

To this army gazing down upon the battlefield, the slaughtered millions will seem almost like a single carcass.

8/ The Rapture will occur when the world feels confident that it can overcome the problems threatening mankind.

Paul gives a very brief but very informative picture of the world scene at the time of the Rapture.

> 2 For yourselves know perfectly that the day of the Lord so cometh as a thief in the night.
> 3 For when they shall say, Peace and safety; then sudden destruction cometh upon them, as travail upon a woman with child; and they shall not escape.
>
> - 1 Thessalonians 5:2–3 -

Why, despite the mounting toll of natural disasters, the contagion of violence and social unrest, and the prospect of even worse calamities in the future, will people be saying, "Peace and safety?" Paul's words are a strong hint that right before Jesus returns, something will happen on the world stage that, with the blaring voice of the media, will be presented to people everywhere as a decisive step forward in meeting all the threats to survival of modern civilization. We can only speculate what the supposed advance will be. Perhaps national leaders will come together and agree on an agenda that they believe will avert catastrophe. Perhaps at the same time they will strengthen the governing power of the United Nations to assure enforcement of this agenda. Again, we can only speculate, but Paul's words clearly anticipate dramatic moves by politicians leading to an illusion shared by all peoples that man's problems will be solved by man himself. This descent of relative calm upon the sea of nations may be the last sign that the Tribulation is near.

Footnotes

[1]Rickard, *Daniel,* 228–279.

[2]Ed Rickard, "Signs during the Apostolic Era," *Bible Studies at the Moorings,* Web (themoorings.org/Bible_prophecy/apostolic_era.html), 6/24/20; Ed Rickard, "Other Signs at the Beginning of the Church Age," *Bible Studies at the Moorings,* Web (themoorings.org/Bible_prophecy/early_centuries.html), 6/24/20.

[3]Berry, 752; *The Analytical Greek Lexicon* (London: Samuel Bagster and Sons, Ltd., n.d.; repr., New York: Harper & Brothers Publishers, n.d.), 141.

[4]Berry, 831; *Lexicon,* 152.

[5]Berry, 831.

[6]R. J. Rummel, *Death by Government* (New Brunswick, N.J.: Transaction Publishers, 1994), 3, 71.

[7]Berry, 96; Arndt and Gingrich, 560.

[8]Berry, 287.

[9]Arndt and Gingrich, 624–625.

[10]Berry, 390.

[11]Ibid., 287.

[12]Arndt and Gingrich, 806–807.

[13]Berry, 95.

[14]Arndt and Gingrich, 735.

Chapter 6

+ Parables of the Kingdom +

In our chapter on seven easy signs of the times, we showed that prophecy foresees the church declining into apostasy before Christ returns. For further evidence of apostasy in the Last Days, let us turn to Matthew 13, which records eight parables of Jesus known as the Parables of the Kingdom. The leading traditional interpretation assumes that they furnish a prophetic overview of the Church Age, and a careful study of them individually would support this interpretation. But such a study is unnecessary to advance our present discussion, since we only need to consider the two parables picturing the church in the Last Days. These are the third, the Parable of the Mustard Seed, and the fourth, the Parable of the Leaven.

Parable of the Mustard Seed

The third is a vignette from gardening.

> 31 Another parable put he forth unto them, saying, The kingdom of heaven is like to a grain of mustard seed, which a man took, and sowed in his field:
> 32 Which indeed is the least of all seeds: but when it is grown, it is the greatest among herbs, and becometh a tree, so that the birds of the air come and lodge in the branches thereof.
>
> - Matthew 13:31–32 -

We argued in an earlier chapter that the plant of phenomenal growth, starting from the smallest of seeds and rising to preeminence in the garden, represents the church, for the church indeed began exceedingly small, as only 120 in the Upper Room. Yet the church—or, more precisely, nominal Christianity—has indeed become the largest religion in the world. Here we will not review the statistics concerning the stature of Christianity among world religions. But we will say again that this is a remarkable prophecy. Two thousand years ago, before the church even existed, Jesus knew that He was founding a religious movement that would continue and prosper until it overshadowed all rivals.

Also in that earlier chapter, we showed that Jesus explained how the professing church would become so large. The dominance of Christianity over other religions would come about through worldwide evangelism. In His last instruction to the disciples, He clearly stated that before He returns, the whole world will hear the gospel.

> But ye shall receive power, after that the Holy Ghost is come upon

you: and ye shall be witnesses unto me both in Jerusalem, and in all
Judaea, and in Samaria, and unto the uttermost part of the earth.

- Acts 1:8 -

The gospel would go even to the uttermost part of the earth. Then we
showed that if the uttermost part is understood as the place furthest
from Jerusalem, the prophecy has been fulfilled. The island closest
to the opposite point on the globe was evangelized in 1826.

Many expositors have leaped to the conclusion that the Parable of
the Mustard Seed paints a glorious future for the church—a future of
steady progress toward the goal of making all men servants of
Christ. This interpretation reinforced the dream of many Christians
in days past that the church would march steadily onward to total
victory over heathenism and unbelief. Every nation would become a
Christian nation, and every citizen of the earth would take Christ as
his sovereign. Then when Christ returned, everyone, everywhere,
would be joyously waiting to receive Him.

The fallacy in this dream is that it does not square with the actual teaching of Scripture. Nowhere in Scripture do we find a prediction that Christianity will flourish until it conquers the
world. Instead, Scripture predicts that when Jesus returns, He will
find the church in a sad state, in a state characterized by weakness
and decay rather than by health and progress.

The weakness of the church in its final days is clearly shown even
in the Parable of the Mustard Seed. It unquestionably anticipates
miraculous growth in the church, but if Jesus meant to portray the
church in its last stages as something beautiful, He certainly chose
strange imagery. Probably He is referring to the plant known as
black mustard (*Brassica nigra*).[1] A mature plant of this species ex-
cites no one's admiration. Its growth is rank. Its form in the
autumn, after spreading upward and outward from a woodlike stem,
is ungainly. The foliage is coarse and weedy. The pretty little flowers
of spring have disappeared. The seedpods are bereft of the color or
lusciousness or pleasant odor that commends other kinds of fruit.[2]

Black mustard is best known in our day as a pest. According to
the *Los Angeles Times,* it is "a terrible invasive species" in places like
California because "it germinates early in winter before native plants
have taken hold, shoots up more than 6 feet tall, hogs the sunlight
with its thick stalks and lays down a deep system of roots that beats
out native plants for water." Even worse, it "is likely to dry up in the
summer months, providing dangerous fuel for wildfires." Also, "because the stalks are taller than grass," mustard can "act as a 'fire
ladder,' carrying flames to taller trees."[3] It certainly appears likely
that in Jesus' choice of a mature mustard plant to represent the end-
time church, He was warning us that a decadent popular Christianity
will displace healthier forms and bring down fires of judgment.

At the very least, His picture of the church in its final stages
leads us to doubt that all will be well. Indeed, to underscore that the

outward success of the church will be accompanied by spiritual decline, He says that "birds ['*peteina*'[4]] of the air" will lodge in its branches. To decipher the riddle, we must accept that in His literary inventions, Jesus is a masterful craftsman. For example, when He uses the same symbol in similar contexts, He retains the same meaning. It is therefore significant that in a companion parable, the Parable of the Sower, fowls (Matt. 13:4; '*peteina*' again[5]) represent, literally, "the wicked" (Matt. 13:19), a term comprehending both the devil and the demonic spirits under his control. We infer that the birds in the Parable of the Mustard Seed represent "the wicked" also. Another proof of Jesus' craftsmanship is that every symbol He chooses is appropriate. The fitness of birds to symbolize spiritual beings who can fly about at great speed thus confirms our interpretation. Jesus' purpose in calling them "birds of the air" may be to connect them with "the prince of the power of the air" (Eph. 2:2).

The birds that roost in the branches of the mustard plant show something evil infiltrating the latter-day church. No doubt they represent demons working through men of influence to introduce corruptions in doctrine and practice. Paul speaks of the false teachings that will someday creep into the church as "doctrines of devils" (1 Tim. 4:1).

We conclude that although the Parable of the Mustard Seed is, on its surface, optimistic, the actual meaning of the parable is that the church in its final stages will lapse into weakness and apostasy.

Parable of the Leaven

Although compressed into a mere twenty-four words, the Parable of the Leaven is full of prophetic teaching.

> Another parable spake he unto them; The kingdom of heaven is like unto leaven, which a woman took, and hid in three measures of meal, till the whole was leavened.
>
> - Matthew 13:33 -

The fourth parable is similar to the third, since both speak of something growing to full extent. R. C. Trench, who wrote *Notes on the Parables of Our Lord,* alleged that the spread of leaven through the lump pictures the spread of the gospel through the world.[6] He said also that the woman who mixes the leaven with the dough is the church. So interpreted, the parable supports the once popular view that the church will eventually convert the whole world to Christ. It is not surprising to find this view in the writings of an Anglican archbishop from the Victorian era. As a loyal member of the British establishment, Trench believed that Britain and the other colonial powers would succeed in bringing all mankind within the bounds of Christian civilization. But today, when the influence of the church is rapidly dwindling, few Christians retain Trench's optimistic vision of its future.

Yet, to reach a valid interpretation of this parable, we should look not to changeable historical circumstances, but to Scripture, for Scripture explains itself. By relying upon its supernatural light, we see that Trench's treatment of the symbols in this parable is untenable. The woman cannot be the church. The lump cannot be the world. And the leaven cannot be the gospel.

The Leaven

Scripture always associates leaven with evil. Before celebrating Passover and the Feast of Unleavened Bread, the people of Israel were required to go through their houses and remove every trace of leaven.

> Seven days shall ye eat unleavened bread; even the first day ye shall put away leaven out of your houses: for whosoever eateth leavened bread from the first day until the seventh day, that soul shall be cut off from Israel.
>
> - Exodus 12:15 -

This ritual depicted their need to remove sin from their lives before they sought fellowship with God.

Paul says,

> 6 Your glorying *is* not good. Know ye not that a little leaven leaveneth the whole lump?
> 7 Purge out therefore the old leaven, that ye may be a new lump, as ye are unleavened. For even Christ our passover is sacrificed for us:
> 8 Therefore let us keep the feast, not with old leaven, neither with the leaven of malice and wickedness; but with the unleavened *bread* of sincerity and truth.
>
> - 1 Corinthians 5:6-8 -

Paul says again,

> 7 Ye did run well; who did hinder you that ye should not obey the truth?
> 8 This persuasion *cometh* not of him that calleth you.
> 9 A little leaven leaveneth the whole lump.
>
> - Galatians 5:7–9 -

We have said already that as a literary craftsman of surpassing genius, Jesus was consistent in His use of imagery. Therefore, to find out the meaning of leaven in His fourth Kingdom Parable, we need only look at how He used leaven elsewhere in His teaching. There are three other occurrences, and in each case, as we will show later in this chapter, the leaven represents something evil that enters and corrupts the work of God. How then could it be anything else in the Parable of the Leaven?

Consider what leaven is. The chemical reactions that cause a lump of dough to rise are the work of minute vegetable organisms called yeast, a type of fungus. A distinctive property of all fungi is their lack of chlorophyll. As nongreen plants, they are incapable of making their own food. They must draw nourishment from other organisms, whether living or dead. Parasitic fungi—those that feed on living organisms—may cause death of the host. Saprophytic fungi—those that feed on dead organic matter, such as the wooden timbers of a house—produce decay. Yeast is a saprophytic fungus that converts bread sugars into alcohol (which disappears during baking) and carbon dioxide, a gas. Notice that the leavening effect of the yeast depends on its destruction of a nourishing and flavorful food substance. As an agent of destruction and decay, leaven is a fitting symbol for something evil. Thus, leaven cannot represent the gospel.

Yet our conclusion raises a natural question. If leaven is truly evil, why does Jesus say that "the kingdom of heaven is like unto" it. The object of comparison is not leaven by itself, however. It is the whole scene showing a woman at work to prepare food. As in all the other Parables of the Kingdom, this scene pictures the future work of building the church during the Church Age. But unlike most of the others, the parable of the leaven passes over the early stages. It says nothing about the woman's labor in preparing, assembling, and mixing good ingredients. Rather, like its companion and closest parallel, the Parable of the Mustard Seed, it focuses on the last stages of church history. Instead of using birds to represent evil, it uses leaven.

The Lump

What is the lump of dough? It is not the world. It is the church. Notice again the passage we just quoted to illustrate the meaning of leaven (1 Cor. 5:6–8). Paul compares his readers—that is, the church—to a lump purged of leaven by the death of Christ.

But if Scripture is consistent in its use of symbols, how can bread represent the church? Jesus said of Himself that He was bread.

> And Jesus said unto them, I am the bread of life: he that cometh to me shall never hunger; and he that believeth on me shall never thirst.
>
> - John 6:35 -

We must remember that Christ is joined to His church in a perfect union often described as a marriage. The church is His bride.

> 7 Let us be glad and rejoice, and give honour to him: for the marriage of the Lamb is come, and his wife hath made herself ready.
> 8 And to her was granted that she should be arrayed in fine linen, clean and white: for the fine linen is the righteousness of saints.
>
> - Revelation 19:7–8 -

Together they are one flesh.

> 29 For no man ever yet hated his own flesh; but nourisheth and cher-
> isheth it, even as the Lord the church:
> 30 For we are members of his body, of his flesh, and of his bones.
> 31 For this cause shall a man leave his father and mother, and shall be
> joined unto his wife, and they two shall be one flesh.
> 32 This is a great mystery: but I speak concerning Christ and the
> church.
>
> - Ephesians 5:29–32 -

Notice what Jesus said concerning His own flesh.

> I am the living bread which came down from heaven: if any man eat
> of this bread, he shall live for ever: and the bread that I will give is my
> flesh, which I will give for the life of the world.
>
> - John 6:51 -

It is therefore not at all strange that in Scripture, the Bride united
with His flesh is also symbolized as bread.

> 16 The cup of blessing which we bless, is it not the communion of the
> blood of Christ? The bread which we break, is it not the communion
> of the body of Christ?
> 17 For we *being* many are one bread, *and* one body: for we are all
> partakers of that one bread.
>
> - 1 Corinthians 10:16–17 -

As we have said before, the symbols that Scripture employs are always appropriate. The underlying thought here is that bread is the
staff of life. Jesus is bread because, through His death, He is the life-
giver to all who believe. The church is bread because it comprises all
those who show Christ to the world and who bring the world to
Christ, where they find life.

The Woman

If the woman in the Parable of the Leaven is responsible for the
church becoming thoroughly infected with evil, she cannot be the
church itself. Rather, she represents all those with special responsibility to oversee and nurture the church—in other words, church
leaders. As we said earlier, the parable gives no attention to her con-
structive work before she adds leaven. The reason is that in the early
stages of church history, the most prominent leaders would be godly
men fulfilling God's program. But Jesus' presentation of the woman
solely as a leavener foretold that soon would come leaders ambitious
not for the gospel, but for worldly success—leaders who would introduce corruptions that would eventually permeate Christendom.

Jesus Himself identified the woman who emerged later in church
history.

> 6 Then Jesus said unto them, Take heed and beware of the leaven of

> the Pharisees and of the Sadducees. . . .
>
> 11 How is it that ye do not understand that I spake *it* not to you concerning bread, that ye should beware of the leaven of the Pharisees and of the Sadducees?
>
> 12 Then understood they how that he bade *them* not beware of the leaven of bread, but of the doctrine of the Pharisees and of the Sadducees.
>
> - Matthew 16:6, 11–12 -

From this we understand that the woman represents all those Pharisees and Sadducees who introduce or promote false doctrine in the church. Who are the Pharisees and Sadducees? In Jesus' day, they were the leaders of Jewish religion. Although both groups sprang from a godly heritage, each had corrupted the truth and were leading people astray.

The party of the Sadducees had adopted a skepticism toward the supernatural. They accepted only the books of Moses as canonical. They disbelieved in angels, in miracles, and in a bodily resurrection. Their counterparts in the world today are the proponents of theological liberalism, a system of religious thought that casts aside the beliefs of historic Christianity. Liberalism treats the Bible as a collection of folk writings rather than as the inspired, inerrant Word of God. It regards Jesus as a good man with a spark of divinity rather than as the only Son of God. And it denies the existence of anything unrecognized by modern science. As liberal preachers and teachers spread their pernicious doctrines, they are taking the role of the woman who mixes leaven into the lump.

The Pharisees in Jesus' day were the conservative party of Jews. They not only tenaciously adhered to all the regulations in the law of Moses; they also imposed many additional regulations and duties upon themselves and their followers. But they failed to prize those virtues most desired by God: faith, justice, and mercy.

> Woe unto you, scribes and Pharisees, hypocrites! for ye pay tithe of mint and anise and cummin, and have omitted the weightier *matters* of the law, judgment, mercy, and faith: these ought ye to have done, and not to leave the other undone.
>
> - Matthew 23:23 -

Worst of all, they failed to comprehend that a man becomes right with God not by his own works, but by divine grace in answer to his repentance.

> 10 Two men went up into the temple to pray; the one a Pharisee, and the other a publican.
>
> 11 The Pharisee stood and prayed thus with himself, God, I thank thee, that I am not as other men *are,* extortioners, unjust, adulterers, or even as this publican.
>
> 12 I fast twice in the week, I give tithes of all that I possess.
>
> 13 And the publican, standing afar off, would not lift up so much as *his* eyes unto heaven, but smote upon his breast, saying, God be merciful to me a sinner.

> 14 I tell you, this man went down to his house justified *rather* than the
> other: for every one that exalteth himself shall be abased; and he that
> humbleth himself shall be exalted.
>
> - Luke 18:10–14 -

Modern Pharisees include all who advocate a theological system that pretends to uphold the Bible, but substitutes human merit for divine merit as the basis of salvation. We find many Pharisees among the Roman Catholics and the cultists. We find them also in the multitudes of nominal Christians who say that they believe the Bible, but also that they plan to reach heaven by observing the Golden Rule. All who teach salvation by works will stand trial as corrupters of the church.

Yet the leaven in the lump is not false doctrine only. Jesus also says,

> In the mean time, when there were gathered together an innumerable multitude of people, insomuch that they trode one upon another, he began to say unto his disciples first of all, Beware ye of the leaven of the Pharisees, which is hypocrisy.
>
> - Luke 12:1 -

Thus, another form of leaven is hypocrisy. Here Jesus omits any reference to the Sadducees, because their religion was at least honest in its unbelief. The Sadducees were vile infidels, but they were not hypocrites. The Pharisees, however, pretended to obey God's Word down to the smallest letter and slightest nuance. But, as Jesus pointed out, while they gave the Lord a tithe from their handfuls of herb pickings (Matt. 23:23 on p. 69), they robbed widows.

> Woe unto you, scribes and Pharisees, hypocrites! for ye devour widows' houses, and for a pretence make long prayer: therefore ye shall receive the greater damnation.
>
> - Matthew 23:14 -

And they slew the righteous.

> 33 *Ye* serpents, *ye* generation of vipers, how can ye escape the damnation of hell?
> 34 Wherefore, behold, I send unto you prophets, and wise men, and scribes: and *some* of them ye shall kill and crucify; and *some* of them shall ye scourge in your synagogues, and persecute *them* from city to city:
> 35 That upon you may come all the righteous blood shed upon the earth, from the blood of righteous Abel unto the blood of Zacharias son of Barachias, whom ye slew between the temple and the altar.
>
> - Matthew 23:33–35 -

Hypocrisy, then, is another form of the evil that will permeate the church. We see it today wherever the private life of a Christian leader is tainted by scandal or corrupt dealings. Any who waves a Bible before his adoring followers and then goes out to seek worldly pleasure, or commit adultery, or forge relationships with unrighteous men of power, or cut shady financial deals, or plot the ruin of a godly critic is a spreader of leaven. He too partakes in the diabolical work of the woman.

Jesus points to yet another source of danger.

> And he charged them, saying, Take heed, beware of the leaven of the Pharisees, and *of* the leaven of Herod.
>
> - Mark 8:15 -

Herod stands in place of all rulers. The leaven of Herod represents any undesirable influence that secular government exerts upon the church. If the will of the state is contrary to the will of God, the church must obey God, or else it will shut souls out of the Kingdom.

Herod tried to silence Christ by sending agents to intimidate Him.

> 31 The same day there came certain of the Pharisees, saying unto him, Get thee out, and depart hence: for Herod will kill thee.
> 32 And he said unto them, Go ye, and tell that fox, Behold, I cast out devils, and I do cures to day and to morrow, and the third *day* I shall be perfected.
> 33 Nevertheless I must walk to day, and to morrow, and the *day* following: for it cannot be that a prophet perish out of Jerusalem.
>
> Luke 13:31–33 -

Had Christ listened to them, leaven would have crept into His ministry.

Today, the church must resist many pressures from the state. One grave threat is the persistent attempt to bring the rearing of Christian children under greater state control. Another is the threat of legal penalties if churches continue to treat homosexuality as sin.

Jesus' use of a woman to depict the various forces arrayed against the purity of the church—the Pharisees, the Sadducees, and Herod—might, to some readers, seem curious. But His choice of imagery is by no means arbitrary. The woman in this parable appears elsewhere in prophecy. As we showed in our discussion of the eighth easy sign of the times—the pope's emergence as a promoter of world government—Revelation 17 speaks of a harlot called Mystery Babylon (Rev. 17:5), who chiefly pictures the Roman Catholic Church that will dominate so-called Christianity and other religions during the early portion of the Tribulation. (The only religion later will be worship of the Antichrist.) She is therefore an embodiment of false Christianity. In relation to the Bride, the embodiment of true Christianity, she is a counterfeit (Rev. 17:1–6 on pp. 33–34). Because of her faithfulness to Christ, the Bride is chaste and blameless, but the woman called Mystery Babylon, because of her traffic with other lovers, is a harlot. Through her fornication with the kings of the earth (v. 2), she has given birth to "abominations" (v. 5).

In its broader meaning, this evil mother pictures all churchmen down through the centuries who have used their influential position in society to accrue power and wealth for themselves. Hence in Jesus' parable, all Pharisees and Sadducees who mix leaven into the lump appear as a woman. Lust for unholy gain drives them to corrupt the church with false doctrine, hypocrisy, and compromising concessions to power-hungry rulers. Such concessions have often in the past led to creation of a state church.

Because leaveners would be a continuing and pervasive source of trouble, Jesus warned, "The kingdom of heaven is like unto leaven, which a woman took, and hid in three measures of meal, till the whole was leavened" (Matt. 13:33). The correct interpretation?

1. The woman in her act of leavening the lump is, as we have said, a symbol of corrupt leaders and teachers.

2. Her act is called hiding because, according to Peter, "there shall be false teachers among you, who privily shall bring in damnable heresies" (2 Pet. 2:1). In other words, false teachers always disguise themselves as the true successors of Jesus.

3. The leaven is described as affecting the whole lump because evil will, in fact, spread throughout the church until at last, in the days before Christ's return, it will reach everywhere. The whole church will be touched by it. It will be pervasive, like the final stages of a terminal cancer.

Warning to men in leadership

The unscrupulous leaders who will dominate the end-time church face an unspeakably gruesome punishment.

42 And the Lord said, Who then is that faithful and wise steward, whom *his* lord shall make ruler over his household, to give *them their* portion of meat in due season?
43 Blessed *is* that servant, whom his lord when he cometh shall find so doing.
44 Of a truth I say unto you, that he will make him ruler over all that he hath.
45 But and if that servant say in his heart, My lord delayeth his coming; and shall begin to beat the menservants and maidens, and to eat and drink, and to be drunken;
46 The lord of that servant will come in a day when he looketh not for *him,* and at an hour when he is not aware, and will cut him in sunder, and will appoint him his portion with the unbelievers.
47 And that servant, which knew his lord's will, and prepared not *himself,* neither did according to his will, shall be beaten with many *stripes.*
48 But he that knew not, and did commit things worthy of stripes, shall be beaten with few stripes. For unto whomsoever much is given, of him shall be much required: and to whom men have committed much, of him they will ask the more.

- Luke 12:42–48 -

45 Who then is a faithful and wise servant, whom his lord hath made

ruler over his household, to give them meat in due season?

46 Blessed *is* that servant, whom his lord when he cometh shall find so doing.

47 Verily I say unto you, That he shall make him ruler over all his goods.

48 But and if that evil servant shall say in his heart, My lord delayeth his coming;

49 And shall begin to smite *his* fellowservants, and to eat and drink with the drunken;

50 The lord of that servant shall come in a day when he looketh not for *him,* and in an hour that he is not aware of,

51 And shall cut him asunder, and appoint *him* his portion with the hypocrites: there shall be weeping and gnashing of teeth.

- Matthew 24:45–51 -

The resurrection and judgment of most of the wicked will take place at the end of Christ's Millennial reign on the earth (Rev. 20:11–15). But Christ will not wait until the end of the Millennium to deal with men who have misused their leadership over the flock of God. The passage cited here shows that He will mete out their punishment when the church comes before His judgment seat.

The servant who misused his authority out of ignorance will be mildly punished. The one who deliberately failed to exercise proper leadership will be severely punished. And the rank hypocrite posing as a servant of God will be cut to pieces and cast into hell.

What church leader aware of this warning would dare step out of line? Only that man whose male egotism led him not just to doubt the Bible, but even to feel cocksure that the Bible could not possibly be true.

Conclusion

Far from teaching that the church will conquer the world, the Parable of the Leaven reveals that the evil world system will conquer the church. Enemies of Christ will lodge corruptions in the church that will progressively diffuse throughout the whole lump. The word "whole" quite pointedly informs us that no part of the church will escape these corruptions. Yet we should not look upon this prophecy as pessimistic, for two reasons.

First, the end-time decline of the church is a necessary prelude to that moment when Christ will come and gather all His saints, both living and dead, who have proved themselves faithful to their Lord. And this event in turn will be a necessary prelude to that later moment when Christ will come with all His saints, riding in battle array behind Him, to deal all His enemies a crushing defeat. So, the apostasy we see now is only a temporary setback on the eve of a glorious victory.

Second, although the general condition of today's church is apostasy, there remains the possibility of local and limited revivals, such as occurred in the nation of Judah during the last fifty years before final destruction of Jerusalem (2 Chron. 34–35).

Footnotes

[1]Henk P. Medema and Lytton John Musselman, "Mustard," Bible Plants, Web (ww2.odu.edu/~lmusselm/plant/bible/mustard.php), 9/26/19.

[2]"Wild Mustard," Survival Weekly, Web (survivalweekly.com/719/wild-mustard/), 9/26/19.

[3]"This Super Bloom Is Pretty Dangerous: Invasive Mustard Is Fuel for the Next Fire," Los Angeles Times, Web (latimes.com/local/lanow/la-me-ln-mustard-fire-santa-monica-mountains-20190425-story.html), 9/26/19.

[4]Berry, 49.

[5]Ibid., 46.

[6]Richard Chenevix Trench, *Notes on the Parables of Our Lord,* popular ed. (n.p., 1861; repr., Grand Rapids, Mich.: Baker Book House, 1948), 43-44.

Chapter 7

+ Pictures of the Last Days +

In a previous chapter we looked at one of the most important signs that the return of Christ is near: the sign of apostasy. Then in the last chapter, when we examined Jesus' overview of the Church Age in His Parables of the Kingdom (Matt. 13), we found that two of these, the Parable of the Mustard Seed and the Parable of the Leaven, give clear pictures of the church of the Last Days and that both see it as fallen into an apostate condition. Let us now look at some other New Testament texts that predict apostasy in the Last Days.

A disappearance of faith from the earth

When Jesus Himself contemplated conditions on the earth at the time of His coming, He asked the question, "When the Son of man cometh, shall he find faith on the earth?" (Luke 18:8b). He would not have asked the question if the right answer was, yes. The question is rhetorical. It is designed to lead the hearer to a particular answer. Since the question raises doubt that faith will be found on the earth, the implied answer is, "Maybe not." Jesus is therefore warning us that in the final stages of church history, the church will sink so low that vital faith will all but disappear.

If we look at His question in context, we find that He had just told the story of a widow who, after suffering some harm at the hands of an adversary, sought the help of a local judge.

> 1 And he spake a parable unto them *to this end,* that men ought always to pray, and not to faint;
> 2 Saying, There was in a city a judge, which feared not God, neither regarded man:
> 3 And there was a widow in that city; and she came unto him, saying, Avenge me of mine adversary.
> 4 And he would not for a while: but afterward he said within himself, Though I fear not God, nor regard man;
> 5 Yet because this widow troubleth me, I will avenge her, lest by her continual coming she weary me.
> 6 And the Lord said, Hear what the unjust judge saith.
>
> - Luke 18:1–6 -

Because the judge did not provide justice at first, the widow went to him time after time until he viewed her as something of a pest. To get rid of her, he finally came to the decision she sought. Jesus offered her as an example for Christians in their prayer life. He said,

> 7 And shall not God avenge his own elect, which cry day and night unto

him, though he bear long with them?
8 I tell you that he will avenge them speedily. Nevertheless when the
  Son of man cometh, shall he find faith on the earth?

- Luke 18:7–8 -

Jesus' gaze forward to the spiritual condition of this world when He
returns implies that He is speaking especially to believers living at
that time. In light of the preceding parable, His words appear intended to teach them two important lessons.

1. They will face a world so abusive of real Christians that they
will be entirely justified in seeking divine vengeance on their enemies.

Yet Jesus is not advising us to pray for God's wrath to be poured
on specific individuals who have wounded us personally. He said
elsewhere,

43 Ye have heard that it hath been said, Thou shalt love thy neighbour,
   and hate thine enemy.
44 But I say unto you, Love your enemies, bless them that curse you, do
   good to them that hate you, and pray for them which despitefully use
   you, and persecute you;
45 That ye may be the children of your Father which is in heaven: for he
   maketh his sun to rise on the evil and on the good, and sendeth rain
   on the just and on the unjust.
46 For if ye love them which love you, what reward have ye? do not even
   the publicans the same?
47 And if ye salute your brethren only, what do ye more *than others?* do
   not even the publicans so?
48 Be ye therefore perfect, even as your Father which is in heaven is
   perfect.

- Matthew 5:43–48 -

The words "avenge" in verses 3, 5, 7, and 8 of Luke 18 represent
slightly different constructions in Greek. All four use a form of the
word *ekdikeo* (εκδικεω), which truly means "avenge." [1] Luke later
uses another form of the same word in his description of events before Christ descends in glory to establish Himself as world ruler.

20 And when ye shall see Jerusalem compassed with armies, then know
   that the desolation thereof is nigh.
21 Then let them which are in Judaea flee to the mountains; and let
   them which are in the midst of it depart out; and let not them that
   are in the countries enter thereinto.
22 For these be the days of vengeance, that all things which are written
   may be fulfilled.
23 But woe unto them that are with child, and to them that give suck, in
   those days! for there shall be great distress in the land, and wrath
   upon this people.
24 And they shall fall by the edge of the sword, and shall be led away
   captive into all nations: and Jerusalem shall be trodden down of the
   Gentiles, until the times of the Gentiles be fulfilled.
25 And there shall be signs in the sun, and in the moon, and in the
   stars; and upon the earth distress of nations, with perplexity; the sea
   and the waves roaring;
26 Men's hearts failing them for fear, and for looking after those things

> which are coming on the earth: for the powers of heaven shall be
> shaken.
> 27 And then shall they see the Son of man coming in a cloud with power
> and great glory.
>
> - Luke 21:20-27 -

In reference to either the whole Tribulation or its horrific climax, Luke anticipates "days of vengeance" (v. 22). "Vengeance" is *ekdikeseos* (εχδιχησεως), another variant of *ekdikeo*.[2] The divine vengeance that Luke foresaw after the Rapture therefore has the same meaning as the vengeance that God promises to provide for His mistreated children in the Last Days. What should we conclude? In Luke 18:7-8, Jesus' message to end-time believers targeted by wicked men must be that if they pray earnestly, from hearts rich in faith, for God to avenge them, He will answer by moving history into the next phase of His divine plan. He will remove them at the Rapture, and immediately afterward He will begin to sweep disaster across a wicked world.

2. Although God speedily avenges His downtrodden people if they "cry day and night unto him," Jesus asks, "When the Son of man cometh, shall he find faith on the earth?" We cannot avoid the conclusion that in the Last Days, there will be few professing Christians with enough faith to implore God for deliverance from their enemies.

Both lessons imply a severely weakened form of Christianity. The organized church will then lack enough leverage in society to stave off persecution. Also, most of those Christians who remain will react to persecution not by looking above with hearts of faith and seeking divine help, but by fending it off by means of compromises in doctrine and practice.

The question in verse 8 at the basis of this bleak picture refers especially to the kind of faith that produces fervent and effective prayer. Do you give prayer a generous portion of your time?

A great falling away

As we pointed out in chapter 5, one strong current in modern Bible study is denial that the Bible tells us anything about the Last Days before Christ's return. There are supposedly no signs of His coming. In this chapter we will continue to build a strong case against this popular way of handling key texts.

Of critical importance is the following passage in Second Thessalonians.

> 1 Now we beseech you, brethren, by the coming of our Lord Jesus
> Christ, and *by* our gathering together unto him,
> 2 That ye be not soon shaken in mind, or be troubled, neither by spirit,
> nor by word, nor by letter as from us, as that the day of Christ is at
> hand.
> 3 Let no man deceive you by any means: for *that day shall not come,*

> except there come a falling away first, and that man of sin be re-
> vealed, the son of perdition;
>
> 4 Who opposeth and exalteth himself above all that is called God, or
> that is worshipped; so that he as God sitteth in the temple of God,
> shewing himself that he is God.
>
> 5 Remember ye not, that, when I was yet with you, I told you these
> things?
>
> 6 And now ye know what withholdeth that he might be revealed in his
> time.
>
> 7 For the mystery of iniquity doth already work: only he who now let-
> teth *will let,* until he be taken out of the way.
>
> 8 And then shall that Wicked be revealed, whom the Lord shall con-
> sume with the spirit of his mouth, and shall destroy with the bright-
> ness of his coming:
>
> - 2 Thessalonians 2:1–8 -

Those who deny any signs during the Church Age find Paul's words extremely troublesome. Why? Because he speaks of something that must happen before the day of Christ. According to Paul, the day of Christ starting with the Rapture will come after a falling away (v. 3). "Falling away" renders the Greek word *apostasia*.[3] In other words, as we showed in our presentation of the sixth easy sign that Christ is coming soon, the Rapture will be preceded by apostasy in the church.

Bible teachers who reject signs have found various ways to skirt the plain sense of this passage. Many agree that an *apostasia* will precede the Day of Christ, but say that the word has been mis-translated as "falling away." Rather, it should be translated "depar-ture," which they give as the root meaning of the word. Moreover, they say that the departure Paul has in mind is the departure of the church at the Rapture, and the meaning of verse 3 is that the Rap-ture will precede the Day of Christ.

The chief difficulty in this interpretation of the verse is that the meaning of a word is determined not by its derivation, but by its us-age. When we investigate how *apostasia* was used in the first cen-tury, we discover that the word meant not simply departure, but de-parture in the sense of betrayal or rebellion. We find this more spe-cific meaning in the only other occurrence of *apostasia* in the New Testament.

> And they are informed of thee, that thou teachest all the Jews which
> are among the Gentiles to forsake [literally, 'teachest apostasy from'[4]]
> Moses.
>
> - Acts 21:21 -

Likewise, the word means "apostasy" in every one of its many occur-rences in the Septuagint (the ancient Greek translation of the Old Testament).[5] Every authoritative Greek dictionary defines *apos-tasia* as "apostasy."[6]

Some Bible teachers who deny the existence of signs adopt yet another interpretation of verse 3. They translate the verse this way:

"For that day will not come, except there come a falling away," wording that leaves us uncertain whether the falling away will come before or during the day. According to these teachers, the meaning Paul intends is that the falling away will occur during the day, serving as evidence that it has already begun. In other words, the sense of the verse is that we should not think the Tribulation has begun until we see one of its opening events, which is apostasy in the church.

But these teachers are ignoring a key word. The Greek text of verse 3 clearly says that in relation to the Day of Christ, the apostasy must come "first." "First" is *proton,* which cannot mean anything else but "first."[7] An event can be the first of two only if it <u>happens</u> first— in other words, only if the first comes <u>before</u> the second. Thus, the word "first" clearly disallows any attempt to place the apostasy at the beginning of the Day of Christ.

Our study of Scripture must proceed with an unbiased openness to what it is really saying. If we try to make it fit preconceived ideas derived from our teachers or based on our preferences, we will never grasp the whole counsel of God. An honest reading of 2 Thessalonians 2:1–8 leaves no doubt that the Rapture will be preceded by general apostasy in the church.

Only a form of godliness

We will next unearth the important teaching in another key text concerning the Last Days.

> 1 This know also, that in the last days perilous times shall come.
> 2 For men shall be lovers of their own selves, covetous, boasters, proud, blasphemers, disobedient to parents, unthankful, unholy,
> 3 Without natural affection, trucebreakers, false accusers, incontinent, fierce, despisers of those that are good,
> 4 Traitors, heady, highminded, lovers of pleasures more than lovers of God;
> 5 Having a form of godliness, but denying the power thereof: from such turn away.
>
> - 2 Timothy 3:1–5 -

The majority view of Bible teachers in my father's generation was that these verses refer especially to our own time. But as we showed in chapter 5, it is the view of many Bible teachers today that they describe the whole Church Age, from Pentecost to the return of Christ. We also showed, however, that Peter explicitly sets the Last Days at a time far in the future (2 Pet. 3:3–7).

So does Paul here in Second Timothy. Remember that Paul himself lived in the Church Age. Yet, in referring to the Last Days, he uses a verb in the future tense. "Perilous times shall come."[8] And he maintains the same tense throughout his discussion of the Last Days; specifically, in verses 2 and 13 of chapter 3 and verses 3 and 4 of chapter 4.[9] He obviously thought that the Last Days had not yet arrived, but would arrive in the future.

The context leaves no doubt that Paul places the Last Days at the end of the Church Age. A few verses later, he says,

> But evil men and seducers shall wax worse and worse, deceiving, and being deceived.
>
> - 2 Timothy 3:13 -

Paul evidently believed that conditions during church history would slide ever deeper into corruption, as more and more people came under the influence of unscrupulous deceivers. Such men, called "evil men and seducers" would "wax worse and worse, deceiving and being deceived." He evidently foresaw a day when the very worst self-deceivers and deceivers of others would control multitudes in the church. Publicly, such men would be convincing examples of real Christians, but privately, they would wallow in the depths of abomination. Paul gives no hint that better leaders would follow the worst. The only trend he foresaw was downward. Thus, the worst must emerge at the very end of church history. We infer that Paul views the end of church history as the last days of special peril. He therefore agrees with many other prophecies that before Christ returns, the church would fall into a condition of general apostasy.

In the next chapter of Second Timothy, Paul gives an expanded picture of the time when the very worst deceivers would arise.

> 3 For the time will come when they will not endure sound doctrine; but after their own lusts shall they heap to themselves teachers, having itching ears;
> 4 And they shall turn away *their* ears from the truth, and shall be turned unto fables.
>
> - 2 Timothy 4:3–4 -

In this graphic description of the poisonous teaching that would plague the church of the Last Days, Paul places the blame where it belongs. False teachers would succeed in becoming influential only because the church would warmly embrace them. Churchgoers would "heap to themselves teachers, having itching ears."

Those who would be intolerant of sound doctrine are compared to dogs. Like dogs, they would follow anyone, regardless of his character, who stoops to scratch them behind the ears. We can carry the analogy a bit further. They would be doglike also in not being fussy about what they eat. They would chew with pleasure on any teaching that gratifies carnal appetites.

Back in chapter 3, after his warning in verse 1 of perilous times in the Last Days, Paul proceeds in the following verses to provide a list of traits that would then be characteristic of religious people (2 Tim. 3:2–5). We find no reference here to murder, rape, or any other high felony, because Paul is speaking about people in general. He is describing not the criminal minority, but the respectable majority—not the atypical, but the average. Ordinary people in ordinary churches would be egotistical ("lovers of their own selves," "boasters," "proud," "heady," "highminded"), irreverent ("blasphemers"), materialistic ("covetous" is, literally, "lovers of money"), and hedonistic ("unholy," "incontinent," "lovers of pleasures"). They would enjoy few loving relationships, for they would be "disobedient to parents" and "without natural affection." Yet they would readily make enemies, for they would be "unthankful," "trucebreakers," and "traitors." And they would treat their enemies ruthlessly, for they would be "fierce" and "false accusers." Being "despisers of those that are good," they would persecute the righteous.

Despite this load of wickedness weighing on their souls, they would pretend to be Christians ("having a form of godliness"). But, as Paul observes, they would know nothing of real Christianity. They would be guilty of "denying the power thereof." A slightly clearer translation would be "rejecting the power thereof."[10] That is, they would reject the power of God to change their lives. Instead of aspiring to holiness through divine grace, they would prefer to remain in their filthiness.

Is this the situation we find in churches today? The answer is clearly, yes. Within my lifetime I have seen within churches generally a drastic loss of good character. Many who profess Christ today are indeed selfish and self-centered, obsessed with gaining more of the world's pleasure and prosperity, difficult to get along with, as prone as unbelievers to quarrel with family and to separate from a spouse. Some years ago, the famous preacher Warren Wiersbe wrote a book entitled *The Integrity Crisis.*[11] He complained that pragmatism, profiteering, and immorality are plaguing the church at the highest levels. Unfortunately, he is right. Yet corruption behind the pulpit is merely a reflection of corruption in the pew. Men of poor character are rising to lead churches and church bodies because men of good character are in short supply.

Paul's admonition to sincere believers in the Last Days is, "From such turn away." He does not mean that we should count ourselves perfect and separate from Christian brothers who happen to be imperfect. No, he means that we should turn away from churches and Christian organizations infected with the kind of moral decay he describes. Comfort, reputation, and every other human consideration might urge us to continue in fellowship with hypocrites, but to maintain fellowship with God, and to defend our families from attacks that would spoil their faith, we must make the break. We must turn away. But where should we go? We must attach ourselves to a band of genuine believers, however small it may be. Then, having placed ourselves in a good church, we must work diligently to keep it a good church. We must do our part to weed out corruption and compromise as soon as they appear.

Only a few left who are looking for His coming

It would be well for us to heed Christ's words in the Olivet discourse.

> Therefore be ye also ready: for in such an hour as ye think not the Son of man cometh.
>
> - Matthew 24:44 -

He is not saying that we cannot predict the exact moment when He will return. Our inability to mark the date does not in any way prevent us from eagerly and joyfully looking forward to the event, and such anticipation expresses itself in a strong hope that He will come at the very next moment. In the forward vision of all Christians who long to see the Lord, the next moment is a time when His return is very possible. They are far from thinking that His return so soon is very unlikely or downright impossible. Yet, according to Jesus, many who will read His words in the Last Days will be confident that they are not living on the verge of His coming. Why will they lack expectancy? For some, the reason might be ignorance. But for the rest, the reason will be either that they are too caught up in this world to want His return, or that they do not believe in a literal Second Coming.

During my lifetime I have seen a sharp decline of interest in Bible prophecy. What is the result of this trend? Many Christians today, especially in the younger generation, are not watching for Christ to return. They are certainly not expecting Him to return at any moment.

What we have discovered, therefore, is yet another sign that Christ's return must be very near. The sign? Fewer and fewer professing Christians are waiting eagerly for this glorious climactic event.

Footnotes

[1] Berry, 287–288; Arndt and Gingrich, 238.

[2] Berry, 303.

[3] Ibid., 731; Arndt and Gingrich, 266.

[4] Ibid., 512.

[5] Arndt and Gingrich, 97.

[6] Ibid.; Joseph Henry Thayer, *A Greek-English Lexicon of the New Testament,* corrected ed. (N.p.: Harper & Bros., 1889; repr., New York: American Book Co., n.d.), 67; *An Intermediate Greek-English Lexicon,* founded upon Liddell and Scott's *Greek-English Lexicon,* 7th ed. (New York: Harper & Brothers, 1889), 107.

[7] Arndt and Gingrich, 732–734.

[8] Berry, 752; *The Analytical Greek Lexicon* (London: Samuel Bagster and Sons, Ltd., n.d.; repr., New York: Harper & Brothers Publishers, n.d.), 141.

[9] Berry, 752–754.

[10] Berry, 752–753; Arndt and Gingrich, 107.

[11] Warren W. Wiersbe, *The Integrity Crisis,* expanded ed. with study guide (Nashville, Tenn.: Oliver-Nelson, 1991).

Chapter 8

+ The Days of Noah +

The apostasy before the Flood

To help us understand the time in which we live, the time known as the Last Days, Jesus used an enlightening comparison. Let us further explore the Olivet Discourse.

> 37 But as the days of Noe *were,* so shall also the coming of the Son of man be.
> 38 For as in the days that were before the flood they were eating and drinking, marrying and giving in marriage, until the day that Noe entered into the ark,
> 39 And knew not until the flood came, and took them all away; so shall also the coming of the Son of man be.
> 40 Then shall two be in the field; the one shall be taken, and the other left.
> 41 Two *women shall be* grinding at the mill; the one shall be taken, and the other left.
>
> - Matthew 24:37–41 -

Jesus compared the days before His coming to the days of Noah, implying that His coming will coincide with judgment and calamity on a scale comparable to the Flood, which destroyed almost all life on the earth. The days of Noah resembled His coming not only in their apocalyptic climax, but also, as Jesus said, in the condition of human society just beforehand. In other words, men in the Last Days will descend to the same deplorable wickedness that God saw in the world before the Flood.

The sin at the root of all sinfulness before the Flood was apostasy—that is, departure from the truth and righteousness that the people had learned from their godly fathers. In the days of Adam's grandson Enos, men began "to call upon the name of the LORD" (Gen. 4:26), but later, 1500 years after man was created, God could find only one man, Noah, who was just and perfect.

> 5 And GOD saw that the wickedness of man *was* great in the earth, and *that* every imagination of the thoughts of his heart *was* only evil continually.
> 6 And it repented the LORD that he had made man on the earth, and it grieved him at his heart.
> 7 And the LORD said, I will destroy man whom I have created from the face of the earth; both man, and beast, and the creeping thing, and the fowls of the air; for it repenteth me that I have made them.
> 8 But Noah found grace in the eyes of the LORD.
> 9 These *are* the generations of Noah: Noah was a just man *and* perfect

in his generations, *and* Noah walked with God.

- Genesis 6:5–9 -

Ultradispensationalism

In recent years, an approach to prophecy has become popular which denies that the Olivet Discourse has anything to say about events just preceding the rapture of the church. A passage generating radically different interpretations is the one just quoted in Matthew 24. Luke offers a parallel passage, which we discussed at some length in chapter 5.

> 34 I tell you, in that night there shall be two *men* in one bed; the one shall be taken, and the other shall be left.
> 35 Two *women* shall be grinding together; the one shall be taken, and the other left.
> 36 Two *men* shall be in the field; the one shall be taken, and the other left.
> 37 And they answered and said unto him, Where, Lord? And he said unto them, Wheresoever the body *is,* thither will the eagles be gathered together.

- Luke 17:34–37 -

Now what do you think these two passages are talking about? The answer that springs to the mind of most believers is, the Rapture. Can anyone offer another interpretation? What you have offered me is the traditional view. But there are Bible teachers today who would disagree with you.

The interpretation of these passages has taken a new turn. At one time, most Bible students believed that "the one . . . taken" will be the privileged one—that he will be taken to heaven while the other will be left behind to suffer the wrath of God. They inferred that Jesus was describing the rapture of the church. Now, however, some Bible teachers hold a different position. They believe that the one taken will go to judgment, while the one left behind will be made a citizen of Christ's Kingdom.

The recent shift of opinion in certain quarters reflects the emergence of a new school of Bible interpretation which many dissenters call ultradispensationalism.[1] Like the older school generally known as dispensationalism, this recent offshoot recognizes that God's program for the Jews stands apart from His program for the gentiles. Yet it goes out of bounds in many claims. For example, its followers view the teachings of Jesus as addressed primarily to Jewish people living under Mosaic law. Such a perspective leads to denial that any of His prophetic discourses speaks to believers during the coming Church Age. Rather, passages such as the two we have quoted lay out the future experience of Jews during the Tribulation, after the church has been removed from the world.

Ultradispensationalists theorize, "The very end of the Tribulation will bring a separation between the godly and the ungodly. God will send His angels to carry away all the ungodly to judgment and eternal damnation. The ungodly will suddenly disappear from the face of the earth, and the godly will remain to pay homage to Christ."

So, ultradispensationalists deny that Matthew 24:37–41 and Luke 17:34–37 are talking about a future rapture of the church. To read any rapture into these passages is, they say, a basic mistake. In their view, these passages are predicting not a rapture, but a judgment. Moreover, they deny any connection between the days of Noah and the Last Days of the Church Age. They say that the days of Noah are a picture of the world during the Tribulation. Are they right? I think not. I think the devil has been working overtime to keep people from understanding these vital passages—passages intended for the instruction of believers living in our time.

Rebuttal

Five reasons demand that we reject the ultradispensational interpretation of Matthew 24:37–41 and Luke 17:26–37.

1. Look at the state of the world at the time previewed in these passages. We see two men in the field. Presumably they are doing some sort of agricultural work. We also see two women grinding at the mill. Again, nothing out of the ordinary. And we see two people in bed asleep. What do these snapshots suggest about life on the earth at this time? They suggest life as usual. We see only the normal activities of people, activities of a kind that flourish in a time of peace and tranquillity.

But it will not be life as usual at the end of the Tribulation. Just consider some of the last plagues.

> 1 And I heard a great voice out of the temple saying to the seven angels, Go your ways, and pour out the vials of the wrath of God upon the earth.
> 2 And the first went, and poured out his vial upon the earth; and there fell a noisome and grievous sore upon the men which had the mark of the beast, and *upon* them which worshipped his image.
> 3 And the second angel poured out his vial upon the sea; and it became as the blood of a dead *man:* and every living soul died in the sea.
> 4 And the third angel poured out his vial upon the rivers and fountains of waters; and they became blood.
> 5 And I heard the angel of the waters say, Thou art righteous, O Lord, which art, and wast, and shalt be, because thou hast judged thus.
> 6 For they have shed the blood of saints and prophets, and thou hast given them blood to drink; for they are worthy.
> 7 And I heard another out of the altar say, Even so, Lord God Almighty, true and righteous *are* thy judgments.
> 8 And the fourth angel poured out his vial upon the sun; and power was given unto him to scorch men with fire.
> 9 And men were scorched with great heat, and blasphemed the name of God, which hath power over these plagues: and they repented not to give him glory.

- Revelation 16:1–9 -

When the First Vial is poured upon the earth, "a noisome and grievous sore" will fall upon all men who wear the mark of the Beast (v.
2). What type of sore it will be, we cannot imagine. But evidently it
will be very painful, and it will afflict most inhabitants of the
earth. Then the second angel will pour out his vial upon the sea,
which will become "as the blood of a dead man" (v. 3). In consequence, every living thing in the sea will die. When the third angel
pours out his vial, all the fountains of water—that is, all the underground sources—will become as blood also. The next angel, the
fourth, will pour out his vial upon the sun. John's alarming obser-
vation that "power was given unto him to scorch men with fire" (v. 8)
suggests a sudden catastrophic rise in the temperature of the earth.

The sensible question is this. When the people of the earth are
suffering from grievous sores, shortages of good water, and burning
heat, will they persist in their regular work? Will men still go out to
the field and tend crops? Will women still go out to the yard and mill
grain? Of course not. Few crops will survive the terrible plagues.
Moreover, few people will feel like working. Sick from sores, thirst,
and heat, most people will lie in misery upon their beds. The few ro-
bust enough to stay active will huddle indoors during the day rather
than face the relentless sun. Consider what Jesus said about the
conditions prevailing at the end of the Tribulation.

> 21 For then shall be great tribulation, such as was not since the begin-
> ning of the world to this time, no, nor ever shall be.
> 22 And except those days should be shortened, there should no flesh be
> saved: but for the elect's sake those days shall be shortened.
>
> - Matthew 24:21–22 -

It is obvious that the wretched climax of this harrowing time will
force suspension of normal activities.

We conclude that the scenes of two in the field and two at the
mill—these being scenes of life as usual—must belong to another period
of history. The attempt by ultradispensationalists to make them fit
the end of the Tribulation is unreasonable.

As a side note, Jesus' prophecy in Luke says that while two are
sleeping in bed, others will be outside hard at work. What knowledge
does the Lord display here that skeptics cannot explain? Unlike everyone else in the ancient world, He understood that the earth is
round and that people live on both sides, with night on one side and
day on the other.

2. The notion that only the wicked will be taken for judgment at
the end of the Tribulation does not agree with the plain teaching of
Scripture. Scripture says that in the transitional period between the
Tribulation and the Millennium, both the wicked and the righteous
will be taken for judgment. What they will face is described in Jesus'
Olivet Discourse.

> 31 When the Son of man shall come in his glory, and all the holy angels

with him, then shall he sit upon the throne of his glory:

32 And before him shall be gathered all nations: and he shall separate them one from another, as a shepherd divideth *his* sheep from the goats:

33 And he shall set the sheep on his right hand, but the goats on the left.

34 Then shall the King say unto them on his right hand, Come, ye blessed of my Father, inherit the kingdom prepared for you from the foundation of the world:

35 For I was an hungred, and ye gave me meat: I was thirsty, and ye gave me drink: I was a stranger, and ye took me in:

36 Naked, and ye clothed me: I was sick, and ye visited me: I was in prison, and ye came unto me.

37 Then shall the righteous answer him, saying, Lord, when saw we thee an hungred, and fed *thee?* or thirsty, and gave *thee* drink?

38 When saw we thee a stranger, and took *thee* in? or naked, and clothed *thee?*

39 Or when saw we thee sick, or in prison, and came unto thee?

40 And the King shall answer and say unto them, Verily I say unto you, Inasmuch as ye have done *it* unto one of the least of these my brethren, ye have done *it* unto me.

41 Then shall he say also unto them on the left hand, Depart from me, ye cursed, into everlasting fire, prepared for the devil and his angels:

42 For I was an hungred, and ye gave me no meat: I was thirsty, and ye gave me no drink:

43 I was a stranger, and ye took me not in: naked, and ye clothed me not: sick, and in prison, and ye visited me not.

44 Then shall they also answer him, saying, Lord, when saw we thee an hungred, or athirst, or a stranger, or naked, or sick, or in prison, and did not minister unto thee?

45 Then shall he answer them, saying, Verily I say unto you, Inasmuch as ye did *it* not to one of the least of these, ye did *it* not to me.

46 And these shall go away into everlasting punishment: but the righteous into life eternal.

- Matthew 25:31–46 -

The people brought to this judgment will be "all nations" (v. 32). We should not, however, imagine that each nation will be judged as a unit. In judging the United States, for instance (assuming the United States still exists), Christ will not relegate all its people to the same destiny. Look at what He approves and what He condemns. He approves acts of personal kindness, and He condemns acts of personal unkindness. So, obviously, as justice would indeed require, He is judging the nations one person at a time. No doubt some in every nation will be placed among the sheep, some among the goats.

Where will the nations be gathered? The place will be the Valley of Jehoshaphat.

1 For, behold, in those days, and in that time, when I shall bring again the captivity of Judah and Jerusalem,

2 I will also gather all nations, and will bring them down into the valley of Jehoshaphat, and will plead with them there for my people and *for* my heritage Israel, whom they have scattered among the nations, and parted my land.

- Joel 3:1–2 -

The name for the place of gathering is probably an ancient name for
the valley directly east of Jerusalem. Gathered by whom? By the
angels. Who will be gathered? All nations. So, at the end of the
Tribulation, both the wicked and the righteous will be taken for
judgment. The idea that only the wicked will be taken, while the
righteous will be excused from judgment and left at their homes, is
utterly false. Yet the angels will no doubt restore the righteous to
their homes after they have heard Christ's invitation to live in His
kingdom.

3. People who favor the ultradispensational interpretation of
Matthew 24:37–41 and Luke 17:26–37 say, "In Matthew 24, look at
the verses preceding verses 40 and 41—at verses 38 and 39." These
ultradispensationalists reason, "The ones taken by the Flood were
destroyed. In a sense, they were taken to judgment. So, the taking
mentioned in the next verse, verse 40, where it says, 'the one shall be
taken,' must be a taking to judgment also."

The hole in this argument is that although verses 39 and 40 may
look similar in an English translation, they do not look similar in the
Greek. The word "took" in verse 39 is entirely unrelated to the word
"taken" in verse 40. The word in verse 39 is *airo,* which means to
take in the sense of forcible removal.[2] The word in verse 40 is, as we
said in an earlier chapter, *paralambano,* which suggests taking to
oneself.[3] It is evident that the words are not close synonyms.
Whereas the one is suitable for describing the destructive effects of a
flood, the other is suitable for describing a rapture.

4. The explanation of verses 40 and 41 in Matthew 24 lies not in
the preceding verse, describing the Flood in Noah's day, but in the
next verses.

> 42 Watch therefore: for ye know not what hour your Lord doth come.
> 43 But know this, that if the goodman of the house had known in what
> watch the thief would come, he would have watched, and would not
> have suffered his house to be broken up.
>
> - Matthew 24:42–43 -

Verse 42 answers the obvious question raised by the prediction that
"the one shall be taken." The question is, by whom? The answer is,
by the thief—in other words, by Christ. When Christ returns to catch
away His church, He will be a thief intruding on the domain of another. The Bible teaches that Satan is presently the ruler and prince
of this world. On the eve of His crucifixion, Jesus said,

> Hereafter I will not talk much with you: for the prince of this world
> cometh, and hath nothing in me.
>
> - John 14:30 -

Paul said,

> 1 And you *hath he quickened,* who were dead in trespasses and sins;
> 2 Wherein in time past ye walked according to the course of this world,

according to the prince of the power of the air, the spirit that now
worketh in the children of disobedience:

- Ephesians 2:1–2 -

Thus, in Matthew 24:40–41, the selective taking of one here and there is not a taking to judgment, but a taking to heaven.

5. Three times in Luke 17:26–37, Jesus says that "the one shall be taken, and the other left." The disciples asked, "Where, Lord?" (v. 37). Jesus answered, "Wheresoever the body is, thither will the eagles be gathered together" (v. 37). As we taught in chapter 5, the meaning is hidden behind symbols. But they are not difficult to interpret. What is the body? The body is the body of Christ. What are the eagles? The eagles are saints in their glorified bodies. What is the gathering? It is not a removal to judgment, but a lifting upward of these eagles to join all the other saints assembling "in the air" (1 Thess. 4:17) before Christ at His return. The lifting will be accomplished at the event known as the Rapture. The host of saints together with Christ will manifest His body.

Footnotes

[1] "What Is Ultra-Dispensationalism?" Got Questions, Web (gotquestions.org/ultra-dispensationalism.html), 5/8/20.

[2] Arndt and Gingrich, 23–24.

[3] Ibid., 624–625.

Chapter 9

✛ Parallels with the Days of Noah ✛

Days of Noah

We showed in an earlier chapter that Jesus in the Olivet Discourse draws a comparison between the days before His return and the days before the Flood.

> 37 But as the days of Noe *were,* so shall also the coming of the Son of man be.
> 38 For as in the days that were before the flood they were eating and drinking, marrying and giving in marriage, until the day that Noe entered into the ark,
> 39 And knew not until the flood came, and took them all away; so shall also the coming of the Son of man be.
>
> - Matthew 24:37–39 -

According to Jesus, the days of Noah had three principal characteristics: 1) eating and drinking; 2) marriage and giving in marriage; 3) ignorance of impending judgment. Jesus' presentation leaves little doubt that this ignorance flowed naturally from everyone's preoccupation with life in the present moment. Especially absorbing were those activities which in all societies have been proven sources of pleasure and satisfaction: namely, eating, drinking, marrying, and giving in marriage.

Likewise in the world today, a desire to enjoy the present moment is the driving force behind what many people think and do, and they are pursuing this goal much as people did before the Flood, but often in perverted ways. Instead of finding satisfaction in healthy amounts of food and drink, they are reluctant to stop before they have gorged themselves. Instead of being content with the sexual intimacy provided by marriage, they are exploring all the dark paths of adultery. Immoral sex and overconsumption at dining tables are becoming addictions. One grievous result, as before the Flood, is that men are so focused on the world today that they are blind to the judgment that will fall tomorrow. Jesus found the same fault in Sodom, where "they did eat, they drank, they bought, they sold, they planted, they builded; But the same day that Lot went out of Sodom it rained fire and brimstone from heaven, and destroyed *them* all" (Luke 17:28–29).

Eating and drinking

Although the poorer classes in many regions of the world live continually on the verge of famine, the more prosperous members of society enjoy the unprecedented wealth created by modern industry and technology. They have plenty of food and drink, as well as plenty of the other necessities. But instead of being content with a good life based on moderation, they are using their wealth to build a lifestyle that includes eating and drinking to excess. We have three kinds of data showing that overindulgence has certainly captured America.

Amount of food consumed. Between 1957 and 2000, per capita food consumption in America (as estimated by the total food marketed for domestic consumption without consideration of wastage) rose from 3000 to 3800 calories.[1] In 2000, consumption of calories was therefore about 27% greater than it was only forty-three years earlier, in 1957. Since then the same measure has diminished slightly, to 3641 calories in 2014.[2] But this small decline does not necessarily mean that Americans are choosing healthier meals. During the same period, from 2000 to 2014, consumption of fruits and vegetables slumped about 10%.[3]

Portion sizes in restaurants. These sizes began to grow in the '70s, rose sharply in the '80s, and continued upward through the '90s. By 2000, the average meal in a restaurant was two to three times the meal size recommended by the USDA (United States Department of Agriculture).[4]

A caloric explosion in restaurant food had become so evident by the turn of the century that it was widely viewed among health professionals as an alarming development. Leading journals published studies giving dramatic evidence of the dangerous trend.

A report in the *Journal of the American Medical Association* noted that between 1977 and 1996, the average serving of a salty snack increased from 1.0 to 1.6 oz., giving 93 more calories. The average serving of a soft drink expanded from 13.1 to 19.9 oz., yielding 49 more calories. Hamburgers added 97 calories by enlarging from 5.7 to 7.0 oz., and french fries added 68 calories when a single serving became 3.6 oz. rather than 3.1 oz.[5]

A thorough study published in the *American Journal of Public Health* came to these conclusions:

> Our data indicate that the sizes of current marketplace foods almost universally exceed the sizes of those offered in the past. When foods such as beer and chocolate bars were introduced, they generally appeared in just one size, which was smaller than or equal to the smallest size currently available. This observation also holds for french fries, hamburgers, and soda, for which current sizes are 2 to 5 times larger than the originals.
>
> Our research also reveals indirect indicators of the increasing availability of larger food portions. In contrast to practices that were common just 15 to 25 years ago, food companies now use larger sizes as selling points . . . . Restaurants are using larger dinner plates, bakers are selling larger muffin tins, pizzerias are using larger pans, and fast-food companies are using larger drink and french fry containers. Identical recipes for cookies and desserts in old and new editions of classic cookbooks such as *Joy of Cooking* specify fewer servings, meaning that

portions are expected to be larger. Another indicator of the trend toward larger portions is that automobile manufacturers have installed larger cup holders in newer models to accommodate the larger sizes of drink cups.[6]

Since 2000, the upward trend in meal size at restaurants has leveled off, but they are still offering food in generous quantities except for menu items aimed at health-conscious consumers. More recent studies show that dining out is still a contributor to the obesity epidemic.[7] They demonstrate also that even though a restaurant meal may fall within an acceptable range for calories, it typically contains very high levels of fat, saturated fat, and sodium.[8]

Incidence of obesity. Public health officials have declared that obesity has reached epidemic proportions in the U.S. In 1976–1980, 47% of adults ages 20–74 were overweight or obese, 15% were obese, and 1% of these were severely obese. By 1999–2000, the same measures had risen to 65%, 31%, and 5%. In just twenty years there had been a 38% increase in the percent overweight and nearly a doubling in the percent obese. By 2015–2016, the comparable figures were still higher, at 71%, 40%, and 8%.[9]

Even more alarming is the sharp upturn in the number of overweight and obese among children and adolescents. The percent overweight or obese in 1999–2000 was 28% and the percent obese was 14%. The latter statistic was triple what it had been 25 years earlier, in 1971–1974, when the same measures were 15% and 5%. By 2013–2014, these had gone up to 33% and 17%.[10]

Gluttony as a worldwide problem. The trend toward overeating is not confined to America. One fairly recent study has established that oversize restaurant meals are now a problem around the world.[11]

We gain a similar picture from other data. When we compare nations by looking at each one's percentage of obese adults, we find that the United States indeed ranks high, with a measure of 36.2% in 2016, but also that many other nations stand at nearly the same level.

They include many Middle Eastern nations—Jordan (35.5%), Saudi Arabia (35.4%), Turkey (32.1%), Egypt (32%), Lebanon (32%), etc. Even among them is Israel (26.1%). Jesus' words cautioning against love of food in the Last Days was certainly relevant to the nations that would then surround the place where He stood.

Yet obesity is also prevalent elsewhere, especially in English-speaking countries, such as New Zealand (30.8%), Canada (29.4%), Australia (29%), and the United Kingdom (27.8%). The percentages are also high throughout Europe, South America (28.9% in Mexico, for instance), Russia, and parts of Africa.[12]

One possible interpretation of such statistics is that they simply reflect a longstanding feature of human society in general—that obesity is commonplace in the richest nations. But this interpretation collapses under decisive evidence that obesity is rapidly increasing everywhere in the world.   Between 1975 and 2016, the global percentage of adults with this condition tripled.[13]

Still today, obesity in a few nations appears to be fairly uncommon, particularly in China (6.2%) and India (3.9%). But even these two nations dramatically illustrate mankind's growing passion for food and drink. In both, the incidence of obesity has jumped tenfold since 1975.[14]

Christian duty.   Are food and drink also becoming an obsession for today's Christians? Habitual overeating is obviously sinful, both because it wastes good money and impairs good health. But to join with others for a sumptuous meal is not necessarily a bad thing. It is appropriate if it happens only once in a while and if its major purpose is to provide a setting for Christian fellowship—at a church potluck, for example—or an occasion for friends and family to share a time of rejoicing, perhaps in celebration of a wedding or holiday. Yet a word of caution. It is easy to use social gatherings as an excuse for gluttony.   There are two simple tests you can use to evaluate your own motives when you sit down to feast with others. Except for the prospect of food, would you be attending this gathering? As you participate, what is the chief object of your attention? Is it mainly the people around you and the meaning of the event, or is it mainly what you are eating now and what you crave in the next round of self-indulgence?

Marrying and giving in marriage

In Matthew 24:38, Jesus says that people in the Last Days will be marrying and giving in marriage just as in the days of Noah. One form of marriage that existed and perhaps was common before the Flood was polygamy (Gen. 4:19). This practice was a sharp deviation from what God intended marriage to be. He wanted a one-body union between two people that would be the fullest possible expression of true love. Since one sign of true love is a longing to spend as much time as possible with the beloved, it follows that the intimacy in godly marriage must be an exclusive relationship. Polygamy was invented by sinful men who were interested more in sex than in love, and women were powerless to stop it. It is significant that Scripture's account of the Flood is at pains to tell us that Noah himself was monogamous (Gen. 7:7).

Just as preoccupation with sexual pleasure corrupted marriage before the Flood, so it is having the same effect today. In this respect also, the Last Days are like the days of Noah. But what we see now may even be worse than any antediluvian plague of sexual sin. Finding pleasure in the present moment has so absorbed modern people that we are seeing an explosion of hedonism in all of its expressions, most notably the pursuit of sex.

One result of mushrooming hedonism is the tottering state of traditional marriage. Statistics prove that the divorce rate in America has exploded. Between 1890 and 1990, it jumped almost tenfold, from .5 divorces per thousand people to 4.7 per thousand.[15] Today the chance a marriage will end in divorce is almost 50%.[16]

Yet many people who divorce do not remarry. Indeed, many people on the contemporary scene do not bother to enter marriage at all. One result is a sharp decline in the marriage rate. It was reported in 2017 that "half of U.S. adults today are married, a share that has remained relatively stable in recent years but is down 9 percentage points over the past quarter century and dramatically different from the peak of 72% in 1960."[17]

Instead, many in today's world prefer cohabitation. A recent study of sexually experienced Americans between ages 18 and 44 found that 17.1% of the women and 15.9% of the men were cohabiting.[18] Of those in the same age group who were married, 67% had cohabited before marriage, and of those who were neither married or cohabiting, 51% of the women and 43% of the men had cohabited with someone in the past.[19] Yet these nonmarital unions are proving to be unstable and impermanent. A growing fad is serial cohabitation; that is, moving from partner to partner.[20] But, sadly, a growing number of teenagers and young adults are rushing down an even darker path. All they want is sex. As a result, they have no interest in establishing a personal relationship that will last beyond tonight and tomorrow. This promiscuity is a fast-spreading plague reaching into every corner of modern society. One proof, as we have already noted, is the explosion of STDs.

Mankind's growing fascination with every kind of sexual sin is one fulfillment of Jesus' prophecy that in the Last Days, people would be slaves to the real or imagined pleasures of earthly life.

Christian duty. As we have stressed elsewhere in this book, the church has a solemn obligation to protect its young people from sexual sin. A strong countermeasure is to discourage dating until they are old enough to consider marriage. Until they reach that age, God has no need to reveal who is their future mate. Other protective countermeasures include keeping the young away from indecent programming in the media and from immodest beachgoers. Yet another is to limit their social interaction as much as possible to other Christian young people, such as they will find at a Christian high school or college.

Ignorance of impending judgment

Today, people are ignorant of impending judgment because they are ignorant of the Bible. There are six reasons for this.

1. Bible ownership has drastically declined.

2. The language is changing, making the traditional versions inaccessible to today's reader.

3. Literacy is declining, with the result that people read less, and what they read is at a lower level. For many, the Bible is hard reading.

4. The Bible has been banished from public schools, and is ignored or mocked in the mass media. Even the posting of the Ten Commandments in a public place has been forbidden.

5. The Bible receives little attention in the home. In the late '70s, 17% of American parents stated that they had read the Bible with their children during the last week.[21] If false claims could have been sifted out, the percent would have been much lower. What would the true percent be today? To guess more than 1% hardly seems realistic.

6. The ruling preoccupation in the lives of most people is TV. What is the purpose of life, according to TV? Is it to please God and escape His judgment? No, it is to have a good time. TV teaches that life is a situation comedy punctuated by compulsive laughter; life is a game of cops and robbers; life is answering some silly questions to win a refrigerator; life is the latest but by no means the last test of the momentous question, who is better at controlling the motions of a ball—Team A or team B?

The evidence that people today do not expect or fear divine judgment is their response to natural disasters. Before God brings total destruction upon a wayward society, He generally gives many warnings so that wicked men can avert destruction if they will but repent. These warning may include a series of lesser calamities, continuing with increasing severity until men heed the warnings and turn to God in repentance. If they fail to repent, destruction will, after their hardness has exhausted God's patience, finally come. The calamities we see today are warnings, but the secular world is blind to their larger significance. The media never considers that the underlying cause might be the angry hand of God. If any news commentator ever suggested that a hurricane or earthquake was a sign of God's displeasure with a sinful world, he would be laughed out of his job. The role of God as overseer of human events occurs to hardly anyone.

From the book of Genesis we glean three more characteristics of the world before the Flood: violence, great wickedness, and apostasy.

Violence

The first violence to pollute the earth was Cain's murder of his brother Abel

> 1 And Adam knew Eve his wife; and she conceived, and bare Cain, and said, I have gotten a man from the LORD.
> 2 And she again bare his brother Abel. And Abel was a keeper of sheep, but Cain was a tiller of the ground.
> 3 And in process of time it came to pass, that Cain brought of the fruit

of the ground an offering unto the LORD.

4 And Abel, he also brought of the firstlings of his flock and of the fat thereof. And the LORD had respect unto Abel and to his offering:

5 But unto Cain and to his offering he had not respect. And Cain was very wroth, and his countenance fell.

6 And the LORD said unto Cain, Why art thou wroth? and why is thy countenance fallen?

7 If thou doest well, shalt thou not be accepted? and if thou doest not well, sin lieth at the door. And unto thee *shall be* his desire, and thou shalt rule over him.

8 And Cain talked with Abel his brother: and it came to pass, when they were in the field, that Cain rose up against Abel his brother, and slew him.

- Genesis 4:1–8 -

Later, Lamech boasted that he had killed a young man.

19 And Lamech took unto him two wives: the name of the one *was* Adah, and the name of the other Zillah. . . .

23 And Lamech said unto his wives, Adah and Zillah, Hear my voice; ye wives of Lamech, hearken unto my speech: For I have slain a man to my wounding, And a young man to my hurt.

24 If Cain shall be avenged sevenfold, Truly Lamech seventy and sevenfold.

- Genesis 4:19, 23–24 -

In the days of Noah, violence had become rife, so much so that the Lord said the earth was filled with it.

The earth also was corrupt before God, and the earth was filled with violence.

- Genesis 6:11 -

It appears that the social fabric had so unraveled that every man sought to gain as much as he could through fighting and feuding.

In our day also, violence of all kinds is escalating, giving us a universal plague of misery and bloodshed. We are living amidst an epidemic of abortion, abusive conduct in the home, angry people going berserk and gunning down people at random, gang warfare, violence in the workplace and in the school, massacres of whole families, domestic and international terrorism, torture and murder by established governments as well as serial murder by lone killers.

Yet, as we noted in chapter 5, the modern era has been especially gruesome in its toll of deaths due to war. Here are some staggering facts. It has been estimated that in all of human history until 1900, about forty million people died in war. Yet in the years from 1900 to 1987, the year when the scholarly work presenting these statistics was published, the number of war casualties was about 38½ million.[22] Undoubtedly by the end of 1999, wars in the twentieth century were more deadly than all the wars in all previous centuries combined.

In every period of history, the number who have died because of genocide, politicide, or mass murder far exceeds the number of war dead. The killing of people by repressive governments is called democide. From 1900 until 1987, the victims of democide numbered 170 million. About 62 million were killed by Russian Communists, 35 million by Chinese Communists, 21 million by German Nazis, ten million by Chinese nationalists, and six million by the Japanese in and before WWII, etc.[23]

Great wickedness

In the time before the Flood, human society sank to such depravity that God could not find any thoughts in the human heart that were not bent on doing evil.

> And GOD saw that the wickedness of man *was* great in the earth, and *that* every imagination of the thoughts of his heart *was* only evil continually.
>
> - Genesis 6:5 -

Man's wickedness had become extraordinary in degree and universal in extent.

How did this plague of wickedness get started, and how did it spread? We know that Adam and Eve originally fell into sin as a result of being tempted by Satan. We know also that Cain murdered his brother at Satan's instigation. A literal translation of Genesis 4:7 (quoted on p. 96) is, "If you do well, is there not acceptance? And if you do not do well, sin is crouching at the door, and its desire [is] toward you, but you should rule over it."[24] The sin crouching at the door pictures the same serpent that tempted Adam and Eve; in other words, Satan. It is only reasonable to suppose that as men scattered over the earth and lost contact with godly ancestors, they experimented with new forms of self-indulgence, thus enlarging Satan's influence over the human race.

But Satan was not alone in seeking to corrupt men. Working under his direction was a horde of demons. We have good reason to believe that their activity was in large measure responsible for the plunge of antediluvian society into great wickedness.

Just as there was an overwhelming presence of evil forces on the earth in Noah's day, so in our day there has been an explosion of demonic activity in America and other formerly Christian nations. Before 1965, occult activity kept mainly underground. The media seldom noticed it and put it in a negative light. Since 1965, there has been a groundswell of interest in the occult.

1. The media have turned a spotlight on the occult, often giving it favorable treatment. The turning point was the seemingly innocuous program *Bewitched* back in the '60s. Now the occult is a regular theme of rock music, videos, and books. Among the top-selling books

for children in recent years is a series featuring a young warlock by the name of Harry Potter.

2. In modern times, a new form of the occult has emerged, packaged in middle-class, quasi-intellectual respectability: the New Age Movement. Bookstores have given it a special place on their shelves. Leading entertainers have promoted it. Yet it is nothing but occultism. People seek paranormal experience and self-evolution to godhood with the aid of spirit guides—that is, demons. Between 1990 and 2000, the number of adherents to New Ageism grew more than threefold, from 20,000 to 68,000.[25] Although the number who identify themselves as New Agers appears to have declined since then, some aspects of its worldview clearly persist as a shaping influence on the thinking of more and more people.[26]

3. Witches and other practitioners of the occult have come out of the closet, openly revealing their allegiance and aggressively recruiting others. In the modern Western world, witchcraft generally takes place in the context of the pagan religion known as Wicca.[27] In 1985, the District Court of Virginia declared that Wicca is a religion entitled to protection under the Constitution and to all the other benefits granted by law to a religion. This ruling was upheld by a Federal Appeals Court.[28] The attraction of Wicca is twofold. It gives immoral sex a religious pretext. Also, it promises to make real all the dark fantasy that the young enjoy as entertainment. Exposure to the occult in their reading and viewing gives them a hankering to sample the real thing. Wicca is among the fastest growing religions in this country, appealing mainly to educated young people. In 2004, Wiccans, pagans, and druids numbered well over 400,000.[29] In 2014, the same religions could claim about 740,000 adherents (0.3% of the U.S. population).[30]

Apostasy

Another characteristic of the days of Noah that we find through the study of Genesis is apostasy. Adam had many sons and daughters, including Abel, the godly son who was slain by his brother Cain, but the Bible has nothing good to say about any of the surviving children except Seth.

> 25 And Adam knew his wife again; and she bare a son, and called his name Seth: For God, *said she,* hath appointed me another seed instead of Abel, whom Cain slew.
> 26 And to Seth, to him also there was born a son; and he called his name Enos: then began men to call upon the name of the LORD.
>
> - Genesis 4:25–26 -

Reading between the lines, we surmise that Enos helped to stir up spiritual revival among the Sethites and perhaps among others as well. It was in the line of Seth rather than in the line of Cain that

Enoch appeared, the man who obtained such favor with God that God took him alive into heaven.

> 22 And Enoch walked with God after he begat Methuselah three hundred
> years, and begat sons and daughters:
> 23 And all the days of Enoch were three hundred sixty and five years:
> 24 And Enoch walked with God: and he *was* not; for God took him.
>
> - Genesis 5:22–24 -

Yet a few centuries later, about 1500 years after man was created, righteousness had nearly disappeared from the face of the earth.

> 5 And GOD saw that the wickedness of man *was* great in the earth, and
> *that* every imagination of the thoughts of his heart *was* only evil
> continually.
> 6 And it repented the LORD that he had made man on the earth, and it
> grieved him at his heart.
> 7 And the LORD said, I will destroy man whom I have created from the
> face of the earth; both man, and beast, and the creeping thing, and
> the fowls of the air; for it repenteth me that I have made them.
> 8 But Noah found grace in the eyes of the LORD.
> 9 These *are* the generations of Noah: Noah was a just man *and* perfect
> in his generations, *and* Noah walked with God.
>
> Genesis 6:5–9

Only one man, Noah, remained who was "just" and "perfect" and who "walked with God" (v. 9). Noah "found grace in the eyes of the Lord" (v. 8), but the rest of mankind earned only the Lord's regret that He had made them (vv. 5–7). The sinful ways of Cain and his descendants had spread to all the descendants of Adam. Corruption had even swallowed up the descendants of Seth, creating a nearly universal departure from truth and righteousness. Apostasy had all but erased godly religion.

The analogy that Jesus drew between the days of Noah and the Last Days implies that the latter will be as apostate as the former. Will true religion disappear completely? In the days before the Flood, many who had once walked in the truth turned away from it, setting their own impulses and opinions above the law of God written on their hearts, preferring the approval of men to the approval of God. Yet the tide of evil did not engulf everyone. When God searched the earth for people He could spare from the general destruction, He found one righteous man, Noah. Besides Noah, God also preserved seven members of the patriarch's family, presumably because they had decided to follow Noah on the path of righteousness. The number found worthy to escape the Flood was exceedingly small— only eight out of the millions then alive on the earth.

Likewise in modern times, we see that the possessors of true faith are becoming alarmingly few. After a long period of spiritual zeal and missionary enterprise, the church has gone into a steep decline. All around us, we see evidence that New Testament Christianity is fading from America and other formerly Christian nations. Even nominal

Christianity is weakening. Between 2009 and 2019, the percentage of American adults who, when asked to name their religion, identified themselves as Christians fell from 77% to 65%.[31] Yet doubtless only a small proportion of these self-identified Christians were born-again believers.

The sharp downward trend will not only continue, but will move ever faster toward the bottom. Yet, as in Noah's day, some will resist the pull of an evil world and stand firm in their commitment to right-eousness. When many others are deserting the ranks of true Chris-tianity, some will remain loyal. How large will the remnant be? We do not know. We need not suppose that the remnant will be exactly eight persons, as in the Old Testament type. Perhaps the number who espouse true faith will be far more. Still today, we find good churches scattered throughout the world. Most of them are small and inconspicuous, hidden from our knowledge. Perhaps the sum total of true believers runs into the millions. But even millions would be a negligible portion of all the people in the world today.

Reconsider Jesus' question, "When the Son of man cometh, shall he find faith on the earth?" (Luke 18:8). This is surely a somber warning that the end-time church will be rotten to the core. But it is also a challenge. It provokes each of us to examine ourselves to see whether we have faith acceptable to God. Although we cannot force any other professing Christian to cast aside mere pretense and es-pouse true faith, we can determine for ourselves to stand among the few who will, with no trace of hypocrisy, answer Jesus' question by affirming, "Yes, I have faith."

Footnotes

[1] "Profiling Food Consumption in America," chapter 2 in *Agriculture Fact Book* (USDA, 2003), Web (usda.gov/factbook/chapter2.pdf), 2004.

[2] "Average Daily Caloric Intake Per Capita in Select Countries 2014," Statista (statista.com/statistics/333901/average-daily-per-capita-caloric-intake-in-select-countries/), 10/21/19.

[3] Jeanine Bentley, *U.S. Trends in Food Availability and a Dietary Assessment of Loss-Adjusted Food Availability, 1970–2014* (USDA, 2017), 6–15.

[4] Jean Carper, "Diet Quick Fix: Eat Half as Much of Everything," USA Week-end.com, Web (usaweekend.com/00_issues/000507/000507eatsmart.html), 5/7/00.

[5] Samara Joy Nielsen and Barry M. Popkin, "Patterns and Trends in Food Portion Sizes, 1977–1998," *Journal of the American Medical Association* 289 (2003): 450–453.

[6] Lisa R. Young and Marion Nestle, "The Contribution of Expanding Portion Sizes to the US Obesity Epidemic," *American Journal of Public Health* 92 (2002), 246–248.

[7] "Restaurant Portion Sizes Contribute to Obesity Epidemic," Here & Now on WBUR, Web (wbur.org/hereandnow/2017/03/29/portion-sizes), 10/22/19.

[8] Laura Schocker, "Restaurant Portion Size: Nearly All Entrees Exceed Nutrition Recommendations," Huffpost, Web (huffpost.com/entry/restaurant-portion-size_n_1534458), 10/22/19.

[9] "Prevalence of Overweight, Obesity, and Severe Obesity among Adults Aged 20 and Over: United States, 1960–1962 through 2015–2016," National Center for Health Statistics, Web (cdc.gov/nchs/data/hestat/obesity_adult_15_16/obesity_adult_15_16.htm),

10/21/19.

[10]"Prevalence of Overweight and Obesity among Children and Adolescents Aged 2–19 Years: United States, 1963–1965 through 2013–2014," National Center for Health Statistics, Web (cdc.gov/nchs/data/hestat/obesity_child_13_14/obesity_child_13_14.htm), 10/21/19.

[11]Mike Pomranz, "Excessive Restaurant Portions Are Not Just an American Phenomenon, Says Study," Food&Wine, Web (foodandwine.com/news/restaurant-portion-sizes-study-global), 10/22/19.

[12]"Prevalence of Obesity among Adults, BMI ≥ 30, Age-standardized Estimates by Country," World Health Organization, 9/22/17, Web (who.int/gho/data/node.main .A900A?lang=en), 5/11/20.

[13]"Global Obesity Levels," ProCon.org, 2020 (obesity.procon.org/global-obesity-levels/), 5/11/20.

[14]"Prevalence of Obesity."

[15]"Marriages and Divorces, 1900–2012," Infoplease.com, Web, (infoplease.com/us/marital-status/marriages-and-divorces-1900-2012), 10/21/19; Jennifer L. Betts, "Historical Divorce Rate Statistics," lovetoknow, Web (divorce.lovetoknow.com/Historical_Divorce_Rate_Statistics), 10/21/19.

[16]"Divorce Statistics: Over 115 Studies, Facts and Rates for 2018," Wilkinson & Finkbeiner: Family Law Attorneys, Web (wf-lawyers.com/divorce-statistics-and-facts/), 10/21/19.

[17]Kim Parker and Renee Stepler, "As U.S. Marriage Rate Hovers at 50%, Education Gap in Marital Status Widens," Pew Research Center, 9/14/17, Web (pewresearch.org/fact-tank/2017/09/14/as-u-s-marriage-rate-hovers-at-50-education-gap-in-marital-status-widens/), 5/14/20.

[18]Colleen N. Nugent and Jill Daugherty, "A Demographic, Attitudinal, and Behavioral Profile of Cohabiting Adults in the United States, 2011–2015," *National Health Statistics Reports; no. 111* (Hyattsville, MD: National Center for Health Statistics, 2018), Web (cdc.gov/nchs/data/nhsr/nhsr111.pdf), 5/14/20.

[19]Scott Stanley and Galena Rhoades, "Cohabitation is Pervasive," Institute for Family Studies, 6/20/18, Web (ifstudies.org/blog/cohabitation-is-pervasive), 5/14/20.

[20]Ibid.

[21]George Gallup, Jr., and David Poling, *The Search for America's Faith* (Nashville, Abingdon, 1980), 51.

[22]Rummel, 3, 71.

[23]Ibid., 4.

[24]Jay P. Green, Sr., *The Interlinear Bible: Hebrew/English*, 3 vols. (Grand Rapids, Mich.: Baker Book House, 1983), 1:9.

[25]"Largest Religious Groups in the United States of America," Adherents.com, Web (adherents.com/rel_USA.html), 10/21/19.

[26]"New Age," *Wikipedia*, Web (en.wikipedia.org/wiki/New_Age), 10/23/19.

[27]"Wicca," *Wikipedia*, Web (en.wikipedia.org/wiki/Wicca#North_America), 10/23/19.

[28]"Religious Discrimination against Wiccans," *Wikipedia*, Web (en.wikipedia.org/wiki/Persecution_of_Wiccans), 8/7/07.

[29]"Largest Religious Groups."

[30]"Religious Landscape Study," Pew Research Center, Web (pewforum.org/religious-landscape-study/), 10/23/19.

[31]"In U.S., Decline of Christianity Continues at Rapid Pace," Pew Research Center, Web (pewforum.org/2019/10/17/in-u-s-decline-of-christianity-continues-at-rapid-pace/), 10/23/19.

Chapter 10

✢ On the Brink of Sorrows ✢

The world is now ripe for all the disasters that will hit the earth directly after the Rapture. After some disciples asked Jesus, "What *shall be* the sign of thy coming, and of the end of the world?" (Matt. 24:3), He sketched out the main forms of judgment that will visit mankind right at the beginning of the Tribulation; in other words, the terrible calamities that will explode soon after God's people are removed from the world scene.

> 7 For nation shall rise against nation, and kingdom against kingdom: and there shall be famines, and pestilences, and earthquakes, in divers places.
> 8 All these *are* the beginning of sorrows.
>
> - Matthew 24:7–8 -

In these verses, Jesus refers to the opening phase of the Tribulation as the beginning of sorrows. The primary sorrows that will then enter human experience and steal away all happiness from a world of sinners are wars, famines, pestilences, and earthquakes.

Wars

Jesus first mentions wars quickly escalating from small-scale (nation against nation) to large-scale (kingdom against kingdom). The bloodshed will begin with the conflict described by the prophet Daniel.

> 40 And at the time of the end shall the king of the south push at him: and the king of the north shall come against him like a whirlwind, with chariots, and with horsemen, and with many ships; and he shall enter into the countries, and shall overflow and pass over.
> 41 He shall enter also into the glorious land, and many *countries* shall be overthrown: but these shall escape out of his hand, *even* Edom, and Moab, and the chief of the children of Ammon.
> 42 He shall stretch forth his hand also upon the countries: and the land of Egypt shall not escape.
> 43 But he shall have power over the treasures of gold and of silver, and over all the precious things of Egypt: and the Libyans and the Ethiopians *shall be* at his steps.
> 44 But tidings out of the east and out of the north shall trouble him: therefore he shall go forth with great fury to destroy, and utterly to make away many.
> 45 And he shall plant the tabernacles of his palace between the seas in the glorious holy mountain; yet he shall come to his end, and none shall help him.
>
> - Daniel 11:40–45 -

The initial act of war will be an attack that the king of the south will direct against the king of the north. We pointed out in chapter 4 that throughout Daniel 11, the king of the north is the ruler of the Seleucid dynasty centered in Syria and the king of the south is the ruler of the Ptolemaic dynasty centered in Egypt. We must therefore conclude that the opening war during the Tribulation will pit Egypt against Syria. It has only been in the last century that fulfillment of this prophecy has become possible. After the ancient kingdoms of Egypt and Syria collapsed, their territories were absorbed by foreign empires, whether Roman, Muslim, or colonial. Neither nation regained the status of a sovereign state until after World War II, Syria in 1945[1] and Egypt in 1952.[2] As a result, the stage is now set for the wars of the early Tribulation.

Likewise, the world is positioned to plunge into all the other troubles that Christ says will erupt after the Rapture.

Famines

One of the disasters that will then strike the world is famine. Do we see any evidence that human society is on the verge of serious food shortages? Until recently, many experts were confident that we are making progress in reducing our vulnerability to famine. In 2002, the UN Food and Agricultural Organization predicted that growth in food production will outstrip population growth for at least the next thirty years.[3]

But optimistic projections are proving incorrect. According to a report in 2019 from the same organization, the number of undernourished people in the world had for decades declined until 2015, when it fell to only 785 million, but since then has increased. In 2018, it was over 820 million. The global percentage has also risen, from 10.6% to 10.8%. A somewhat larger number of people worldwide now suffer what is termed "a moderate level of food insecurity." When they are counted along with the severely malnourished, the total number is about two billion people, or about 26% of the world's population.[4]

A report in 2016 stated that 24% of children worldwide under five suffered from stunted growth (low height) and 8% were wasted (low weight for height). An estimated 16% of all newborns had low birth weight.[5] Why is providing enough food for the world proving such a difficult task? Several factors are involved.

1. We continue to see rapid growth in world population. In 2019, it was about seven billion, seven hundred million and was growing at a rate of about eighty-two million per year.[6] Experts predict that it will reach eight billion by 2025.[7] They expect the growth rate to decline by midcentury, leaving world population at about 9.7 billion by

2050 and 11.2 billion by 2100.[8] Yet any guess as to future growth
rates must make questionable assumptions.

2. Another pressure on food supply is the loss of arable land—
that is, good farmland—as a result of soil erosion, soil degradation,
and the expansion of cities. Success in converting wild ground into
either crop fields or pastures caused steady growth in the amount of
agricultural land until about 1990. But since then, it has barely increased. The current projection of many experts is that it will peak
between 2020 and 2040, although some see a decline after 2020.[9]

3. In the years following the 1960s, agricultural productivity was
able to keep pace with population growth. The reason was that productivity received a strong boost from the so-called Green Revolution,
which refers to farmers replacing natural varieties of food plants with
high-yielding varieties developed through selective plant breeding.
Yet this revolution has had a side effect which jeopardizes sustain-
able agriculture. Planting genetically identical plants has resulted in
reduction of available genetic diversity. It has been estimated that
75% of the genetic diversity in crop plants has disappeared during
the last century.[10] One consequence is loss of adaptability to diseases, pests, and environmental change. An optimistic outlook is
hard to justify for yet another reason. Further gains in productivity
through selective breeding are unlikely, because there are limits to
genetic improvement. Just as a horse cannot be bred beyond a certain largeness or smallness, so plants cannot be bred beyond a certain level of productivity.

Nevertheless, another factor continues to support growth in productivity worldwide. Yields are still improving due to the spread of
modern agricultural techniques. Yet the impact of this factor on future production is impossible to predict because of its dependence on
many uncertain economic and political factors.[11]

4. If you read carefully any optimistic assessment of future food
output, you will find that it assumes unlimited supplies of motive
power and fertilizer. But such an assumption is untenable. What
powers farm machinery? It is fuel derived from petroleum. Where do
agricultural chemicals come from? They are petrochemicals, made
by reacting atmospheric nitrogen with hydrogen derived from natural
gas (methane) or coal.[12] It is evident that modern agriculture is critically dependent on fossil fuels. A drastic reduction in the supply of
petroleum or natural gas would quickly lead to a comparable reduction in the supply of food.

How much crude oil remains in the ground? It is a question that
does not permit a certain answer, but many experts agree that from
the beginning of time until 2018, man extracted between 1.1 and 1.5
trillion barrels, leaving perhaps 1.5 trillion barrels in reserve. In
other words, about half of the earth's supply of crude oil is now gone.
In 2018, the rate of oil consumption was about one hundred million
barrels per day, and usage was expected to increase steadily in

coming years. Therefore, at present rates of increasing consumption, the entire supply will be exhausted in another forty years or so. But perhaps as much as 35% of present oil reserves lies in regions where, for political or other reasons, retrieval may prove difficult.[13]

What will farmers do when shortages force them away from dependence on fossil fuels? Various processes have been invented to generate methane from a renewable source, such as manure, but none so far appears to be remotely cost-effective.[14] Switching to ethanol, fuel cells, or batteries would take enormous time and investment as well as a plentiful supply of needed resources—all these being requirements on a scale that is probably unrealistic. If advanced technology cannot furnish practical alternatives to fossil fuels, the world has little surviving capacity for more primitive means of food production. Labor-intensive small farms disappeared long ago from prosperous nations. The number of draft horses and mules is rapidly dwindling. Nonmechanized farm equipment survives only in museums. It would take considerable time and trouble to revive antiquated methods. Even if accomplished, farmers would still lack adequate supplies of effective fertilizer and pesticide.

5. Also limiting future supplies of food is the amount of available fresh water. The World Resources Institute reported in 2019 "that 17 countries, which are home to a quarter of the world's population, face 'extremely high' water stress"—in other words, critical shortages.[15] As population growth and industrialization continually raise the demand for water, the supply continually diminishes through exhaustion or pollution of freshwater sources. Water shortages are especially severe in places like the Middle East and India, but they affect America as well. Groundwater throughout the United States except in the Pacific Norwest is currently being depleted at a rate somewhat greater than the rate of recharge.[16] One culprit is urban sprawl, which is replacing soft ground with impervious surfaces which cast off the water instead of soaking it up

Pestilences

Let us consider the third kind of calamity that will afflict the early Tribulation period: pestilences (Matt. 24:7–8). Jesus speaks of these pestilences as though they will suddenly emerge or suddenly affect many more people. The vulnerability of global society to pestilences is growing every day, as it is to every other kind of disaster.

Many of the most dangerous pestilences are communicable diseases caused by bacteria or viruses. In their genetic makeup, the microbes of a given kind are highly variable, and new varieties are continually appearing through mutation. This is not true evolution, because the new varieties do not display either new powers or new complexity. They are essentially the same as the old, except for slight structural differences that may make them resistant to drugs effective

against the old varieties. The battle against these diseases is therefore always shifting from one strain of microbe to another, and as we
will see, each new strain may be harder and more expensive to eliminate than the one preceding it. More and more scientists are afraid
that in man's fight against the worst communicable diseases, he may
soon exhaust his arsenal of practical countermeasures.

STDs. One development making global society more vulnerable
to pestilences is the breakdown of morals. The result has been an
explosion of sexually transmitted diseases (STDs). The STD receiving
the most public attention is AIDS (acquired immunodeficiency syn-
drome), caused by HIV (human immunodeficiency virus). Since
1981, when the disease was first described, about seventy-five million people have become infected worldwide, and about thirty-two
million have died, leaving about forty-three million victims alive today.[17] Of these cases, 54% are in sub-Saharan Africa, where a com-
bination of ignorance, poverty, and rampant immorality have made it
impossible to bring the epidemic under control.[18] In several countries, more than 20% of the population have the disease.[19]

Among the countries where the disease is still spreading is China,
which has about one million cases.[20] Over one million cases affecting about 1% of the population now exist in Russia, which has one of
the fastest growing epidemics in the world.[21] Victims in the U.S.
number about 1,100,000 people—one in seven being unaware of his
condition[22]—and about forty thousand new cases are diagnosed each
year.[23] The yearly growth worldwide is about 1.7 million cases.[24]

The specter hanging over the battle against AIDS is the emergence of drug-resistant varieties of HIV. The story here is the same
as we find in all other attempts to overcome disease with drugs.
Failure to administer them to a patient until his disease is fully
eradicated increases the probability that a drug-resistant strain will
appear and become dominant. In many countries where AIDS is
prevalent, lapses in treatment are common, because medical services
are inadequate or patients lack commitment to taking a medicine
faithfully. As a result, dozens of drug-resistant strains of HIV have
appeared, accounting for more than 10% of the new cases in twelve
countries.[25] In poor countries, a second line of treatment drugs is
often unavailable because of the high cost. Even in wealthier nations, the high cost of second-line drugs or (if they fail) of third-line
drugs could easily become prohibitive.

Not only AIDS, but also every other sexually transmitted disease
is becoming epidemic. Fifty years ago, the only two of significance
were syphilis and gonorrhea. But now more than thirty-five different
STDs have been identified, and the prevalence of nearly all is on the
rise.[26]

The most common is human papillomavirus (HPV), which affects
"79 million Americans, most in their late teens and early twenties."[27]

Medical treatment cannot rid the body of the responsible virus, although a vaccine can give some protection from the cancers which are a common side effect.[28]

Another prevalent STD is genital herpes, which has about 140 million victims worldwide.[29] In America, more than one sixth of people aged fourteen to forty-nine have this sexually transmitted infection,[30] yet close to 90% are unaware of being victims.[31] Since it emerged from obscurity in the 1980s, no cure has been found.[32]

The STD most commonly reported to the Centers for Disease Control (CDC, an American government agency) is Chlamydia.[33] The number of cases on record in 2018 was about 1.8 million.[34]

Even syphilis, once thought to be near extinction, is making a strong comeback. The rates of both syphilis and gonorrhea are increasing every year, with gonorrhea now exceeding a half million cases.[35] In its report on current levels of chlamydia, gonorrhea and syphilis in 2017, CDC stated that all three reached "record highs," posing "a substantial health challenge" for the United States.[36] After the upward surge in rates persisted in 2018, the CDC announced that in the last five years, just since 2014, they had observed a 19% increase in chlamydia, a 63% increase in gonorrhea, and a 71% increase in syphilis.[37]

Altogether, about twenty million new STD infections appear each year, half of these affecting young people between ages fifteen and twenty-four.[38] To put this estimate in proper perspective, however, we must remember that "many cases of chlamydia, gonorrhea, and syphilis continue to go undiagnosed and unreported, and data on several additional STDs, such as human papillomavirus and herpes simplex virus, are not routinely reported to CDC. As a result, national surveillance data captures only a fraction of America's STD burden."[39]

Do you catch the mind-boggling implications of these statistics from the CDC? This year, about ten million new cases of STD will appear among young people between ages fifteen and twenty-four, although we have only about forty million young people in this age group. It follows that a large fraction of American young people must be contracting an STD or multiple STDs before they become adults.

The recent flood of STDs is clearly a divine judgment on our licentious society. It is evident that instead of protecting the precious young lives God has entrusted to us, America has allowed them to be corrupted by forces seeking to overthrow Biblical beliefs and values.

We in the Christian community should not look with complacency on the epidemic of STDs, as if our own young people were immune. On the contrary, we must redouble our efforts to safeguard them. How? By forbidding premature dating, by preventing close friendships with worldly young people, by always providing adequate supervision, and by teaching our young people the Biblical principles and the practical wisdom they will need to make a good choice of a life partner.

Tuberculosis. Perhaps the most dangerous disease confronting mankind is tuberculosis. It has been a terrible scourge on the human race almost since the beginning of time. Tubercular decay is evident in the spinal tissue of Egyptian mummies predating 2000 BC.[40] TB is deadly, killing about 70% of all victims without recourse to modern medicine.[41] Even today, despite apparent progress in the war against TB, it ranks as one of the top ten causes of death among people worldwide. In fact, it is the leading cause of death traceable to a single infectious agent.[42]

Tuberculosis is a severe threat for two reasons: 1) the disease is highly contagious, the microbes moving easily from person to person through the air;[43] 2) TB bacteria are already present in one out of three people.[44] A body with a strong immune system can seal off a small number of resident bacteria. The result is a latent infection that cannot be passed to others. But if a body's defenses are weak, resident bacteria can generate a life-threatening, communicable disease.[45]

One vaccine has long been available for prevention of the disease, but it is only 0% to 80% effective for adults. Pharmaceutical companies see little incentive for developing alternatives because the disease is presently epidemic only in poor countries. In wealthy countries, where the disease is uncommon, there is little demand for a vaccine and, in consequence, little opportunity for profits.[46]

Worldwide, TB accounts for about 1.6 million deaths per year.[47] Still, an ordinary case of TB is easily overcome with such drugs as isoniazid and rifampicin,[48] but improper or incomplete treatment of the disease—a common misfortune in poorer countries—can spell disaster, for it may allow the microbe to develop resistance. Some years ago, there emerged a form of TB that cannot be overcome by usual drug therapy. It was called MDR-TB, which means multidrug resistant TB. The new cases of this illness that now appear each year number about 460,000.[49] Coping with it is far more risky and costly than remedies effective against TB in the past. The second-line drugs have serious side effects, and a cure takes months or years to accomplish at a cost of about three hundred thousand dollars.[50] It is evident that a large-scale outbreak of MDR-TB would overwhelm our medical system.

Yet even worse forms of TB are now on the scene. About thirty-nine thousand people worldwide are infected with extensively drug-resistant TB, called XDR-TB,[51] which resists some second-line drugs as well as the first-line drugs.[52] This form of TB arises when cases of MDR-TB are mishandled.[53] Treatment costs are astronomical, exceeding seven hundred thousand dollars for a single case.[54] As we might have expected, however, not all cases of XDR-TB receive perfect medical care either, and the result has been a still worse form of the infection known as extremely drug-resistant TB (XXDR-TB) or totally drug-resistant TB (TDR-TB). So far, only a few cases have appeared worldwide.[55]

Should any of the drug-resistant strains of TB escape into general circulation, we would return to the days when TB was incurable, for treating so many victims would overburden our resources. A recent study found "an alarming situation of XDR-TB patients in China with a high mortality rate" and "a sizable proportion of newly transmitted cases."[56]

These are ominous words as we consider social conditions during the Tribulation. The worldwide incidence of TB has been gradually diminishing in modern times, currently at a rate of about 2% each year.[57] But the slow advance against this enemy has required a costly, organized effort by the medical community employing sophisticated weapons. But what will happen when medical care is disrupted by wars and natural disasters? TB will rage out of control. As we said, the mortality rate for TB is about 70%.

Influenza. Let us look at some other diseases that could run amok as society crumbles under divine judgment. One of the chief threats is the viral disease influenza. Several pandemics in the past have killed millions of people, the worst being Spanish flu in 1918, which took a toll of more than fifty million lives.[58] The most recent pandemic, caused by so-called swine flu, hit in 2009 and caused roughly 400,000 deaths worldwide, mainly among people under sixty-five years of age.[59]

Influenza is an especially dangerous pestilence for three reasons.

1. Although some strains of flu can be treated with antivirals that reduce the effects, there is no cure.[60] The only effective weapon is preventive vaccines.[61]

2. Flu is highly communicable through airborne transmission of the germs.[62]

3. New strains of the disease are always appearing.

Seasonal flu is caused by influenza viruses of types A or B. Although both types undergo genetic changes, only the A viruses are capable of mutating to the extent that immune systems of people worldwide cannot recognize and eliminate the new strain.[63] Pandemics are therefore "global outbreaks of a new influenza A virus."[64]

Some strains produce a very high mortality rate. An especially worrisome case is bird flu, which sometimes spreads to people who have had close contact with birds or bird droppings. Although communication of the infection to other people rarely happens, this disease remains a cause of major concern because it kills about 60% of its victims.[65]

If bird flu or any similar plague broke loose on the scale of a pandemic, modern society would be helpless to stop it, for several reasons:

1. Population growth worldwide has led to high population density. The crowding of people allows easier transmission of disease.

2. Modern transportation and the lowering of international barriers have made travel between nations commonplace. Again, the spread of disease can therefore be more rapid.

3. The delivery of medical care is concentrated in large hospitals, where victims of a pandemic cannot be treated without exposing others.

4. The time lag for development and distribution of new vaccines and other combative drugs is generally greater than for global spread of the disease.

Once the Tribulation begins, all these factors will still exist, and another will also come into play. Medical services everywhere will be severely weakened, so that an effective campaign to save lives will be impossible.

Let us consider some more diseases that could particularly endanger mankind during the Tribulation.

Other zoonoses. Zoonoses are diseases caused by germs that cross over from animals to man. Among them are Spanish flu, which evidently came from birds,[66] and swine flu, which indeed came from pigs.[67] The cause of the disease need not be an influenza virus, however. Several epidemics in recent years have been the deadly work of some coronavirus. SARS, emerging in 2003, produced only about 800 deaths, and MERS in 2013 only about 900.[68] In both cases, the infectious agents came from bats, although the route of transmission to man may have gone through other species.[69] Much worse, of course, has been the coronavirus responsible for COVID-19, which people first contracted from an unknown source.[70] Another grievous scourge, this one due to invasive ebolaviruses, is Ebola. Bats again have been the ultimate suppliers of the germs. The deaths it has produced since 1976 amount to well over 13,000.[71]

Zoonotic diseases could become a particular danger after divine judgment falls on the earth. The many upheavals will doubtless weaken the barriers that normally limit contacts between man and beast.

Malaria. Overall, the fight against malaria, caused by a unicellular organism carried by mosquitoes, has succeeded in gradually reducing the number of victims. Although the number of deaths increased in 2014–2016, returning to 2010 levels,[72] this upward trend halted in 2017, when deaths worldwide diminished slightly to about 435,000.[73] Yet the whole tally of cases in the same year, 219 million,[74] is a clear reminder that malaria is one of the major health threats to mankind.

A look at malaria is relevant to our discussion because, as one expert observed recently, it lurks as a special danger when people are displaced from their homes.[75] In the wars that will rage during the Tribulation, many people will be robbed of their homes when they flee from invaders, or when their homes are destroyed by shellings or bombings. Instead of spending the night inside structures with walls and closed windows, they will sleep out in the open or in unprotected tents. There they will be easy prey for mosquitoes.

Smallpox. In 1980, the 33rd World Health Assembly declared that this deadly viral disease had been eradicated.[76] Outbreaks of smallpox had long plagued countries around the world, with fatalities among the afflicted amounting to about 30% for adults and even more for babies.[77] Today, however, only small samples of the virus remain in two research facilities, one in America and one in Russia.[78] Yet it is unquestionably possible that some countries in the past may have secretly preserved stocks of the virus as a potential weapon; also, that some of this remnant could someday fall into the hands of bioterrorists. The American government judged this threat plausible enough to work out a detailed plan of response to any outbreak of the disease.[79] During the Tribulation, not only would bioterrorism of this kind be more likely, but also to limit its destructive effects would be more difficult.

Cholera. This bacterial disease of the small intestine has long been prevalent wherever people lack access to clean water.[80] This is already a pervasive problem. According to the World Bank, 29% of the world's people do not have access to safe drinking water, 39% have no facilities to give their hands a proper washing, and 55% lack sanitary treatment of waste water.[81]

About 21,000 to 143,000 cases of cholera out of 1.3 to 4.0 million total cases worldwide lead to death.[82] It has been suggested that the disease will become an even more serious threat as a result of rising sea levels.[83] Environmental and social breakdown during the Tribulation will certainly degrade water supplies and make cholera an ever-present danger.

The modern world recognizes the horrible toll of lives and the major social disruption that could follow a deadly pandemic, and much is being done to fend off the danger. Yet all this effort alters man's predicament only by giving it a veneer of safety. In the aftermath of any severe shock to global society, such as from the major wars and other catastrophes that will occur during the early Tribulation, our defenses against pestilences would crumble, allowing them to sweep away untold millions into eternity.

Earthquakes

According to Jesus' Olivet Discourse, the fourth calamity that will come during the opening phase of the Tribulation is earthquakes (Matt. 24:7–8). The phrase "in divers places" (that is, in "in different places") strongly suggests that earthquakes will become far more frequent, and since Jesus treats them as major disasters causing great sorrow, we may assume that they will be more severe also. The failure of the United States Geological Survey to detect any definite rise in either the frequency or severity of earthquakes since 1972 is not inconsistent with our view that the Tribulation is imminent.[84] It merely confirms that the Tribulation has not yet begun.

The number of casualties when earthquakes occur in divers places will no doubt be overwhelming, of a magnitude possible only under the conditions of life in modern society, which is daily becoming more vulnerable to earthquakes as it is to every other kind of disaster. Listen to this report from the Seismological Society of America. "The annual death toll from earthquakes has increased fourfold between the 17th and 20th centuries and is likely to increase dramatically in the 21st century. . . . With the dramatic increase in urban population, it is possible that very large earthquakes could cause up to one million deaths."[85]

The growth of urban areas with high population density is not the only factor making modern society more prone to earthquake damage. Another is our irrational insistence on building cities in places prone to earthquakes. In America, there are two fault systems known to be capable of producing great disasters. One is the San Andreas fault in California, which runs for eight hundred miles beneath a densely populated region.[86] Excavations by geologists have shown that "San Andreas quakes with a magnitude 7.5 or higher have struck Southern California on average once in 105 years."[87] The last one occurred 162 years ago—"which suggests that L.A. could soon experience another major hit."[88] A similar threat hangs over Northern California. A study done by the United States Geological Survey projects a 62% chance that a major quake will hit near San Francisco before 2033.[89]

The other potential source of tremendously damaging earthquakes in the U.S. is the New Madrid fault below the Mississippi Valley. Here is a recent government report. "In the winter of 1811–12, the central Mississippi Valley was struck by three of the most powerful earthquakes in U.S. history. . . . Damage was reported as far away as Charleston, South Carolina, and Washington, D.C., [and] church bells [rang] in Boston, Massachusetts, 1,000 miles away."[90]

The casualties were light because, "in 1811, the central Mississippi Valley was sparsely populated. Today, the region is home to millions of people, including those in the cities of St. Louis . . . and Memphis. Adding to the danger, most structures in the region were not built to withstand earthquake shaking, as they have been in California and Japan. Moreover, earthquake preparations also have lagged far behind."[91]

"The probability of a moderate earthquake occurring in the New Madrid seismic zone in the near future is high. Scientists estimate that the probability of a magnitude six to seven earthquake occurring in this seismic zone within the next twenty-five years is higher than 90%."[92]

Just since 2000, we have seen dramatic proof of mankind's growing vulnerability to vast devastation in the wake of a terrible earthquake. What is the worst natural disaster ever to hit the Western Hemisphere? The worst was the earthquake that overwhelmed Haiti in 2010. The Haitian government put the number of deaths at more than 220,000, although some experts have labeled this an exaggeration. Still, the casualties were far greater than any previous disaster on the Western side of the globe.[93]

What is the worst natural disaster to hit the human race since the Flood? Several disasters of overwhelming magnitude have befallen China within recorded history. More than once, river flooding has extinguished about a million lives.[94] The worst earthquake on record was the enormously catastrophic one that leveled the Chinese province of Shaanxi in 1556. It is estimated that more than 830,000 people died.[95] Another five earthquakes in world history are blamed for more than two hundred thousand deaths.[96] The worst of these may have been the one that triggered the Indian Ocean tsunami in 2004. By some calculations, the death toll approached 300,000.[97]

Disclaimers

Let me say that I do not claim perfect statistics. I have as much as possible used conservative estimates from trustworthy sources. What is important, however, is not the exact numbers, but the undeniable trends they illustrate.

Let me attach another disclaimer. As we investigate the dangerous trends in the world today, we are not saying that they will lead to the horrors of the Tribulation as a natural development. Rather, we are saying that global society is becoming fragile. When the time of judgment arrives, God will hit this world with severe shocks, such as major wars, that will overwhelm man's weakening defenses against calamity and leave him helpless to avert horrible devastation. Indeed, the world's vulnerability to huge disasters, such as will occur during the Tribulation, is growing every day.

Larger significance

Why are all these data concerning the state of today's world relevant to Biblical signs of the times? Because God designed this world to support human civilization for the sole purpose of enabling Him to set apart a people for Himself. To make this planet a comfortable place for men to inhabit any longer than His plan required would have opposed His purpose, for the most efficient gathering of souls, with the highest ratio of saved to lost, would be accomplished by bringing history to a climax in environmental and social chaos—exactly the kind of chaos that we see emerging everywhere today. Trouble pushes men toward God, whereas a world satisfying to self pushes them away.

Footnotes

[1] "Syria," *Wikipedia*, Web (en.wikipedia.org/wiki/Syria), 11/12/19.

[2] "Egypt," *Wikipedia*, Web (en.wikipedia.org/wiki/Egypt), 11/12/19.

[3] "World Agriculture 2030: Main Findings," Food and Agriculture Organization of the United Nations, 2002, Web (fao.org/english/newsroom/news/2002/7833-en.html), 8/20/19.

[4] "The State of Food Security and Nutrition in the World, 2019," Food and Agriculture Organization of the United Nations, 2019, Web (fao.org/state-of-food-security-nutrition/en/), 8/26/19.

[5] "The State of the World's Children: 2016 Statistical Tables," United Nations Children's Fund (UNICEF), 2016, Web (data.unicef.org/resources/state-worlds-children-2016-statistical-tables/), 8/20/19.

[6] "Current World Population," Worldometers, Web (worldometers.info/world-population/), 8/26/19.

[7] "World Population Day: July 11, 2018," United States Census Bureau, Web (census.gov/newsroom/stories/2018/world-population.html), 8/20/19.

[8] "The Future of Food and Agriculture: Trends and Challenges," Food and Agriculture Organization of the United Nations (Rome, 2017), 12, Web (fao.org/3/a-i6583e.pdf), 8/20/19.

[9] Max Roser and Hannah Ritchie, "Yields and Land Use in Agriculture: Empirical View," Our World in Data, Web (ourworldindata.org/yields-and-land-use-in-agriculture), 8/26/19.

[10] "Harvesting Nature's Diversity," Food and Agriculture Organization of the United Nations, Web (www.fao.org/3/v1430e/V1430E04.htm), 8/26/19.

[11] "The Future of Food and Agriculture: Alternative Pathways to 2050," Food and Agriculture Organization of the United Nations, 2018, 76–77, Web (http://www.fao.org/ 3/I8429EN/i8429en.pdf), 8/26/19.

[12] "The Facts: Nitrogen Fertilizer," Crop Nutrition, Web (cropnutrition.com/the-facts-nitrogen-fertilizer), 8/26/19.

[13] Julianne Geiger, "How Much Crude Oil Has the World Really Consumed?" Oilprice, Web (oilprice.com/Energy/Crude-Oil/How-Much-Crude-Oil-Has-The-World-Really-Consumed.html#), 9/2/19.

[14] Irina Slav, "Is Renewable Hydrogen a Threat to Natural Gas?" Oilprice, Web (oilprice.com/Energy/Energy-General/Is-Renewable-Hydrogen-A-Threat-To-Natural-Gas.html), 9/2/19.

[15] "Updated Global Water Risk Atlas Reveals Top Water-Stressed Countries and States," World Resources Institute, Web (wri.org/news/2019/08/release-updated-global-water-risk-atlas-reveals-top-water-stressed-countries-and-states),9/2/19.

[16] Ben Mandler, "Groundwater Use in the United States," American Geosciences Institute, Web (americangeosciences.org/geoscience-currents/groundwater-use-united-states), 9/2/19.

[17] "Fact Sheet-Global Aids Update 2019," UNAIDS, Web (unaids.org/en/resources/fact-sheet), 8/12/19.

[18] Ibid.

[19] "List of Countries by HIV/AIDS Adult Prevalence Rate," *Wikipedia*, Web (en.wikipedia.org/wiki/List_of_countries_by_HIV/AIDS_adult_prevalence_rate), 9/30/19.

[20]"HIV/AIDS in China," *Wikipedia,* Web (en.wikipedia.org/wiki/HIV/AIDS_in_ China), 9/30/19.

[21]"HIV/AIDS in Russia," *Wikipedia,* Web (en.wikipedia.org/wiki/HIV/AIDS_in_ Russia), 9/30/19.

[22]"Statistics," American Sexual Health Association, Web (ashasexualhealth.org/ stdsstis/statistics), 8/12/19.

[23]"HIV in the United States and Dependent Areas," Centers for Disease Control and Prevention, Web (cdc.gov/hiv/statistics/overview/ataglance.html), 8/12/19.

[24]"Global Aids Update 2019."

[25]"Alarming Surge in Drug-Resistant HIV Uncovered," Nature, Web (nature.com/ articles/d41586-019-02316-x), 8/12/19.

[26]"Sexually Transmitted Diseases," Office of Disease Prevention and Health Promotion, Web (healthypeople.gov/2020/topics-objectives/topic/sexually-transmitted-diseases), 9/30/19.

[27]"Genital HPV Infection–Fact Sheet," Centers for Disease Control and Prevention, Web (cdc.gov/std/hpv/stdfact-hpv.htm), 10/1/19.

[28]Ibid.

[29]"Statistics," ASHA.

[30]"Genital Herpes: Basic Fact Sheet," Centers for Disease Control and Prevention, Web (cdc.gov/std/herpes/stdfact-herpes.htm), 9/30/19.

[31]"Statistics," ASHA.

[32]"Genital Herpes," *Wikipedia,* Web (en.wikipedia.org/wiki/Genital_herpes), 9/30/19.

[33]"Sexually Transmitted Disease Surveillance 2018," Centers for Disease Control and Prevention, Web (cdc.gov/std/stats18/default.htm), 10/17/19.

[34]Ibid.

[35]Ibid.

[36]"CDC Fact Sheet: Reported STDs in the United States, 2017," Centers for Disease Control and Prevention, Web (cdc.gov/nchhstp/newsroom/docs/factsheets/ std-trends-508.pdf), 9/30/19.

[37]"Sexually Transmitted Disease."

[38]"Statistics," ASHA.

[39]"Reported STDs in the United States."

[40]"Tuberculosis," *Wikipedia,* Web (en.wikipedia.org/wiki/Tuberculosis#History), 10/7/19.

[41]*Global Tuberculosis Report 2018* (Geneva: World Health Organization, 2018), 6.

[42]Ibid., 1.

[43]"How TB Spreads," Centers for Disease Control and Prevention, Web (cdc.gov/ tb/topic/basics/howtbspreads.htm), 10/7/19.

[44]"Fact Sheet on Tuberculosis (TB)," World Health Organization TB Department, Web (who.int/3by5/TBfactsheet.pdf), 10/7/19.

[45]"Latent TB Infection and TB Disease," Centers for Disease Control and Prevention, Web (cdc.gov/tb/topic/basics/tbinfectiondisease.htm), 10/7/19.

[46]"Tuberculosis Vaccines," *Wikipedia,* Web (en.wikipedia.org/wiki/Tuberculosis_ vaccines), 10/8/19.

[47]*Global Tuberculosis Report 2018,* 1.

[48]Ibid., 6.

[49]Ibid., 1.

[50]"The Costly Burden of Drug-Resistant TB in the U.S.," Centers for Disease Control and Prevention, Web (cdc.gov/nchhstp/newsroom/docs/factsheets/costly-burden-dr-tb-508.pdf), 10/7/19.

[51]*Global Tuberculosis Report 2018,* 2.

[52]Ibid., 47.

[53]"Drug-Resistant TB," Centers for Disease Control and Prevention, Web (cdc.gov/ tb/topic/basics/drtb/default.htm), 10/7/19.

[54] "The Costly Burden."

[55] "Drug-Resistant TB: Totally Drug-Resistant TB FAQ," World Health Organization, Web (who.int/tb/areas-of-work/drug-resistant-tb/totally-drug-resistant-tb-faq/en/), 10/7/19.

[56] Chengli Bei, et al., "Mortality and Associated Factors of Patients with Extensive Drug-Resistant Tuberculosis: an Emerging Public Health Crisis in China," *BMC Infectious Diseases,* 18 (2018): 261; Web (ncbi.nlm.nih.gov/pmc/articles/PMC5992859/), 10/7/19.

[57] *Global Tuberculosis Report 2018,* 1.

[58] "Spanish Flu," History, Web (history.com/topics/world-war-i/1918-flu-pandemic), 10/8/19.

[59] "2009 H1N1 Pandemic (H1N1pdm09 Virus)," Centers for Disease Control and Prevention, Web (cdc.gov/flu/pandemic-resources/2009-h1n1-pandemic.html), 10/8/19.

[60] "Flu Treatment," Centers for Disease Control and Prevention, Web (cdc.gov/flu/treatment/index.html), 10/8/19.

[61] "Preventive Steps," Centers for Disease Control and Prevention, Web (cdc.gov/flu/prevent/prevention.htm?CDC_AA_refVal=https%3A%2F%2Fwww.cdc.gov%2Fflu%2Fconsumer%2Fprevention.htm), 10/8/19.

[62] "How Flu Spreads," Centers for Disease Control and Prevention, Web (cdc.gov/flu/about/disease/spread.htm), 10/8/19.

[63] "How the Flu Virus Can Change: 'Drift' and 'Shift,'" Centers for Disease Control and Prevention, Web (cdc.gov/flu/about/viruses/change.htm), 10/8/19.

[64] "Pandemic Influenza," Centers for Disease Control and Prevention, Web (cdc.gov/flu/pandemic-resources/index.htm), 10/8/19.

[65] "Frequently Asked Questions about Bird Flu," WebMD, Web (webmd.com/cold-and-flu/flu-guide/what-know-about-bird-flu#1), 10/8/19.

[66] Douglas Jordan with Terrence Tumpey and Barbara Jester, "The Deadliest Flu: The Complete Story of the Discovery and Reconstruction of the 1918 Pandemic Virus," Centers for Disease Control and Prevention, Web (cdc.gov/flu/pandemic-resources/reconstruction-1918-virus.html), 4/30/20.

[67] Adrian J. Gibbs, John S. Armstrong, and Jean C. Downie, "From Where Did the 2009 'Swine-Origin' Influenza A Virus (H1N1) Emerge?" *Virology Journal* 6 (2009): 207, Web (virologyj.biomedcentral.com/articles/10.1186/1743-422X-6-207), 5/4/20.

[68] Tara C. Smith, "The Animal Origins of Coronavirus and Flu," *Quanta Magazine,* 2/25/20, Web (quantamagazine.org/how-do-animal-viruses-like-coronavirus-jump-species-20200225/), 3/13/20.

[69] Ibid.

[70] "2019–2020 Coronavirus Pandemic," *Wikipedia,* Web (en.wikipedia.org/wiki/2019-20_coronavirus_pandemic), 4/12/20.

[71] "Ebola Virus Disease," *Wikipedia,* Web (en.wikipedia.org/wiki/Ebola_virus_disease), 3/13/20.

[72] "Malaria Progress Has Levelled but New Drugs Are Due," Fight Against Malaria, Web (fightagainstmalaria.com/malaria-progress-stalls-first-time-since-2000/), 10/8/19.

[73] *World Malaria Report 2018* (Geneva: World Health Organization, 2018), xiii, Web (apps.who.int/iris/bitstream/handle/10665/275867/9789241565653-eng.pdf), 11/4/19.

[74] Ibid.

[75] Rune Bosselmann, Director of TANA Netting, "Malaria Progress."

[76] "History of Smallpox," Centers for Disease Control and Prevention, Web (cdc.gov/smallpox/history/history.html), 10/14/19; "Smallpox," *Wikipedia,* Web (en.wikipedia.org/wiki/Smallpox), 10/15/19.

[77] Ibid.

[78] Ibid.

[79] "The Threat," Centers for Disease Control and Prevention, Web (cdc.gov/smallpox/bioterrorism/public/threat.html), 10/15/19; "Preparedness," Centers for Disease Control and Prevention, Web (cdc.gov/smallpox/bioterrorism/public/preparedness.html), 10/15/19.

[80] "Water Overview," The World Bank, Web (www.worldbank.org/en/topic/water/overview), 9/2/19.

[81] "Cholera," *Wikipedia*, Web (en.wikipedia.org/wiki/Cholera), 10/15/19.

[82] "Cholera, 1/17/19," World Health Organization, Web (who.int/news-room/fact-sheets/detail/cholera), 10/15/19.

[83] "Cholera," *Wikipedia.*

[84] "Why Are We Having So Many Earthquakes?" United States Geological Society, Web (usgs.gov/faqs/why-are-we-having-so-many-earthquakes-has-naturally-occurring-earthquake-activity-been?qt-news_science_products=0#qt-news_science_products), 9/23/19.

[85] "Seismological Society of America Scientists Foresee Earthquakes with Fatality Counts Exceeding One Million," *Ascribe Higher Education News Service,* 5/2/03.

[86] Britt Norlander, "Waiting for the Big One: Two New Studies Show That When It Comes to a Major Earthquake, California Could Be a Time Bomb," *Science World,* 10/13/03.

[87] Ibid.

[88] Ibid.

[89] Ibid.

[90] Eugene Schweig, Joan Gomberg, and James W. Hendley II, "The Mississippi Valley—'Whole Lotta Shakin' Goin' On,'" *Fact Sheet 168–95,* United States Geological Society, 1995, Web (pubs.er.usgs.gov/publication/fs16895), 9/23/19.

[91] Ibid.

[92] Ibid.

[93] Stephanie Pappas, "Top 11 Deadliest Natural Disasters in History," Live Science, 4/2/18, Web (livescience.com/33316-top-10-deadliest-natural-disasters.html), 9/23/19; "The Top 10 Deadliest Earthquakes in History," Asia-Pacific on NBCNews.com, 2019, Web (nbcnews.com/id/42029974/ns/world_news-asia_pacific/t/top-deadliest-earthquakes-history/#.XYp6WJNKgo8), 9/24/19.

[94] Pappas.

[95] Ibid.; "The Top 10."

[96] "The Top 10."

[97] Ibid; Pappas.

Chapter 11

✣ The Worthiness Test ✣

Importance of watchfulness

The command to watch for the Lord's return is a major theme of the New Testament. The word "watch" occurs in such a context twelve times.

> 35 Let your loins be girded about, and *your* lights burning;
> 36 And ye yourselves like unto men that wait for their lord, when he will return from the wedding; that when he cometh and knocketh, they may open unto him immediately.
> 37 Blessed *are* those servants, whom the lord when he cometh shall find watching: verily I say unto you, that he shall gird himself, and make them to sit down to meat, and will come forth and serve them.
> 38 And if he shall come in the second watch, or come in the third watch, and find *them* so, blessed are those servants.
> 39 And this know, that if the goodman of the house had known what hour the thief would come, he would have watched, and not have suffered his house to be broken through.
> 40 Be ye therefore ready also: for the Son of man cometh at an hour when ye think not.
>
> - Luke 12:35–40 -

There are also many texts that give the same command without actually using the word "watch."

> Looking for that blessed hope, and the glorious appearing of the great God and our Saviour Jesus Christ.
>
> - Titus 2:13 -

The closing words of the Bible frame the prayer that should always be on our lips.

> He which testifieth these things saith, Surely I come quickly. Amen. Even so, come, Lord Jesus.
>
> - Revelation 22:20 -

To insure watchfulness, the Bible teaches that the Lord's return is imminent—that is, so far as we know, He could come at any moment.

> Let your moderation be known unto all men. The Lord *is* at hand.
>
> - Philippians 4:5 -

> For yet a little while, and he that shall come will come, and will not tarry.
>
> - Hebrews 10:37 -

> Behold, I come quickly: hold that fast which thou hast, that no man
> take thy crown.
>
> - Revelation 3:11 -

Why is watching for His return important? For two reasons.

1. It keeps Christ in the center of our thoughts. There is a great danger that we will become so preoccupied with serving Christ that we will forget the One we are serving. Remember Mary and Martha.

> 38 Now it came to pass, as they went, that he entered into a certain vil-
>   lage: and a certain woman named Martha received him into her
>   house.
> 39 And she had a sister called Mary, which also sat at Jesus' feet, and
>   heard his word.
> 40 But Martha was cumbered about much serving, and came to him,
>   and said, Lord, dost thou not care that my sister hath left me to serve
>   alone? bid her therefore that she help me.
> 41 And Jesus answered and said unto her, Martha, Martha, thou art
>   careful and troubled about many things:
> 42 But one thing is needful: and Mary hath chosen that good part, which
>   shall not be taken away from her.
>
> - Luke 10:38–42 -

Imagine having Jesus Christ as a guest in your living room and spending all your time in the kitchen. But that is exactly what we are prone to do. Although we faithfully go about the tasks of a Christian—assisting ministries in the church, witnessing to the lost, teaching our children Biblical principles—we may fail to sit down at the feet of Jesus. We may spend little time talking with Jesus Himself. We should be confiding in Him, earnestly seeking His counsel, treasuring His every word, and lavishing our love and praise upon Him.

One good way to keep our focus on Christ is to remember that we might see Him at any moment. Suddenly, without warning, our bodies will be changed, and in that moment of transformation we will receive the capacity to hear a trumpet that mere mortals cannot hear. From its sound of stupendous majesty, racing from sky to sky, will emerge another sound, the voice of Christ inviting us to ascend into His presence. Then we will joyfully depart from this world of corruption and meet Him face to face. The meeting we long for could be just minutes away. How important it is, then, that we keep our love for Christ warm and fresh, lest we become like the church at Ephesus.

> 2 I know thy works, and thy labour, and thy patience, and how thou
>   canst not bear them which are evil: and thou hast tried them which
>   say they are apostles, and are not, and hast found them liars:
> 3 And hast borne, and hast patience, and for my name's sake hast la-
>   boured, and hast not fainted.
> 4 Nevertheless I have *somewhat* against thee, because thou hast left thy
>   first love.
> 5 Remember therefore from whence thou art fallen, and repent, and do
>   the first works; or else I will come unto thee quickly, and will remove

thy candlestick out of his place, except thou repent.

- Revelation 2:2-5 -

The Ephesians were busy doing God's work, but their labor was dry duty, empty of love. We will not neglect to love Christ if we are always looking for Him.

2. The second reason we must watch is that we must not forget how close we are to being judged. The first event after the Rapture will be the Judgment Seat of Christ. According to Paul, that prospect put terror in his heart.

> 10 For we must all appear before the judgment seat of Christ; that every one may receive the things *done* in *his* body, according to that he hath done, whether *it be* good or bad.
> 11 Knowing therefore the terror of the Lord, we persuade men; but we are made manifest unto God; and I trust also are made manifest in your consciences.

- 2 Corinthians 5:10-11 -

If God's anointed apostle to the gentiles was afraid of the accounting he must give to Christ, how should we feel? Watchfulness, if combined with recognition that Christ will judge us soon after we meet Him, will deter us from sin. Time and time again, the New Testament warns us that we will fall into sin if we forget how close we are to being judged.

Let us examine some of these warnings:

> 8 Be ye also patient; stablish your hearts: for the coming of the Lord draweth nigh.
> 9 Grudge not one against another, brethren, lest ye be condemned: behold, the judge standeth before the door.

- James 5:8-9 -

The word "grudge" would be better translated "groan" or "grumble." James is talking about complaining, or gossip, or any use of the tongue to run down a brother. He tells us to be careful. If the Lord comes while we are waging a campaign against our brother, we will go straight to judgment and be condemned. What is the right way to handle any complaint or grievance? The Bible is very clear. We should go to the person who has offended us and talk to him before we talk to anybody else. Let him satisfy us without damage to his own reputation.

> 15 Moreover if thy brother shall trespass against thee, go and tell him his fault between thee and him alone: if he shall hear thee, thou hast gained thy brother.
> 16 But if he will not hear *thee, then* take with thee one or two more, that in the mouth of two or three witnesses every word may be established.
> 17 And if he shall neglect to hear them, tell *it* unto the church: but if he neglect to hear the church, let him be unto thee as an heathen man and

a publican.

- Matthew 18:15–17 -

According to James in the text we have just quoted, the best way to keep sweetness among ourselves is to remember that the judge stands at the door. One danger in not being watchful is that we lose a great incentive to control our tongues. We let poisonous words come out and breed conflict.

Consider another warning.

> 44 Therefore be ye also ready: for in such an hour as ye think not the Son of man cometh.
> 45 Who then is a faithful and wise servant, whom his lord hath made ruler over his household, to give them meat in due season?
> 46 Blessed *is* that servant, whom his lord when he cometh shall find so doing.
> 47 Verily I say unto you, That he shall make him ruler over all his goods.
> 48 But and if that evil servant shall say in his heart, My lord delayeth his coming;
> 49 And shall begin to smite *his* fellowservants, and to eat and drink with the drunken;
> 50 The lord of that servant shall come in a day when he looketh not for *him*, and in an hour that he is not aware of,
> 51 And shall cut him asunder, and appoint *him* his portion with the hypocrites: there shall be weeping and gnashing of teeth.

- Matthew 24:44–51 -

Here is urgent divine counsel to pastors and church leaders. Jesus says that if they neglect to be watchful—if they forget that they will soon meet Christ in judgment—they may start abusing the flock entrusted to them. Abuse of power by church leaders has been a recurring problem in church history. Every new movement of God tends to stagnate within a few generations. One reason is that leaders eventually arise who are more interested in career than in Christ, in enlarging their own fame and power than in enlarging the kingdom of God. Jesus calls such a man an evil servant, and the destiny He decrees for such a man is the most terrible we find in Scripture. A Christian leader who is a rank hypocrite mistreating his people and serving his own pleasure will be torn limb from limb and cast into hell.

Pretribulational rapture

See yet another warning.

> 34 And take heed to yourselves, lest at any time your hearts be overcharged with surfeiting, and drunkenness, and cares of this life, and *so* that day come upon you unawares.
> 35 For as a snare shall it come on all them that dwell on the face of the whole earth.
> 36 Watch ye therefore, and pray always, that ye may be accounted worthy to escape all these things that shall come to pass, and to stand before the Son of man.

- Luke 21:34–36 -

This is an amazing text. As we read it, we feel that we can almost hear Jesus' voice speaking directly to us, in our generation.

Yet perhaps you have ignored it because, like many today, you have no interest in prophecy. As we showed in chapter 2, such an interest is rapidly disappearing from evangelical churches. When I was young, prophecy was a major theme of both teaching and preaching. Many people devoted summer vacations to attending Bible conferences on prophecy. They devoured books on the subject and eagerly tuned in such radio Bible teachers as M. R. DeHaan, who faithfully expounded the prophetic Scriptures. Today, prophecy has become the province of weird televangelists, who drum up enthusiasm by making sensational but unscriptural claims. But we cannot afford to neglect prophecy. We see its importance in how much of the Bible is devoted to it. Between one fourth and one third of the Bible has prophecy as its subject.

Nor can we afford to misinterpret prophecy. As we showed in chapter 8, a popular view today is that the passage just quoted in Luke 21 and many other prophecies of Jesus concerning the end times are referring to events during the Tribulation. We labeled this view "ultradispensationalism." If I am describing what you were taught, I respect your position. As a Baptist, I believe in soul liberty. But I beg to differ with you. It is evident that God has given us this passage as a warning of vital importance. Therefore, you would be wise to consider my arguments against ultradispensationalism. In the same earlier chapter, I show that the ultradispensational view of Jesus' sayings does not stand up to scrutiny. The root problem is that it fails to compare Scripture with Scripture.

Before we can heed the warning in Luke 21:34–36, we must, however, understand it. Let us approach it with some Biblical common sense. What is "that day which as a snare will come on all them that dwell on the face of the whole earth?" What are "all these things that shall come to pass?" The answer is in the preceding verses 25 to 28.

> 25 And there shall be signs in the sun, and in the moon, and in the stars; and upon the earth distress of nations, with perplexity; the sea and the waves roaring;
> 26 Men's hearts failing them for fear, and for looking after those things which are coming on the earth: for the powers of heaven shall be shaken.
> 27 And then shall they see the Son of man coming in a cloud with power and great glory.
> 28 And when these things begin to come to pass, then look up, and lift up your heads; for your redemption draweth nigh.
>
> - Luke 21:25–28 -

Jesus is obviously talking about the coming period of earth's history when God will pour out His wrath on the whole world—the period that believers today call the Tribulation. But Jesus promises that His people will not have to go through it. A few verses later, in verse 36,

He says that they will "escape all these things that shall come to pass"; literally, "escape these things all which are about to come to pass."[1] Back in verse 28, in reference to the same deliverance, the text says that it will happen "when these things begin to come to pass." The clear meaning is that God will deliver His people just when the world descends into all-consuming trouble. In other words, believers will miss the whole Tribulation. How will they escape? The answer should be obvious to every reader. The only way to escape worldwide calamity is to leave the world. We should be able to agree that Jesus in these verses is teaching the rapture of the church. Indeed, this is one of numerous passages undergirding the doctrine of a pretribulational rapture.

The marks of a true Christian

Now be patient. We have to lay the groundwork for a momentous conclusion—a life-changing conclusion, I hope, for some of you. Despite the obvious importance of this passage in Luke 21, many preachers steer away from it, because it raises hard questions. For example, Jesus clearly teaches that to participate in the Rapture, we must pass a worthiness test. He says, "Watch ye therefore, and pray always, that ye may be accounted worthy to escape all these things" (v. 36). The meaning is not that we should be praying always for God to find us worthy, but that we should make ourselves worthy by praying always.   The test of worthiness is therefore exactly this: whether we are always watching and praying rather than letting ourselves be absorbed by worldly pleasures and cares. But wait a minute. You do not have to pass a worthiness test to become a Christian. If you did, salvation would not be by faith, but by works. Thus, from the teaching that only the worthy will be taken at the Rapture, some people have drawn false conclusions. They have decided that it will be only a partial rapture, a rapture not of the whole church, but of a few saints selected for their outstanding godliness. Just the worthiest Christians will be taken, they say.

But the people holding this view have failed to study the mind of Jesus. Everywhere in His teaching, Jesus treats faith and works as inseparable. A good example is the following:

> 21 Not every one that saith unto me, Lord, Lord, shall enter into the kingdom of heaven; but he that doeth the will of my Father which is in heaven.
> 22 Many will say to me in that day, Lord, Lord, have we not prophesied in thy name? and in thy name have cast out devils? and in thy name done many wonderful works?
> 23 And then will I profess unto them, I never knew you: depart from me, ye that work iniquity.
>
> - Matthew 7:21–23 -

Here, Jesus speaks as though eternal destiny depends on works,

does He not?   Those admitted to heaven have done the will of the
Father. Those barred from heaven have practiced iniquity. But what
He means is clarified by James.

> 20 But wilt thou know, O vain man, that faith without works is dead?
> 21 Was not Abraham our father justified by works, when he had offered
>   Isaac his son upon the altar?
> 22 Seest thou how faith wrought with his works, and by works was faith
>   made perfect?
> 23 And the scripture was fulfilled which saith, Abraham believed God,
>   and it was imputed unto him for righteousness: and he was called the
>   Friend of God.
> 24 Ye see then how that by works a man is justified, and not by faith
>   only.
>
> - James 2:20–24 -

We find in this passage that true faith always produces good works.
We find elsewhere in Scripture that truly good works, pleasing to
God, are impossible without faith.

> 8 For by grace are ye saved through faith; and that not of yourselves: *it
>   is* the gift of God:
> 9 Not of works, lest any man should boast.
> 10 For we are his workmanship, created in Christ Jesus unto good
>   works, which God hath before ordained that we should walk in them.
>
> - Ephesians 2:8–10 -

So, when Jesus calls someone a worker of iniquity, He means that he
lacks not only works, but also faith, for a true man of faith is never a
worker of iniquity, in the sense that iniquity controls his life. Rather,
he is a man who does the Father's will.

Let us reexamine Luke 21:34–36 in the light of these principles.
When Jesus says that we must pass a worthiness test to participate
in the Rapture, He means that this worthiness test is also a test of
our salvation.   Works are not the means of our salvation, but the
proof of our salvation. At the time when He returns for the church, a
saved man will be watching for Him and praying always.   No real
Christian will instead have a heart overcharged with surfeiting,
drunkenness, and cares of this life. "Overcharged" means "weighed
down." Jesus is describing someone whose heart has sunk into the
world of self instead of rising into the world of eternity. Do you understand the terrible implications of our conclusion? Viewed in this
way, the words of this passage fall like a bombshell on the contemporary church, which is overrun by professing Christians absorbed in
unspiritual lifestyles.   Jesus is saying that such people are self-
deceived if they think they have a place reserved at the Rapture.

Laodiceans

A similar warning for our benefit is found in the last of the letters
recorded in the opening chapters of Revelation, the letter to Laodicea.

It describes a people who sound exactly like many Christians in the modern world. They are smug about their Christianity. They imagine that no one could stand higher in God's estimation than they do. But they are self-deceived.

> 14 And unto the angel of the church of the Laodiceans write; These things saith the Amen, the faithful and true witness, the beginning of the creation of God;
> 15 I know thy works, that thou art neither cold nor hot: I would thou wert cold or hot.
> 16 So then because thou art lukewarm, and neither cold nor hot, I will spue thee out of my mouth.
> 17 Because thou sayest, I am rich, and increased with goods, and have need of nothing; and knowest not that thou art wretched, and miserable, and poor, and blind, and naked:
> 18 I counsel thee to buy of me gold tried in the fire, that thou mayest be rich; and white raiment, that thou mayest be clothed, and *that* the shame of thy nakedness do not appear; and anoint thine eyes with eyesalve, that thou mayest see.
> 19 As many as I love, I rebuke and chasten: be zealous therefore, and repent.
> 20 Behold, I stand at the door, and knock: if any man hear my voice, and open the door, I will come in to him, and will sup with him, and he with me.
> 21 To him that overcometh will I grant to sit with me in my throne, even as I also overcame, and am set down with my Father in his throne.
> 22 He that hath an ear, let him hear what the Spirit saith unto the churches.
>
> - Revelation 3:14–22 -

As we will show later, the church of Laodicea pictures a typical evangelical church in the Last Days, just before Christ returns. It is a church that is outwardly prosperous. Its people even have the audacity to boast that they have need of nothing. Perceiving the bustling success of their church as a sign of God's favor, they freely thank God for His special blessings upon them. In their hearts they feel secure in their salvation, and they have no doubt that they will go to heaven. If they believe in the Rapture, they expect to be included.

But what is their true condition? Jesus says that despite the size and wealth of Laodicean churches, He does not take any pleasure in them. They are, in fact, disgusting, like the taste of lukewarm water. The terms He uses to describe their members show clearly that, with few exceptions, they are not born again. In reality, they are wretched and miserable. That is, they are still in bondage to sin.

> 23 But I see another law in my members, warring against the law of my mind, and bringing me into captivity to the law of sin which is in my members.
> 24 O wretched man that I am! who shall deliver me from the body of this death?
>
> - Romans 7:23–24 -

Although it is a believer speaking here, he is talking about man's

natural condition apart from the Holy Spirit. Wretchedness and misery are the lot of every unsaved man. The Laodiceans are also poor.
That is, they lack the true riches of an inheritance in heaven.

> The eyes of your understanding being enlightened; that ye may know
> what is the hope of his calling, and what the riches of the glory of his in-
> heritance in the saints, . . .
>
> - Ephesians 1:18 -

They are blind. That is, they walk in darkness and know not the
light of Christ.

> 6 If we say that we have fellowship with him, and walk in darkness, we
> lie, and do not the truth:
> 7 But if we walk in the light, as he is in the light, we have fellowship
> one with another, and the blood of Jesus Christ his Son cleanseth us
> from all sin.
>
> - 1 John 1:6–7 -

They are naked. That is, they are not clothed with the righteousness
of Christ.

> And to her was granted that she should be arrayed in fine linen,
> clean and white: for the fine linen is the righteousness of saints.
>
> - Revelation 19:8 -

To be wretched, miserable, poor, blind, and naked—these are terms
describing unsaved people. The point is, evangelical churches in the
Last Days will be filled with unsaved people who are oblivious to their
true spiritual condition.

What will happen to them? They will suffer the fate described in
verse 16 of Revelation 3. Jesus says that He will spew them out of
His mouth. The obvious meaning is that He will judge them to be
strangers to His body, with no right to be included among the raptured saints. As a result, they will not escape the horrors of history's
final hour. Some, as a result of being left behind, will repent. These
are the ones mentioned in verse 19. Yet when they finally live in a
manner pleasing to God, they will suffer terrible persecution. We will
show later that the Tribulation will produce a host of martyrs.

Dare I assume that I am not a typical Laodicean? Dare you assume that you are not? Because we are all human, with an immense
capacity for self-deception, we must all examine ourselves to see
whether we are truly saved.

> Examine yourselves, whether ye be in the faith; prove your own
> selves. Know ye not your own selves, how that Jesus Christ is in you,
> except ye be reprobates?
>
> - 2 Corinthians 13:5 -

How do we know? The telltale sign that end-time Laodiceans will be
playacting at their religion is given in Revelation 3:15–16. Their

works will be neither cold nor hot, but lukewarm. They will be exactly the kind of people that Jesus describes when He reveals who will be excluded from the Rapture (Luke 21:34–36 on p. 121). Although they may profess a relationship with Christ, they will be preoccupied with life in this world. Instead of praying and watching, they will devote themselves to earthly pleasures and cares.

Three miseries of the self-deceived

According to Jesus' words in the same passage, the lives of worldlings who miss the Rapture will center on three things: surfeiting, drunkenness, and cares of this life. The result? Instead of escaping from the Tribulation, they will be its victims. It will descend upon them by surprise and swallow them up.

What is meant by "surfeiting"? The English word is a poor attempt to translate *kraipale* (κραιπαλή).[2] Scholars agree that in its core meaning, the Greek word suggests unpleasant sensations in a person's head. One authority defined it as "both *carousing, intoxication,* and its result *drunken headache, hangover,* since it means *dizziness, staggering,* when the head refuses to function."[3] Another says, "In the medical writings it is used of *drunken nausea* or *headache.*"[4] Yet another points out that it is a compound of two roots, the Greek words "head" and "toss about."[5]

The second preoccupation Jesus predicts in the lives of many in the Last Days is "drunkenness," another reference to their use of intoxicating beverages. The unavoidable question is why Jesus referred to both surfeiting and drunkenness if both terms name essentially the same vice. Was not the mention of only one sufficient to convey His intended meaning? Perhaps He used both for the sake of emphasis. But since they are not exact synonyms, it is more likely that He used both to give us a larger picture of how alcohol hurts people. Although the terms overlap in meaning, they highlight slightly different evils on the world scene. The first, because it vividly describes the immediate physical and neurological effects of drinking, points to all the harm that an inebriated person can do to himself and others. The second, because it serves as Jesus' description of people left behind at the Rapture, suggests a habitual practice. Therefore, it points to the vice known as alcoholism, which causes decay of both mind and body.

There is no doubt that today's world is madly in love with alcohol, as well as with many other mind-altering chemicals. One recent study found that the total volume of alcohol consumed per year around the world increased 70% between 1990 and 2017.[6] In the same period, global population increased only 29%.[7] Yet these statistics do not mean that drinking more alcohol is a uniform trend. On the contrary, the percentage of drinkers in all countries actually decreased between 2000 and 2016.[8] But at the same time there was an even sharper increase in per capita consumption of alcohol by those who were still drinkers.

For a proper understanding of Luke 21:34–36, we must see the sharp contrast between this passage and Matthew 24:37–39 (quoted on p. 90). Although both provide Jesus' description of the masses who will be unprepared for His return, they look at the spiritually ignorant from different perspectives. In Matthew 24, where Jesus likens the days before His coming to the days of Noah, He says that the Flood took most people by surprise because their attention was wholly given to such everyday pleasures as eating, drinking, marrying, and giving in marriage. In essence, they just wanted to enjoy life. Likewise in the Last Days, people will attach no importance to things spiritual. They too will be seeking a world-centered happiness. But whereas in Matthew 24, Jesus tells what they will be seeking, in Luke 21 He tells what they will find. Their compulsive pursuit of worldly pleasure will take them at last to a life of misery. Instead of boundless joy in eating and drinking, they will, if they surrender their hearts to food and drink, find only surfeiting and drunkenness. Also, instead of perfect happiness in marriage, they will find only cares of this life if they become obsessed with searching for a perfect sexual partner of their own choosing, without God's help, or even for a perfect family of their own making, without God's help.

Christian duty. Have Christians stood firm in opposition to alcoholic beverages? A generation ago, Christians were strongly opposed to them. My mother was a member of the WCTU (the Women's Christian Temperance Union), the driving force behind Prohibition. Back in the '50s, I knew the president of this organization. She belonged to a good fundamental church. But today, the standards against drinking are crumbling away. At one time, Christians would not go to a restaurant that served alcohol. That standard has evaporated, has it not? Now, in some evangelical circles, drinking itself has become acceptable. This is an alarming trend in light of Jesus' warning to us who live in the Last Days that we should stay away from drunkenness. Even opposition to psychoactive drugs is weakening in the Christian world. Professing Christians here and there have argued that it makes sense to legalize marijuana for treatment of certain medical conditions. But any church that wishes to remain a good influence on society and to avoid sliding into Laodicea must stand firm in opposition to use of both alcohol and drugs.

Another misery that Jesus says will be pervasive in the Last Days, even hitting many false Christians, is cares of this life. Also, when we see Matthew 24:37–39 and Luke 21:34–36 as contrastive parallels, He suggests how these cares will enter their experience. The source will be a devotion of self to enjoying the kind of intimate personal relationships that are normally provided by marriage and family. It may seem to you that anyone who at least succeeds in building a marriage and family must be climbing fairly high on the scale of happiness, but despite the great advantages in marriage, the dominant view of Scripture is that it embroils us in trouble and sorrow.

> 28 But and if thou marry, thou hast not sinned; and if a virgin marry, she hath not sinned. Nevertheless such shall have trouble in the flesh: but I spare you.
> 29 But this I say, brethren, the time *is* short: it remaineth, that both they that have wives be as though they had none;
> 30 And they that weep, as though they wept not; and they that rejoice, as though they rejoiced not; and they that buy, as though they possessed not;
> 31 And they that use this world, as not abusing *it:* for the fashion of this world passeth away.
> 32 But I would have you without carefulness. He that is unmarried careth for the things that belong to the Lord, how he may please the Lord:
> 33 But he that is married careth for the things that are of the world, how he may please *his* wife.
>
> - 1 Corinthians 7:28–33 -

So, it is not surprising that in the two passages where Jesus foresees the obsessions of unsaved people on the eve of His return, He appears to set marriage parallel to cares of this world. He knew that marriage-centered cares would be especially severe in the Last Days, because the institution of marriage would then break down, making it hard for families to remain whole and happy. And for the many people who would then cast aside marriage and pursue sex instead, the cares of life would eventually mount to a terrible climax of disease and unbearable loneliness.

There are crucial applications even for saved people. Do not let the difficulty of finding a good mate in perilous times pull you down into deep sadness. If you do marry but discover afterward that your mate has serious flaws, do not let disappointment and discontent become the theme of your thoughts. If you are cast aside by a mate who proves faithless, do not surrender to anger and bitterness. On the other hand, if you have a good marriage, do not let family life become an idol, drawing your heart away from the worship and service of God. Nor should you let family life become an obsession, robbing you of time for fruitful ministry outside your family. In summary, do not let anything in your life as a partner or parent chase from your mind a wholesome meditation on "the blessed hope" of Christ's return. Remember, Scripture suggests that the worldly cares distracting us from being watchful will include cares of marriage and family.

Meager harvest

From the letter to Laodicea, we learn that many members of today's large evangelical churches are not really saved. The picture that this letter furnishes of an end-time church is consistent with

Jesus' warnings that few will be taken at the Rapture. More than once, He compared the time right before the Tribulation to the days of Noah (Luke 17:26–27, quoted on p. 43; Matt. 24:37–39, quoted on p. 90). How many in Noah's day did God deem worthy to save from the Flood? Only eight out of the millions or billions who may have been alive at that time. Also, on one occasion Jesus used a sobering question to alert us that the harvest of souls at the Rapture will be exceedingly small.

> I tell you that he will avenge them speedily. Nevertheless when the Son of man cometh, shall he find faith on the earth?
>
> - Luke 18:8 -

The question is rhetorical; in other words, it suggests the right answer. By asking it, Jesus implied that the presence of faith at His return is rather doubtful. So, there will be either none with faith or very few with faith.

Now we come to the most important question you will ever face—the most important because it is equivalent to asking whether you are saved. This is it. Are you ready for Christ to come? Are you watching for Him always? Are you praying always? Or have you turned your eyes downward to see only the things of this world? Are you living mainly for the sake of the next good meal, the next good time, the next good video? Is your mind largely centered on family cares and other problems? Or is one theme of your thoughts the hope of soon meeting the precious person of Christ?

Think on these things, brethren. I have discharged my responsibility by preparing you for this question as well as I could, and by putting the question to you as clearly as I could. You will never ponder a more important question.

Footnotes

[1]Berry, 305.

[2]Ibid.

[3]Arndt and Gingrich, 449.

[4]Marvin Vincent, *Word Studies in the New Testament,* 4 vols., 2nd ed. (N.p.: [c. 1888]; repr., McLean, Va.: MacDonald Publishing Co., n.d.), 1:420

[5]Joseph Henry Thayer, *A Greek-English Lexicon of the New Testament,* corrected ed. (N.p.: Harper & Bros., 1889; repr., New York: American Book Co., n.d.), 358.

[6]Maria Cohut, "Global Alcohol Intake Has Increased by 70%, Study Warns," MedicalNewsToday, 5/9/19, Web (medicalnewstoday.com/articles/325135), 5/20/20.

[7]"Current World Population," Worldometer, 5/20/20, Web (worldometers.info/world-population/#table-historical), 5/20/20.

[8]*Global Status Report on Alcohol and Health 2018* (Geneva: World Health Organization, 2018), 44, 46, Web (who.int/substance_abuse/publications/global_alcohol_report/en/), 5/18/20.

Chapter 12

✛ Church of Philadelphia ✛

Seven churches of Asia

Chapters 2 and 3 in the Book of Revelation contain letters from Christ to seven churches in Asia Minor. All seven of these churches ceased to exist long ago, when the Muslims overran that part of the world. Yet a leading traditional view is that in addition to representing actual churches in the first century, they are also symbols with prophetic meaning. After all, we find them in a book devoted to prophecy.

A common view is that these Asian churches divide church history into seven periods. The first church, Ephesus, corresponds to the apostolic period. The last church, Laodicea, corresponds to the modern period. And the other five churches are a chronological sequence of intervening periods spanning almost two thousand years.

The great difficulty in this view is that Christ strongly implies that four churches other than Laodicea will exist when He returns. To show which of the seven will have an end-time presence, we will review the contents of each letter.

The letter to Ephesus makes no mention whatever of Christ's coming.

> 1 Unto the angel of the church of Ephesus write; These things saith he that holdeth the seven stars in his right hand, who walketh in the midst of the seven golden candlesticks;
> 2 I know thy works, and thy labour, and thy patience, and how thou canst not bear them which are evil: and thou hast tried them which say they are apostles, and are not, and hast found them liars:
> 3 And hast borne, and hast patience, and for my name's sake hast laboured, and hast not fainted.
> 4 Nevertheless I have *somewhat* against thee, because thou hast left thy first love.
> 5 Remember therefore from whence thou art fallen, and repent, and do the first works; or else I will come unto thee quickly, and will remove thy candlestick out of his place, except thou repent.
> 6 But this thou hast, that thou hatest the deeds of the Nicolaitans, which I also hate.
> 7 He that hath an ear, let him hear what the Spirit saith unto the churches; To him that overcometh will I give to eat of the tree of life, which is in the midst of the paradise of God.
>
> - Revelation 2:1–7 -

Instead, we find an ominous warning. If the people in Ephesus fail to repent, Christ will remove their candlestick, or lamp stand, out of its place (v. 5). In other words, if they refuse to rekindle their first love,

He will extinguish their witness, and their church will cease to exist. In fact, no church we could identify as Ephesian remains in the modern world.

Smyrna is the second of the seven churches in Asia.

> 8 And unto the angel of the church in Smyrna write; These things saith the first and the last, which was dead, and is alive;
> 9 I know thy works, and tribulation, and poverty, (but thou art rich) and *I know* the blasphemy of them which say they are Jews, and are not, but *are* the synagogue of Satan.
> 10 Fear none of those things which thou shalt suffer: behold, the devil shall cast *some* of you into prison, that ye may be tried; and ye shall have tribulation ten days: be thou faithful unto death, and I will give thee a crown of life.
> 11 He that hath an ear, let him hear what the Spirit saith unto the churches; He that overcometh shall not be hurt of the second death.
>
> - Revelation 2:8–11 -

Here likewise, we find no allusion to the return of Christ. Whether Smyrna will still exist in the end times is left uncertain.

But in the letter to each remaining church, we find easy clues that it will last to the end of our present age. The next is Pergamos.

> 12 And to the angel of the church in Pergamos write; These things saith he which hath the sharp sword with two edges;
> 13 I know thy works, and where thou dwellest, *even* where Satan's seat *is:* and thou holdest fast my name, and hast not denied my faith, even in those days wherein Antipas *was* my faithful martyr, who was slain among you, where Satan dwelleth.
> 14 But I have a few things against thee, because thou hast there them that hold the doctrine of Balaam, who taught Balac to cast a stumblingblock before the children of Israel, to eat things sacrificed unto idols, and to commit fornication.
> 15 So hast thou also them that hold the doctrine of the Nicolaitans, which thing I hate.
> 16 Repent; or else I will come unto thee quickly, and will fight against them with the sword of my mouth.
> 17 He that hath an ear, let him hear what the Spirit saith unto the churches; To him that overcometh will I give to eat of the hidden manna, and will give him a white stone, and in the stone a new name written, which no man knoweth saving he that receiveth *it.*
>
> - Revelation 2:12–17 -

To this church, the third, Jesus says, "Repent; or else I will come unto thee quickly, and will fight against them with the sword of my mouth" (v. 16). "Quickly" means that He will come sooner than they expect. He plainly warns them that unless they repent and cast out false teachers, He Himself will take up the fight against these evildoers when He returns. Thus, He must believe that the church of Pergamos will still exist.

We find the same expectation in the letter to the church of Thyatira.

> 18 And unto the angel of the church in Thyatira write; These things saith the Son of God, who hath his eyes like unto a flame of fire, and his feet *are* like fine brass;

19 I know thy works, and charity, and service, and faith, and thy patience, and thy works; and the last *to be* more than the first.

20 Notwithstanding I have a few things against thee, because thou
sufferest that woman Jezebel, which calleth herself a prophetess, to
teach and to seduce my servants to commit fornication, and to eat
things sacrificed unto idols.

21 And I gave her space to repent of her fornication; and she repented
not.

22 Behold, I will cast her into a bed, and them that commit adultery with
her into great tribulation, except they repent of their deeds.

23 And I will kill her children with death; and all the churches shall
know that I am he which searcheth the reins and hearts: and I will
give unto every one of you according to your works.

24 But unto you I say, and unto the rest in Thyatira, as many as have
not this doctrine, and which have not known the depths of Satan, as
they speak; I will put upon you none other burden.

25 But that which ye have *already* hold fast till I come.

26 And he that overcometh, and keepeth my works unto the end, to him
will I give power over the nations:

27 And he shall rule them with a rod of iron; as the vessels of a potter
shall they be broken to shivers: even as I received of my Father.

28 And I will give him the morning star.

29 He that hath an ear, let him hear what the Spirit saith unto the
churches.

- Revelation 2:18–29 -

Jesus says, "But that which ye have already hold fast till I come" (v.
25). Thus, He clearly envisions this church continuing until the
Rapture. He says, moreover, "Behold, I will cast her [Jezebel, the
false prophetess who led many in Thyatira astray] into a bed, and
them that commit adultery with her into great tribulation, except
they repent of their deeds" (v. 22). This appears to be a warning of
what will befall the wicked in Thyatira after His return. The children
of Jezebel will then undergo the agonies of the Tribulation (v. 23).

Beginning with the letter to the fifth church, Sardis, the references to Christ's coming become very explicit.

1 And unto the angel of the church in Sardis write; These things saith
he that hath the seven Spirits of God, and the seven stars; I know thy
works, that thou hast a name that thou livest, and art dead.

2 Be watchful, and strengthen the things which remain, that are ready
to die: for I have not found thy works perfect before God.

3 Remember therefore how thou hast received and heard, and hold fast,
and repent. If therefore thou shalt not watch, I will come on thee as a
thief, and thou shalt not know what hour I will come upon thee.

4 Thou hast a few names even in Sardis which have not defiled their
garments; and they shall walk with me in white: for they are worthy.

5 He that overcometh, the same shall be clothed in white raiment; and I
will not blot out his name out of the book of life, but I will confess his
name before my Father, and before his angels.

6 He that hath an ear, let him hear what the Spirit saith unto the
churches.

- Revelation 3:1–6 -

The Lord takes for granted that Sardis will exist at His return. The only doubt is whether Sardis will be ready. He warns them that if they fail to watch, He will come like a thief and catch them unawares (v. 3). Yet He expects that He will find some in Sardis who are worthy to be taken into His presence, where they will "walk . . . in white" (v. 4).

The prognosis is much better for Philadelphia. In his letter to this church, which we will quote later, He issues no warning of chastisement or rebuke when He returns, but only the promise that He will keep it "from the hour of temptation, which shall come upon all the world, to try them that dwell upon the earth" (Rev. 3:10). Obviously, then, one of the churches remaining in the world at Christ's coming will be Philadelphia.

The last letter is the one to Laodicea.

> 14 And unto the angel of the church of the Laodiceans write; These things saith the Amen, the faithful and true witness, the beginning of the creation of God;
> 15 I know thy works, that thou art neither cold nor hot: I would thou wert cold or hot.
> 16 So then because thou art lukewarm, and neither cold nor hot, I will spue thee out of my mouth.
> 17 Because thou sayest, I am rich, and increased with goods, and have need of nothing; and knowest not that thou art wretched, and miserable, and poor, and blind, and naked:
> 18 I counsel thee to buy of me gold tried in the fire, that thou mayest be rich; and white raiment, that thou mayest be clothed, and *that* the shame of thy nakedness do not appear; and anoint thine eyes with eyesalve, that thou mayest see.
> 19 As many as I love, I rebuke and chasten: be zealous therefore, and repent.
> 20 Behold, I stand at the door, and knock: if any man hear my voice, and open the door, I will come in to him, and will sup with him, and he with me.
> 21 To him that overcometh will I grant to sit with me in my throne, even as I also overcame, and am set down with my Father in his throne.
> 22 He that hath an ear, let him hear what the Spirit saith unto the churches.

> - Revelation 3:14–22 -

The most alarming prophecy in all seven letters is the Lord's threat to spue the complacent Laodiceans out of His mouth (v. 16). This decisive and violent act of rejection makes no historical sense unless we associate it with a single event. He seems to be announcing a judgment that He will bring upon them at the time of His coming. Specifically, most Laodiceans will be denied the privilege of being lifted up at the Rapture. Instead, they will be rejected as mere pretenders of true faith. Yet even among these left behind will be some that the Lord, in His grace and mercy, will love nevertheless (v. 19). Upon these He will bring a stern hand of discipline, designed to produce repentance unto salvation. His return will presumably mark the moment in history when His chastening of the wayward Laodiceans will begin.

It is now evident what the seven churches in Asia truly represent. That each stands for something beyond itself is undeniable, for, as we said earlier, all the actual churches in the cities bearing the names given in Revelation 2 and 3 disappeared long ago, yet Christ treats them as though they would endure through the centuries. That the Book of Revelation seeks to give a comprehensive picture of the future is undeniable as well. So, we may suppose that He singles out the seven churches in Asia for special instruction because they represent the entire spectrum of churches that would emerge during the Church Age. What the Lord says to each of the seven churches in Asia applies equally to all similar churches in the future.

The Lord apparently conceives of the whole church as divided sevenfold into distinct branches or streams or types. Perhaps not all seven have always existed. Yet at any given time in church history, every true work of God belongs to one of the seven.

Also, in His letters to these churches, He apparently addresses them in chronological sequence, showing the order of their appearance on the world scene. First to appear would be Ephesus. Next would be Smyrna. Then would come Pergamos, Thyatira, Sardis, Philadelphia, and, lastly, Laodicea.

So, the common belief that these churches represent ages of church history has a kernel of truth in it. Yet if they were actually church ages, which of the seven could look forward to the Rapture? Only the last, Laodicea. Yet this is the church that Christ will especially repudiate. As we will see, the clearest promise of the Rapture is given to the preceding church, Philadelphia. The seven churches are in fact seven types of churches that have emerged at different times in history.

Proof that the promise to Philadelphia speaks of a rapture

The Lord's message to Philadelphia is especially enlightening to readers living on the verge of Christ's return.

7 And to the angel of the church in Philadelphia write; These things saith he that is holy, he that is true, he that hath the key of David, he that openeth, and no man shutteth; and shutteth, and no man openeth;

8 I know thy works: behold, I have set before thee an open door, and no man can shut it: for thou hast a little strength, and hast kept my word, and hast not denied my name.

9 Behold, I will make them of the synagogue of Satan, which say they are Jews, and are not, but do lie; behold, I will make them to come and worship before thy feet, and to know that I have loved thee.

10 Because thou hast kept the word of my patience, I also will keep thee from the hour of temptation, which shall come upon all the world, to try them that dwell upon the earth.

11 Behold, I come quickly: hold that fast which thou hast, that no man take thy crown.

12 Him that overcometh will I make a pillar in the temple of my God, and he shall go no more out: and I will write upon him the name of my God, and the name of the city of my God, *which is* new Jerusalem,

> which cometh down out of heaven from my God: and *I will write upon him* my new name.
> 13 He that hath an ear, let him hear what the Spirit saith unto the churches.

> - Revelation 3:7–13 -

In verse 10, we find wording similar to the wording in Luke 21:34–35, describing the Tribulation. The former speaks of "the hour of temptation, which shall come upon all the world, to try them that dwell upon the earth." The latter refers to "that day" which "as a snare shall . . . come on all them that dwell on the face of the whole earth." In the letter to Philadelphia, the Lord seems to be assuring the saints of this church that the Tribulation will not start before they have been caught up to heaven. Proof that Jesus is pointing to the Rapture comes by investigating the door open before Philadelphia. Two arguments establish that it is heaven's door.

1. Jesus says to Philadelphia, "Behold, I have set before thee an open door, and no man can shut it" (v. 8). A few verses later we read of another open door. John writes,

> After this I looked, and, behold, a door *was* opened in heaven: and the first voice which I heard *was* as it were of a trumpet talking with me; which said, Come up hither, and I will shew thee things which must be hereafter.

> - Revelation 4:1 -

By passing through this door "in heaven"—that is, in the sky—John entered the heaven where God dwells. Thus, the immediate context assures us that the door mentioned in Revelation 3:8 must also be a door to heaven. Lest we shrink from this conclusion, the two references to an open door are prefaced by the same word, "behold." The word signifies that the sight about to be described is extraordinary. If the open door in Revelation 3:8 is merely a figure of speech, introducing this figure with a word suggesting that the door is able to excite wonder is certainly overdramatic.

Biblical prophecy frequently represents the coming of Christ for His saints as the opening of a door or doors. Among the many texts referring to a door or doors through which the saints will enter the heavenly realm is the following:

> So likewise ye, when ye shall see all these things, know that it is near, *even* at the doors.

> - Matthew 24:33 -

"It" can be translated "he."[1] The idea is that "all these things" will be signs that Christ is about to open the doors and admit His people into His presence. Passage through a door into heaven also appears in the Parable of the Virgins.

> And while they went to buy, the bridegroom came; and they that

were ready went in with him to the marriage: and the door was shut.

- Matthew 25:10 -

The bridegroom represents Christ, and the virgins admitted to the feast represent the Church. The event Jesus is describing is the Rapture, here also associated with the opening of a door. James warns that after the saints pass through a door into heaven, they will come before the Judgment Seat of Christ.

> 8 Be ye also patient; stablish your hearts: for the coming of the Lord draweth nigh.
> 9 Grudge not one against another, brethren, lest ye be condemned: behold, the judge standeth before the door.

- James 5:8–9 -

2. In Revelation 3:7, Jesus says that He can open the door because He carries the key of David. It is evident that the Lord is speaking here in riddles. What this key signifies is clarified in the Book of Isaiah.

> 20 And it shall come to pass in that day, that I will call my servant Eliakim the son of Hilkiah:
> 21 And I will clothe him with thy robe, and strengthen him with thy girdle, and I will commit thy government into his hand: and he shall be a father to the inhabitants of Jerusalem, and to the house of Judah.
> 22 And the key of the house of David will I lay upon his shoulder; so he shall open, and none shall shut; and he shall shut, and none shall open.
> 23 And I will fasten him as a nail in a sure place; and he shall be for a glorious throne to his father's house.
> 24 And they shall hang upon him all the glory of his father's house, the offspring and the issue, all vessels of small quantity, from the vessels of cups, even to all the vessels of flagons.
> 25 In that day, saith the LORD of hosts, shall the nail that is fastened in the sure place be removed, and be cut down, and fall; and the burden that was upon it shall be cut off: for the LORD hath spoken it.

- Isaiah 22:20–25 -

The prophecy concerns a transfer of high office from one man to another. Eliakim the son of Hilkiah would be made the king's steward, and in that capacity he would carry the key of the house of David—that is, the key giving him access to the king's treasure house. Jesus' words in Revelation 3:7 deliberately echo verse 22 here in Isaiah 22. In claiming possession of the key of David, Jesus means that only He can admit us to the treasure house of the heavenly King. Only He can open to us all the riches of heaven.

Revelation 3:7 does not speak explicitly of a door. It speaks only of a key enabling Christ to open and shut. Yet the next verse, verse 8, speaks of a door standing open before the church of Philadelphia. Twice, first in relation to the key and then in relation to the door, Christ says that no man can shut what He opens. Clearly, then, the key He is talking about is the key that fits the door. Since it is the key to the treasures of heaven, the door that it opens must be the door to heaven.

We are now ready to interpret the riddle. In Revelation 3:10 Jesus warns of the hour of "temptation" (also translatable as "trial" or "testing"[2]) that will fall on "all the world." He is clearly referring to a time of universal trouble on the earth, yet He promises to keep Philadelphia from it. How else could Jesus keep Philadelphia from universal trouble on the earth except by removing them from the earth? Heaven's door open before them is an obvious reference to their avenue of escape. Presumably, then, He is alerting Philadelphia that He intends to snatch them away into heaven—in other words, to rapture them.

The true identity of Philadelphia

Yet Philadelphia is not the only church that will exist when Christ returns. We have shown from the letters in Revelation that Pergamos, Thyatira, Sardis, and Laodicea will exist also. Ephesus will not exist, for it will have receded into the distant past. Whether Smyrna will survive to the end of the age is left uncertain. Although Philadelphia is the only church as a whole that Jesus promises to rescue from the hour of temptation, He reveals that among those taken to heaven will be some from Sardis (Rev. 3:4 on p. 133). We may therefore presume that some from the other remaining churches will be taken as well.

So, what is Philadelphia? It is critically important to understand what Philadelphia represents. A convincing answer requires that we identify all seven churches. As we have said, these seven stand for the different streams or branches of Christianity that have developed over the centuries. They are seven types of churches. We will now go further and say that the types are comprehensive. In their portrayal of the churches that have appeared in history, they show the whole spectrum. In other words, there have been seven types of churches, no more and no less. How do we know that seven is the real sum of types? Because seven is the number that represents perfection or completeness. Creation was perfect and complete in seven days.

If the seven churches in Asia symbolize seven branches of Christianity, what specifically are these branches?

Ephesus, first to appear in the Church Age, must be the apostolic church, which no longer exists.

Smyrna represents the kind of church that faces severe persecution. Churches fitting this pattern have existed throughout church history since the first or second century, and they still exist today. Examples in the past include the Waldensians, the Anabaptists, and the Bohemian Brethren (Hussites). In the modern world, the primary examples have been hidden enclaves of fellowshipping believers in Muslim and Communist countries. These enclaves may meet informally without a pastor, and any denominational lines that divided the people previously may become blurred. If Smyrna exists at Christ's return, we may presume that all of its members with true understanding of the gospel will be raptured, since they have identified with Christ at great personal cost, proving that their hearts truly belong to Him. Christ's warning that Smyrna would undergo "tribulation" is perhaps a suggestion that during the actual period known as the Tribulation, Smyrna will be the only church still on the earth.

Pergamos represents churches that exalt experience over the written Word. They first emerged in the Montanist movement of the second century and they have reemerged in the Pentecostal and Charismatic movements of our day. All are tongues-speaking churches. Notice that the Lord is severely critical of this stream of Christianity.

Thyatira represents churches that are ecclesiastical in government, liturgical in worship, and medieval in superstition. These arose in the fourth century after Christianity won the patronage of the Roman emperor. Among them is a certain Jezebel that the Lord hates. The original Jezebel slew the true prophets of God (1 Kings 18:4, 13). In Jesus' letter, she stands for the papal church, which has a long history of persecuting true believers. The toll martyred by Rome runs into millions. (Please understand that this interpretation does not support hatred of Catholics. We should love Catholics no less than we love others. Christ does not censure the people in Catholic churches, but the religious system that enthralls them and keeps them away from Biblical truth.) The two modern churches that embody Thyatira are the Roman Catholic and Eastern Orthodox.

Sardis embraces the churches that came out of the Reformation, including Episcopalian, Lutheran, and all known as Presbyterian or Reformed. Since they have always had an excessive respect for human learning and human tradition, they have found it difficult to resist becoming intellectual, cold, and worldly. Also, most adopted a form of theology which has blinded them to the meaning of prophecy. Therefore, the Lord rebukes them for being ignorant of their place in history and for failing to watch.

The roots of Philadelphia go back to the seventeenth century, when the first Baptist churches appeared. The Moravian movement and the Great Awakening in the eighteenth century, as well as the many revivals in the nineteenth century, made Philadelphia a strong presence in the Christian world. One offshoot of this tradition has been the modern fundamentalist movement in America. The churches embodying Philadelphia have been distinctive in several respects.

1. In government, they have been largely independent of outside control.

2. They have been extremely missionary-minded. In fact, the standard view, seeing the churches as representing seven consecutive

periods in the Church Age, is that Philadelphia corresponds to the age of great missionary enterprise, from 1800 to 1950 and afterward.

3. They have been very interested in prophecy and generally, from the late 1800s onward, have believed that they existed in the Last Days.

4. They have been marked by a keen interest in Bible study. A wealth of good Christian books has come out of this tradition, more so than from any other tradition except perhaps Sardis.

5. They have been unusual in their commitment to both personal and ecclesiastical separation. The well-known rules against worldly practices belong especially to the Philadelphian churches.

6. The laity have always played an especially prominent role. Among the Moravians, every man was a preacher, and throughout the history of Philadelphia, many of its foremost preachers lacked formal theological training. Some, like D. L. Moody, even lacked ordination.

We are left with Laodicea. We said earlier that many students of prophecy have identified it as the whole church in the Last Days. This is not exactly right, because Jesus suggested that other churches would also exist then. But it is right in some measure, because Laodicea is a church that exists only in the Last Days. It is, to be specific, the modern evangelical church. Although wealthy and outwardly successful, it has abandoned the virtues of its predecessor, Philadelphia. It is lukewarm about missions, about prophecy, about Bible study, about separation, about lay involvement in ministry. Its members prefer to be spectators, and they see no contradiction between their profession of faith and their worldly lifestyle.

How did we arrive at these identifications? Each letter is full of pointers, which we will examine fully in the Appendix. Here, we will be content to show how we discovered the identity of Thyatira.

In His salutation to each church, Jesus presents Himself in a manner that will correct their view of Him. He shows them how their view is deficient. To Thyatira He says, "And unto the angel of the church in Thyatira write; These things saith the Son of God, who hath his eyes like unto a flame of fire, and his feet *are* like fine brass" (Rev. 2:18). Why? Because this is the church that has delighted in images of Christ—icons, crucifixes, and other pictorial representations. Jesus wants them to know that all their artwork is unacceptable. Its blindness to His true splendor does not encourage a proper reverence for the Son of God.

Just as the opening words of each letter point to the intended church, so also do the closing words, which reveal the rewards awaiting its people if they remain faithful to the Lord. He fashions the promise to suit their special mentality. He says to Thyatira, "And he that overcometh, and keepeth my works unto the end, to him will I give power over the nations: And he shall rule them with a rod of iron; as the vessels of a potter shall they be broken to shivers: even as I received of my Father. And I will give him the morning star" (Rev. 2:26–28). He offers them power and splendor. Why? Because a high standing in the world is what Thyatira has always wanted. This church has built the most beautiful houses of worship and composed the most beautiful music. Its leaders have striven for temporal power, and in some countries have succeeded in winning state recognition of their religious body as the official church. Some of its leaders have even used empowerment by the state to suppress and persecute other churches..

Is your church Philadelphia?

We have argued that only five of the seven churches will certainly exist at the Rapture. To four of these, Jesus issues a strong warning to repent. To none of these four does He hold out the hope of being raptured, except to tell Sardis that a few will be taken. Yet to the fifth church, Philadelphia, He has nothing critical to say, and assurance of their inclusion in the Rapture is His main message. What must we conclude? The right church to be in when Christ comes is Philadelphia.

To determine whether yours is a church of Philadelphia, you must apply two tests. First, does it fit into the tradition that Philadelphia represents? That is, does it preserve historic fundamentalism? Second, does it possess the virtues that Scripture ascribes to Philadelphia?

Let us start by applying the first test. Does your church truly fit into the fundamentalist tradition?

1. Is it independent?
2. Does it have a zeal for missions?
3. Do your people have a serious interest in prophecy, and have they allowed the Holy Spirit to teach them the great prophetic truths of vital importance today?
4. Do your people diligently study the Bible? Is understanding the Bible so important to them that they view coming to classes and preaching services as a high priority? Do they read Christian books?
5. Are they committed to separated living? Or has worldly lust drawn them into lives under the world's influence?
6. Do they view Christian work as a responsibility of the pastors, or do they view it as a responsibility they all share? Are they Sunday morning Christians, or are they actively involved in the ministries of the church?

Now we come to the second test. Scripture has much to say about the qualities that will distinguish the saints taken at the Rapture. Let us see whether your church measures up.

7 And shall not God avenge his own elect, which cry day and night unto
   him, though he bear long with them?
8 I tell you that he will avenge them speedily. Nevertheless when the Son

of man cometh, shall he find faith on the earth?

- Luke 18:7–8 -

Watch ye therefore, and pray always, that ye may be accounted worthy to escape all these things that shall come to pass, and to stand before the Son of man.

- Luke 21:36 -

From these passages read in conjunction, we surmise that the chief evidence of worthiness will be perseverance in prayer and in personal communion with God despite ever-mounting distractions. We find also that the saints prepared for Christ's coming will be characterized by watchfulness.

42 Watch therefore: for ye know not what hour your Lord doth come. . . .
44 Therefore be ye also ready: for in such an hour as ye think not the Son of man cometh.

- Matthew 24:42, 44 -

35 Watch ye therefore: for ye know not when the master of the house cometh, at even, or at midnight, or at the cockcrowing, or in the morning:
36 Lest coming suddenly he find you sleeping.
37 And what I say unto you I say unto all, Watch.

- Mark 13:35–37 -

Another trait will be purity.

2 Beloved, now are we the sons of God, and it doth not yet appear what we shall be: but we know that, when he shall appear, we shall be like him; for we shall see him as he is.
3 And every man that hath this hope in him purifieth himself, even as he is pure.

- 1 John 3:2–3 -

Yet another will be holiness.

Follow peace with all *men,* and holiness, without which no man shall see the Lord:

- Hebrews 12:14 -

Yet another will be sobriety.

5 Ye are all the children of light, and the children of the day: we are not of the night, nor of darkness.
6 Therefore let us not sleep, as *do* others; but let us watch and be sober.

- 1 Thessalonians 5:5–6 -

12 Teaching us that, denying ungodliness and worldly lusts, we should live soberly, righteously, and godly, in this present world;
13 Looking for that blessed hope, and the glorious appearing of the great God and our Saviour Jesus Christ;

- Titus 2:12–13 -

> But the end of all things is at hand: be ye therefore sober, and watch
> unto prayer.
>
> - 1 Peter 4:7 -

Sobriety is a serious outlook on life, an outlook refusing to see life as the pursuit of fun and games.

Christ's commendation of Philadelphia in Revelation 3:8 (p. 133) further broadens the concept of worthiness. The worthy in this church will be notable for three virtues.

1. They will have "a little strength ['*dunamis,*' ordinarily translated 'power'[3]]." Since these words are meant as a tribute, we infer that He is talking about the power of godliness. The Philadelphians' possession of this power will set them apart from others in the Last Days who will have only the form of godliness.

> 1 This know also, that in the last days perilous times shall come.
> 2 For men shall be lovers of their own selves, . . . ;
> 5 Having a form of godliness, but denying the power thereof: from such
> turn away.
>
> - 2 Timothy 3:1–2, 5 -

Through the Holy Spirit, who is the source of spiritual power, Philadelphia will exhibit a character antithetical to the character of false Christians. The terms describing them will be exact opposites of the terms Paul uses in 2 Timothy 3. Instead of being lovers of self, for example, they will be lovers of God. Yet even so, their strength will be little, no doubt in comparison with the church after Pentecost. Perhaps the Lord is suggesting also that this will not be a large church.

2. Philadelphia will keep the Word of God. They will revere every word of it as inerrant truth. They will reject corrupt texts and versions. They will renounce hermeneutical approaches which belittle the supernatural. And they will study the Scriptures diligently as their rule of doctrine and practice.

3. Philadelphia will not deny the name of Christ. They will uphold His name in two ways. (1) Under persecution, they will not shrink from identifying themselves as Jesus' disciples. (2) They will renounce a perverted form of the gospel that will be popular in the Last Days, when many will use Christianity as a cloak for worldly and corrupt lifestyles. The true requirement for salvation is belief in Jesus' name, and His name is the Lord Jesus Christ (John 1:12; 3:18; Acts 2:21; 4:12; Rom. 10:13; 1 John 5:13). Philadelphia will not demean His name by allowing the unruly to imagine that they can claim Him as Savior without treating Him as Lord.

Brotherly love within the church

One quality never mentioned in the letter to Philadelphia must nevertheless be the most outstanding quality of this church, for the name Philadelphia means "brotherly love."[4] Now the warning in James takes on added significance.

> 8 Be ye also patient; stablish your hearts: for the coming of the Lord draweth nigh.
> 9 Grudge not one against another, brethren, lest ye be condemned: behold, the judge standeth before the door.
>
> - James 5:8–9 -

"Grudge"—which refers to voicing groans or complaints against another person[5]—surely signifies an absence of godly love. With the prospect of soon meeting our Judge, let us therefore be diligent to make real and maintain our love for each other.

How can we do that? True brotherly love is distinguished by the following three characteristics, although these are hardly a full description.

1. It refrains from exercising any personal right that may weaken or do harm to a brother.

> Wherefore, if meat make my brother to offend, I will eat no flesh while the world standeth, lest I make my brother to offend.
>
> - 1 Corinthians 8:13 -

A junior or senior in high school may be mature enough to begin serious dating, but his or her church may strongly encourage postponement of dating until a few years later. Why would any church set such a standard? To protect its young people from all the damage often done in today's world by pairing off too soon. Even a member of the youth group who thinks he is ready to date will be glad to comply if he is spiritually minded. He will uphold the standard for the sake of friends who otherwise might go to ruin.

2. It gives sacrificially of time and resources to meet a brother's need.

> But whoso hath this world's good, and seeth his brother have need, and shutteth up his bowels *of compassion* from him, how dwelleth the love of God in him?
>
> - 1 John 3:17 -

A church should have a deacon board keeping close tabs on every member who is elderly, disabled, unemployed, or disadvantaged. Then whenever a need is detected, they should step in with appropriate help.

3. It refrains from all speech that will defile, discourage, or defame a brother.

> Let no corrupt communication proceed out of your mouth, but that which is good to the use of edifying, that it may minister grace unto the

hearers.

- Ephesians 4:29 -

Everywhere in society today, speech is becoming more crude and unkind. The media are full of people sniping at each other while puffing up their own egos, and the world on the screen is not only reflecting, but also shaping daily life. Nasty words are becoming a cultural norm. But whenever someone steps inside the door of a church, he should find a different world—a world where people actually use words that are gracious, encouraging, and, above all, loving.

Brotherly love reaching outward

Any true believer does not find it difficult to comprehend and accept his duty to love other believers. But brotherly love of the kind suggested by the name Philadelphia has yet another dimension. We should love not only our actual brothers in Christ; we should also love our potential brothers in Christ. In other words, we should love all our brothers in the family of mankind. How else could we provide any witness effective in leading some to salvation? Jesus said that our love for fellowmen should extend even to our worst enemies.

43 Ye have heard that it hath been said, Thou shalt love thy neighbour, and hate thine enemy.
44 But I say unto you, Love your enemies, bless them that curse you, do good to them that hate you, and pray for them which despitefully use you, and persecute you;

- Matthew 5:43–44 -

When setting the standard for neighborly love, He could not have raised it any higher.

And the second is like unto it, Thou shalt love thy neighbour as thyself.

- Matthew 22:39 -

It should be obvious, therefore, that a church of Philadelphia will be as outstanding for love reaching outward as for love kept within. What should be the proof of our love for people unconnected to our church and like churches? The Biblical answer is that we should make our love visible through good works.

Let your light so shine before men, that they may see your good works, and glorify your Father which is in heaven.

- Matthew 5:16 -

12 Having your conversation honest among the Gentiles: that, whereas they speak against you as evildoers, they may by your good works, which they shall behold, glorify God in the day of visitation. . . .
15 For so is the will of God, that with well doing ye may put to silence the ignorance of foolish men:

- 1 Peter 2:12,15 -

Indeed, down through history Christians have been outstanding for bringing assistance to people with every kind of need.

In the early centuries of the church, Christians started the first real hospitals.[6] Even today, in most communities with a historic Christian presence, many hospitals bear the name of a Christian denomination. During the Middle Ages, Christians founded the first universities.[7] In America, they began the first schools and colleges.[8] Other kinds of charitable institutions, such as orphanages and asylums for the mentally disturbed, originated in the efforts of Christians.[9] Democratic forms of government, protecting the common man from the outrages of tyranny, first appeared in nations where the gospel was deeply rooted. All the worthwhile movements for social justice that have emerged in the last three centuries—the crusades to abolish slavery and child labor, for example—have been spearheaded by Christians.[10] As they have always been, so Christians are prominent today in every effort to fight hunger, famine, and disease and to alleviate the effects of war and natural disaster.

Yet the need to show love has two sides. On one side, we should be busy in helping others. On the other side, we must be careful to avoid projecting a negative image to a watching world. In our political affiliations and endeavors, we must never give the world reason to label us as white supremacists, racists, right-wing bigots, or anything else that suggests hatred rather than love. We must be careful in all political judgments to show the heart of Christ.

Persecution

Despite the godly character of the Philadelphians, they will not be well-liked in the world. In Jesus' letter to them (quoted on pp. 135–136), He said that one source of persecution will be a "synagogue of Satan" (v. 9). This alarming description may have more than one reference. The first must be to an actual synagogue of Jews that persecuted the original church of Philadelphia. They were Jews by birth, but since they lacked a right relationship with God, they were not Jews in God's estimation.

> 28 For he is not a Jew, which is one outwardly; neither *is that* circumcision, which is outward in the flesh:
> 29 But he *is* a Jew, which is one inwardly; and circumcision *is that* of the heart, in the spirit, *and* not in the letter; whose praise *is* not of men, but of God.
>
> - Romans 2:28–29 -

Rather, since they did the will of their father, the devil (John 8:44), they were a synagogue of Satan.

What is the synagogue of Satan that will trouble Philadelphia on the eve of Christ's return? The word "synagogue" can be used for any group of people.[11] Perhaps the group or assembly of Satan will be a church whose members consider themselves the people of God, but are self-deceived. In reality, they do Satan's bidding. If this interpretation is correct, Jesus is predicting that a significant body of false Christians will cast reproach on Philadelphia and hinder its work in every way possible, probably calling it a deviant or cultic form of religion.

However, another possible interpretation is that Jesus was speaking of figures in secular society who are pawns of Satan—figures like influential people in politics, the media, and the world of scholarship. Their false claim to be Jews must then be understood figuratively—as a pretense to be the truly righteous. With Satan's backing, they will employ innuendo, ridicule, false accusation, fake expertise, legal maneuvering, incessant drumbeating of propaganda, and every other available weapon to oppose Philadelphia as it seeks to advance the cause of true Christianity.

But whoever stands against Philadelphia, the outcome is certain. The Lord declares that when the time of judgment arrives, He will show His approval of this church by requiring all its detractors to bow down and kiss the feet of the saints they so viciously maligned (v. 9).

Elsewhere in the letter to Philadelphia we learn more about the circumstances that will especially trigger persecution by the synagogue of Satan. The door (v. 8) may have double meaning. Besides being the door to heaven, perhaps also it bears a more familiar sense. A figure we often use in our thinking about spiritual decisions is the door of opportunity. Thus, the door that Christ can open and no one can shut may refer to a special opportunity that Christ will provide for Philadelphia to prosper in a difficult period of history. The synagogue of Satan will oppose it vigorously. But despite all the obstacles that Satan and his human instruments will throw in the path of Philadelphia, it will go forward to success, as measured by eternal results. No one will be able to stop it.

A muted but instructive picture of the people who will belong to Philadelphia appears in the closing promise. Jesus says that when the people of this church are raptured into His presence, they "shall go no more out" (v. 12). He apparently means that to maintain their purity and integrity, they will never again have to separate themselves from corrupt religion. All the churches within the historical stream of Philadelphia originated by separating themselves from churches on a downward slide: the Moravians from the Lutherans, the Wesleyans from the Anglicans, the fundamentalists from the liberals. The letter to Philadelphia suggests that this church will retain its separatist leanings even throughout the Last Days. It will be a haven for people who, in obedience to the command we find in 2 Timothy 3:5 (pp 136, 137), have moved from church to church in an effort to find a true work of God. Before finding Philadelphia, however, they may repeatedly go through the bitter experience of false Christians labeling them as fanatics or Pharisees.

Footnotes

[1] Alfred Marshall, translator, *The Nestle Greek Text with a Literal English Translation,* republished as *The Interlinear Greek-English New Testament,* in *The Zondervan Parallel New Testament in Greek and English* (Grand Rapids, Mich.: Zondervan Bible Publishers, 1975), 82; *Analytical Greek Lexicon,* 169.

[2] Berry, 863; Arndt and Gingrich, 646.

[3] Berry, 863; Arndt and Gingrich, 206–207.

[4] Berry, 863; Arndt and Gingrich, 866.

[5] Berry, 811; Arndt and Gingrich, 773.

[6] Henry C. Sheldon, *History of the Christian Church,* vol. 2: *The Mediaeval Church* (New York: Thomas Y. Crowell and Co., 1895; repr. Peabody, Mass.: Hendrickson Publishers, 1988), 2:268; Frederick Spanheim, *Ecclesiastical Annals, from the Commencement of Scripture History to the Epoch of the Reformation,* trans. George Wright, 2nd ed. (London: Gilbert & Rivington, 1840), 412–413; Kenneth Scott Latourette, *A History of Christianity* (New York: Harper & Brothers Publishers, 1953), 538, 558, 569.

[7] Latourette, 496.

[8] Clifton Johnson, *Old-Time Schools and School-Books* (n.p.: The Macmillan Company, 1904; repr. 1935; repr. Detroit: Gale Research Company, 1982), 1–14; George Brown Tindall and David Emory Shi, *America: A Narrative History,* 9th ed. (New York and London: W. W. Norton & Company, 2013), 154–155.

[9] Roger Steer, *George Müller: Delighted in God!* (Wheaton, Ill.: Harold Shaw Publishers, 1975), 61–68; Edwin Hodder, *The Life and Work of the Seventh Earl of Shaftesbury, K.G.* (London: Cassell & Company, Ltd., 1887), 330–332.

[10] Earle E. Cairns, *The Christian in Society,* rev. ed. of *Saints in Society* (Chicago: Moody Press, 1973), 68–119; John H. Overton, *The English Church in the Nineteenth Century* (1800–1833) (London: Longmans, Green, & Co., 1894), 76–79; Latourette, 1019, 1032; Hodder, 70–90, 215–234, 242–248, 367–379.

[11] Berry, 863; Arndt and Gingrich, 790–791.

Chapter 13

✦ Revival? ✦

As we have noted previously, the closing words of the Bible prescribe the desire that we should always keep central in our hearts.

> He which testifieth these things saith, Surely I come quickly. Amen. Even so, come, Lord Jesus.
>
> - Revelation 22:20 -

Without a continuing vibrant hope that we will soon see Christ, all the troubles of life in a sinful world will make it hard for us to produce the fruit of the Spirit, especially joy.

> 22 But the fruit of the Spirit is love, joy, peace, longsuffering, gentleness, goodness, faith,
> 23 Meekness, temperance: against such there is no law.
>
> - Galatians 5:22–23 -

It is therefore obvious that we should often be asking the Lord to come soon and take us at the Rapture.

But this is a prayer that unfortunately can develop a bad twist. It is good to seek escape from all the wickedness of this world. It is good to want face-to-face fellowship with Christ. And it is good to desire the privilege of living in a perfect society cemented together by godly love. But it is not good to pray for Christ's coming if we are expressing a desire that terrible divine judgment will soon be unleashed on this evil world. Nowhere in Scripture are we authorized to pray for sinners to be summarily killed and sent to hell. Our petitions raised to God's throne must always conform to God's will. What is His will concerning sinners?

> The Lord is not slack concerning his promise, as some men count slackness; but is longsuffering to us-ward, not willing that any should perish, but that all should come to repentance.
>
> - 2 Peter 3:9 -

We argued in the last chapter that members of the church of Philadelphia will be outstanding for godly love expressed not only toward each other, but also toward the whole world of human beings outside the church. What is love's prayer for the lost? It is that they will be saved, not that they will be damned as soon as possible.

In other words, while Philadelphia is imploring God to send Christ soon, it will also be imploring Him with no less fervor to grant a new season of prosperity to gospel witness around the world. The

familiar word for multitudes coming to Christ in a brief time frame is
"revival." Prayer for revival will therefore be a distinguishing mark of
Philadelphia. It will be entirely appropriate for them to ask for revival
not only before the Rapture, but also afterward.

While praying for revival, they should be doing whatever they can
to make it happen. They should be developing new programs of out-
reach and sending new laborers into the field. Though small perhaps
in relation to more popular churches, they will not withdraw into self-
satisfied isolation. Rather, they will mount aggressive campaigns on
the field of spiritual warfare.

Earlier we discussed Jesus' promise to Philadelphia.

> I know thy works: behold, I have set before thee an open door, and
> no man can shut it: for thou hast a little strength, and hast kept my
> word, and hast not denied my name.
>
> - Revelation 3:8 -

We said that the open door primarily refers to the door of heaven.
Jesus is promising to take Philadelphia at the Rapture. But we said
also that a secondary reference is to the door of opportunity. To encourage a zeal for ministry, Jesus is promising them divinely empow-
ered success.

A sad reality as we look about us today is that few churches remain that can rightly claim to be part of Philadelphia. What we see
may therefore suggest that God will indeed grant revival before the
Rapture—perhaps not on a mammoth scale like the Great Awakening, yet on a scale large enough so that Philadelphia will again be a
visible presence in the religious world. We should pray that it will
gain prominence not only in America, but also in nations worldwide,
so that its disappearance at the Rapture will have a worldwide
impact.

The great barrier to praying for revival is lack of faith. We are
prone to doubt that a few mere words—much less the words of a single, weak human being—could change the course of history. But
prayers for revival appear in Scripture.

> 6 Wilt thou not revive us again: that thy people may rejoice in thee?
> 7 Shew us thy mercy, O LORD, and grant us thy salvation.
> 8 I will hear what God the LORD will speak: for he will speak peace unto
>   his people, and to his saints: but let them not turn again to folly.
> 9 Surely his salvation is nigh them that fear him; that glory may dwell
>   in our land.
>
> - Psalm 85:6–9 -

> 19 Thou, O LORD, remainest for ever; thy throne from generation to
>   generation.
> 20 Wherefore dost thou forget us for ever, and forsake us so long time?
> 21 Turn thou us unto thee, O LORD, and we shall be turned; renew our
>   days as of old.
>
> - Lamentations 5:19–21 -

> O LORD, I have heard thy speech, *and* was afraid: O LORD, revive thy work in the midst of the years, in the midst of the years make known; in wrath remember mercy.
>
> - Habakkuk 3:2 -

Surely these prayers, as well as all the other prayers in Scripture for God's blessing upon His people, were intended as an example for us.

Chapter 14

✛ The Rapture and Its Aftermath ✛

In previous chapters we have looked at the many precious promises in Scripture that all true believers will escape the horrors descending upon this wicked world during the Tribulation. They will not be left to endure any of the famines, pestilences, and earthquakes that will then strike the earth. They will not see any of the wars that will eventually exalt the Antichrist to world leadership. Before the age of nightmares begins, God will remove all His children from this world. Their path of escape will be the Rapture.

When we understand the full measure of evil that we will miss by God's gracious intervention, we can only give Him thanks. Moreover, we can look forward to the Rapture with even keener anticipation, especially as we see world events moving rapidly and steadily down the path toward all those climactic scenes described in Revelation.

But we would be wise to avoid the misconceptions about the Rapture that are now widespread, due either to false teachers or to careless treatments in popular fiction.

The Event Itself

What exactly will a saint hear and see and do when he goes through the experience of being raptured? In two passages written by Paul, we find the fullest descriptions of Christ descending from heaven to snatch away His people from the earth.

> 51 Behold, I shew you a mystery; We shall not all sleep, but we shall all be changed,
> 52 In a moment, in the twinkling of an eye, at the last trump: for the trumpet shall sound, and the dead shall be raised incorruptible, and we shall be changed.
> 53 For this corruptible must put on incorruption, and this mortal *must* put on immortality.
> 54 So when this corruptible shall have put on incorruption, and this mortal shall have put on immortality, then shall be brought to pass the saying that is written, Death is swallowed up in victory.
>
> - 1 Corinthians 15:51–54 -

> 15 For this we say unto you by the word of the Lord, that we which are alive *and* remain unto the coming of the Lord shall not prevent them which are asleep.
> 16 For the Lord himself shall descend from heaven with a shout, with the voice of the archangel, and with the trump of God: and the dead in Christ shall rise first:
> 17 Then we which are alive *and* remain shall be caught up together with

> them in the clouds, to meet the Lord in the air: and so shall we ever
> be with the Lord.
>
> - 1 Thessalonians 4:15–17 -

In a literal translation of the latter text, Paul says, "Himself the Lord
with a shout of command with voice archangel's and with trumpet of
God shall descend from heaven." [1]

Yet these passages do not give the most informative reply to the
question we are seeking to answer. The fullest insight on a saint's
experience when his life transitions from earth to heaven comes from
a past event that apparently was intended to provide clues about the
Rapture. At the beginning of Revelation 4, just a few verses after the
Lord promised the church of Philadelphia that they would be removed from this world before the Tribulation, John himself was taken
out of this world.

> 1 After this I looked, and, behold, a door *was* opened in heaven: and
> the first voice which I heard *was* as it were of a trumpet talking with
> me; which said, Come up hither, and I will shew thee things which
> must be hereafter.
> 2 And immediately I was in the spirit: and, behold, a throne was set in
> heaven, and *one* sat on the throne.
>
> - Revelation 4:1–2 -

From what happened to John we garner three facts concerning the
future experience of every saint living at the return of Christ.

First, John heard a trumpetlike voice. Here in this text is a point
of agreement with the other two texts we quoted. In their anticipation of the Lord coming to remove His people, all three state that the
sound then blasting from above will be like a trumpet. Who will hear
this mighty thunderclap of music? Presumably, only the saints.
When Jesus Himself spoke of the Rapture, He compared His coming
to a thief's invasion of a house during the night. A thief is at pains to
assure that no one being robbed will hear him. Likewise, it is prob-
able that when the Rapture occurs, the whole unbelieving world will
be blind and deaf to the event.

Second, John heard the heavenly voice issue a command, "Come
up hither," followed by words giving the purpose of his ascent: "I will
shew thee things which must be hereafter." It therefore seems likely
that the command Jesus issues as He descends as a thief will also be
a summons to His presence; again, "Come up hither." And it seems
likely that other words will follow, giving each saint a fuller perspective on what is happening.

Third, after hearing the heavenly voice, John was "immediately . .
. in the spirit," a state that no doubt prefigures our future transformation into glorified bodies. The picture is evidently intended to
show us when we will undergo this momentous change. It will directly follow the trumpetlike voice.

Yet John was not transformed. He retained an earthly body

incapable of entering heaven. It is therefore at this point in the narrative that his experience ceases to parallel the future experience of
raptured saints. For the rest of the story, we must consult one of the
Pauline texts already quoted. From First Thessalonians 4:17, we
learn that all the saints will be caught up together into the clouds,
where, in the airy skies above the earth, they will meet the Lord. The
place of assembly will evidently be in the same realm as the clouds,
which is the lower atmosphere.

The future intrusion of Christ into our dying world will happen
suddenly, at a time no one can predict. The lesson for us? The
prospect of His coming must always be near the forefront of our
minds. To make sure we are prepared for that breathtaking moment,
what must we do? We must keep our hearts pure. When the trumpet sounds, it will be too late to take care of unconfessed sin. If any
weighs upon our conscience, our joy in meeting Christ will be diminished by shame—or even worse, by fear. Remember the words of
James, "Grudge not one against another, brethren, lest ye be condemned: behold, the judge standeth before the door" (Jas. 5:9).

Misconceptions about the Rapture

All babies and little children will be taken.

A myth popularized by the authors of the *Left Behind* series is
that besides adult believers, the Rapture will take every child in the
world under the age of accountability. I do not know who originated
this idea, but it is certainly not what Christians in the past believed.
The position of historic fundamentalism has been that Christ will
take all children with at least one saved parent, but not all the children of the world. Notice some of the strange implications of this
new teaching. If all children will be taken, then presumably all un-
born babies will be taken as well. Suddenly, every pregnant woman
in the world will be delivered of her baby. Of all the crises that fiction
writers have imagined in the aftermath of the Rapture, none quite
compares with the medical crisis that would ensue if all the women of
the world with suddenly terminated pregnancies rushed in panic to
find out what happened and to seek help as their bodies made the
adjustment.

Why will many of the world's babies and children be omitted from
the Rapture? Because they do not belong to the body of Christ.
Wherever the Rapture is discussed in Scripture, it is defined in the
same way, as a future gathering of the church.

> 14 For if we believe that Jesus died and rose again, even so them also
>   which sleep in Jesus will God bring with him.
> 15 For this we say unto you by the word of the Lord, that we which are
>   alive *and* remain unto the coming of the Lord shall not prevent them
>   which are asleep.
> 16 For the Lord himself shall descend from heaven with a shout, with

> the voice of the archangel, and with the trump of God: and the dead in Christ shall rise first:
> 17 Then we which are alive *and* remain shall be caught up together with them in the clouds, to meet the Lord in the air: and so shall we ever be with the Lord.
>
> - 1 Thessalonians 4:14–17 -

The "we" that will be caught up (v. 17) are the same "we" who believe in Jesus (v. 14). A passage in Paul's next epistle reinforces our conclusion.

> Now we beseech you, brethren, by the coming of our Lord Jesus Christ, and *by* our gathering together unto him,
>
> - 2 Thessalonians 2:1 -

The Rapture is "our gathering together unto him," and those who will be included are called the "brethren"—that is, brethren in Christ. Furthermore, as we have shown repeatedly throughout this book, the Rapture is described in many passages as a privilege for the worthy— for those who are found watching (Luke 21:36), who are faithful in prayer (Luke 18:7–8), who stand fast in the faith of their spiritual fathers (Rev. 3:11), and who have separated themselves from a fleshly lifestyle (Luke 21:34–36). Possession of all these attributes is limited to people whose lives have been transformed by the power of God and who are indwelt by the Spirit of God—in other words, people saved by the grace of God. Only they belong to the true church of Jesus Christ. Only they constitute the bride of Christ. When Christ comes to steal some away from this world, He will come as the bridegroom seeking His bride. He will take no one who stands apart from His bride.

For two reasons, we can state confidently that the church does not include all the babies and children of the world.

1. The true church of Jesus Christ includes everyone who is saved. But once saved, always saved. You cannot lose your salvation. Therefore, children who have never professed Christ cannot be considered saved, because many will never put their faith in Christ. Indeed, many grow up to reject Him.

2. The church includes all sinners saved by grace, but God does not reckon babies and children under the age of accountability as sinners. As Paul states or implies repeatedly in his Epistle to the Romans, sin is not reckoned where there is no knowledge or true understanding of the law.

> For until the law sin was in the world: but sin is not imputed when there is no law.
>
> - Romans 5:13 -

> 7 What shall we say then? *Is* the law sin? God forbid. Nay, I had not known sin, but by the law: for I had not known lust, except the law had said, Thou shalt not covet.
> 8 But sin, taking occasion by the commandment, wrought in me all

manner of concupiscence. For without the law sin *was* dead.

- Romans 7:7–8 -

From God's judicial perspective, all babies and children under the age of accountability are reckoned innocent, even though they were born with a sin nature. God is just, is He not? If human law spares young minors from prosecution for crime, on the grounds that they are too young to be held responsible, would divine law be any less just or merciful? Before God, the very young are not sinners. Yet one consequence is that they cannot be counted among those who have been forgiven by faith in Christ.

What then happens to babies and children when they die? We must make a distinction between the children of believers and the children of unbelievers. The overwhelming majority view of the church has always been that the dead children of unbelievers do not go to hell, because when they die, they are still in a state of innocence. Scripture declines to tell us what will happen to them. It's not our story, as it were. But doubtless they will at some time appear before God in judgment and be admitted to eternal bliss. The exact shape of their destiny, whether it will differ in any fashion from ours, is beyond our knowledge and unknowable.

Yet when we consider the children of believers, we can speak with confidence about their destiny. A child with at least one saved parent is considered sanctified, in the sense that God chooses to treat him or her as belonging to Christ.

For the unbelieving husband is sanctified by the wife, and the unbelieving wife is sanctified by the husband: else were your children unclean; but now are they holy.

- 1 Corinthians 7:14 -

If the child dies, he or she goes to heaven. Proof that a Christian child is secure comes from the story of David's grief after his loss of an infant child.

18 And it came to pass on the seventh day, that the child died. And the servants of David feared to tell him that the child was dead: for they said, Behold, while the child was yet alive, we spake unto him, and he would not hearken unto our voice: how will he then vex himself, if we tell him that the child is dead?

19 But when David saw that his servants whispered, David perceived that the child was dead: therefore David said unto his servants, Is the child dead? And they said, He is dead.

20 Then David arose from the earth, and washed, and anointed *himself,* and changed his apparel, and came into the house of the LORD, and worshipped: then he came to his own house; and when he required, they set bread before him, and he did eat.

21 Then said his servants unto him, What thing *is* this that thou hast done? thou didst fast and weep for the child, *while it was* alive; but when the child was dead, thou didst rise and eat bread. And he said,

22 While the child was yet alive, I fasted and wept: for I said, Who can tell *whether* GOD will be gracious to me, that the child may live?

> 23 But now he is dead, wherefore should I fast? can I bring him back
> again? I shall go to him, but he shall not return to me.
>
> - 2 Samuel 12:18–23 -

David declared that the child now rested in the same place where he
would go after death—in the abode of the righteous dead. In Old
Testament times, that abode was known as Abraham's bosom, which
was separated from the abode of the wicked by a great gulf. But
since the Cross, the abode of the righteous dead is heaven. If believers in David's time had the privilege of being reunited after death
with any dead children, we must suppose that God has granted the
same privilege to believers in the Church Age. It would be absurd to
suppose that God has arbitrarily changed His policy, so that the dead
children of believers now go to hell.

No, He grants them life forever. The reason is that parents are
one body in God's sight.

> Know ye not that your bodies are the members of Christ? shall I then
> take the members of Christ, and make *them* the members of an harlot?
> God forbid. What? know ye not that he which is joined to an harlot is
> one body? for two, saith he, shall be one flesh.
>
> - 1 Corinthians 6:15 -

Also, the one body created by marriage includes all the young children. This way of thinking may seem strange to us, but it is Biblical.
Levi is credited with a righteous act done by his grandfather Abraham.

> And as I may so say, Levi also, who receiveth tithes, payed tithes in
> Abraham. For he was yet in the loins of his father, when Melchisedec
> met him.
>
> - Hebrews 7:9–10 -

Why does credit go to Levi? Because, in a sense, he was then one
body with his grandfather. Actually, it is not at all unnatural to
think of our children as one body with us, for as long as they are
young, their bodies cannot survive unless we use our bodies to care
for them and provide their needs. There is, in other words, a total
dependency of their bodies upon ours.

It follows that if a parent is joined to the body of Christ, any
young child is joined to His body also. A child does not cease to be
one body with his parents until he is old enough to care for himself,
an age which by God's design coincides with the attainment of moral
understanding. Then comes a severance, and he must accept responsibility both for his own bodily welfare in this world and his destiny in the world to come. Then he must establish his own relationship with Christ if he wishes to gain eternal life.

He faces the same requirement if he wishes to participate in the
Rapture. Unless by faith he joins himself to Christ, he will be left behind. But all younger children of at least one believing parent will
surely be taken. It is preposterous to suppose that God would leave

them here as helpless orphans when He makes so many promises to care for the children of the righteous.

> His seed shall be mighty upon earth: the generation of the upright shall be blessed.
>
> - Psalm 112:2 -

> *Though* hand *join* in hand, the wicked shall not be unpunished: but the seed of the righteous shall be delivered.
>
> - Proverbs 11:21 -

> In the fear of the LORD *is* strong confidence: and his children shall have a place of refuge.
>
> - Proverbs 14:26 -

Yet, despite the words in First Corinthians 7 (p. 156), the unsaved spouse of a saint will not be taken at the Rapture, although he or she is in some sense sanctified, or set apart, as a result of union with a child of God. That is the dire warning implicit in Jesus' prediction that when He comes to steal away His church, two will be in a bed but only one will be taken; the other will be left behind (Luke 17:34). The Rapture will break up marriages.

When the saints suddenly disappear, any vehicles they have been driving or piloting will go out of control and crash.

This claim by *Left Behind* made good entertainment, but misrepresented God. Supposedly, there will be chaos on the roads, and many airplanes will go into a nosedive, dragging many down to their destruction. Nonsense. God will not bring death on those who have entrusted their lives to a believer. The angels will descend on this world in force at the time of the Rapture, and they will assure that no one's departure will create a hazard for the people left behind. They will shepherd to safety all who are traveling in vehicles driven or piloted by a saint who vanishes.

To leave them untended, their fate controlled by chance, would defeat one of God's purposes in the Rapture. God's removal of His beloved children to a place of safety will tell unbelievers that the world is ripe for judgment. Since it will demonstrate that there is a righteous Judge, the event will also tell unbelievers that they had better repent of their sins. To give this message a chance to change lives, God in His mercy will not permit the judgment that He has decreed for lost humanity to fall instantly. Rather, it will develop over time. Letting people die because of the Rapture would therefore be counterproductive. God wants the Rapture to be a means not of killing people, but of alerting them to their need of salvation.

It is my personal belief, without any Scriptural foundation except general teaching on the loving character of God, that He will also make some provision for any animals who depend on believers for care and feeding.

Raptured saints will leave behind their garments and everything else they were carrying.

Here is another prediction with a prominent place in *Left Behind*. Supposedly, when the saints rise, all their garments and jewelry, all the contents of their pockets, and all handheld items like purses will remain on the earth. Onlookers will see these belongings strewn on the ground or draped over a seat. But this is another simplistic idea serving to make the story more sensational. If in fact the Rapture will create piles of forsaken belongings, what will happen to them? The first person to find any abandoned heap will be strongly tempted to sort through the mess in search of valuables. Pockets will be examined, purses and wallets opened. Unless the person is a close relative, anything he takes for himself will be stealing. In other words, the Rapture will lead to widespread thievery. Yet if true, this will happen only because God created the opportunity. We must remember, however, that God tempts no man. "Let no man say when he is tempted, I am tempted of God: for God cannot be tempted with evil, neither tempteth he any man" (Jas. 1:13).

For yet another reason it is unlikely that cast-off clothes will mark every saint's place of ascent. God will not force the unsaved world to recognize the disappearance of saints as a divine miracle. He wants people to come to Him by faith, not under coercion by unanswerable evidence. He will therefore allow Satan to spread semi-plausible explanations for the Rapture. As we will argue later, the devil's principal story will be that saints have been removed by aliens. But it will be hard to believe that aliens were both willing and able to undress all their victims first. Therefore, it is likely that when a saint is called above, all things on his body will be either destroyed or transformed to something heavenly.

After the Rapture, believers in Christ will not be joined to His body.

Earlier we refuted some of the positions associated with the school of Bible interpretation which we called ultradispensationalism. Among those who reject this school are many who hold to dispensationalism in a more moderate form. Yet with few exceptions, all dispensationalists agree that there will be a change in divine dispensations when the church departs from the world. Presently, we are in the Church Age, a dispensation under the covenant ratified by the blood of Christ. It is their belief that when the church is raptured at the outset of the Tribulation, the Church Age will cease and a new dispensation will begin.

The text they most often cite as support for their position is Paul's

prediction that after the age of the gentiles, God will shape the experience of the Jews so that the whole surviving nation will be saved.

> 25 For I would not, brethren, that ye should be ignorant of this mystery,
> lest ye should be wise in your own conceits; that blindness in part is
> happened to Israel, until the fulness of the Gentiles be come in.
> 26 And so all Israel shall be saved: as it is written, There shall come out
> of Sion the Deliverer, and shall turn away ungodliness from Jacob:
> 27 For this *is* my covenant unto them, when I shall take away their sins.
>
> - Romans 11:25–27 -

The same dispensationalists suppose that the time God has appointed for accomplishing His purpose is the Tribulation; furthermore, that since God will restore the Jews to a central role in His
program for history, He will revive in some measure the Mosaic dispensation, the one that governed ancient Israel from the time of
Moses until the time of Christ. How much the new dispensation will
replicate the Mosaic is a matter of some debate, but mainstream dispensationalists agree that it will supplant the Church Age. Some go
so far as to deny that any gentiles will be saved after the Rapture,
and most who avoid this extreme nevertheless insist that all gentile
believers during the Tribulation will be saved only in the same sense
that believing Jews in Old Testament times were saved. No convert
will at the moment of salvation be incorporated into Christ's body.[2]

I do not accept such a gloomy outlook for gentiles, although I myself am a dispensationalist. In my commentary on Daniel, I strongly
support the dispensational tenet that Israel will be the main focus of
God's dealings with mankind both during the seventieth week of
Daniel (the last seven years before Christ's return in glory) and during the Millennial Kingdom. There can be no doubt that Israel will
have a prominent place in God's program even at the beginning of the
Tribulation, for He will then set His seal upon 144,000 chosen from
the twelve tribes (Rev. 7:3–8).

But whether the Rapture will close the Church Age depends on
how the Church Age is defined. If it means the span of history when
God sets Israel aside from spiritual blessing and spreads the offer of
salvation to all peoples of the world, then indeed the Church Age will
end at the Rapture, and the Tribulation will amount to a new dispensation based on a change in divine policy. God will continue His
work of saving gentiles, but also He will again treat Israel as His chosen people. But rather than see the Tribulation as a new dispensation, a better perspective is to see it as a transitional period between
preceding and following dispensations, between the Church Age and
the Millennial Kingdom. It will therefore display distinctive features
of both. As in the Church Age, believers will still be joined to Christ's
body and indwelt by the Holy Spirit.

Against the view of many dispensationalists that the Rapture will
bring a return in some degree to a Jewish-centered Mosaic
dispensation which will not allow believers to be full-fledged Chris-

tians, I will urge six objections.

1. God's activity during the Tribulation will not be limited to special dealings with the Jews. He Himself characterizes one phase of the Tribulation as "the hour of temptation, which shall come upon all the world, to try them that dwell upon the earth" (Rev. 3:10). In other words, during this period of history He will be at work not only among the Jews, but also among all the other races of mankind. He will vigorously stir their hearts to consider the terrible consequences of sin. His purpose will be twofold. He will be allowing the wicked to ripen in their wickedness before they are taken to judgment, but also He will be drawing to Himself multitudes that He has chosen in scattered places. The Tribulation will be the setting of a worldwide divine campaign to bring gentiles as well as Jews to salvation.

2. After the Cross, God will not revive either fully or partially the Mosaic dispensation or any other that existed before the Cross. Many of the laws and ceremonies appropriate for Israel were merely pictures of the coming Redeemer's person and work. Now that He has come, and now that His work has been finished, reintroduction of a pre-Christian economy would obscure what is plain and darken what is bright. Comments by the writer of Hebrews make it clear that the old covenant at the basis of the Mosaic system will not be revived.

> 1 Then verily the first *covenant* had also ordinances of divine service, and a worldly sanctuary. . . .
> 6 Now when these things were thus ordained, the priests went always into the first tabernacle, accomplishing the service *of God.*
> 7 But into the second *went* the high priest alone once every year, not without blood, which he offered for himself, and *for* the errors of the people:
> 8 The Holy Ghost this signifying, that the way into the holiest of all was not yet made manifest, while as the first tabernacle was yet standing:
> 9 Which *was* a figure for the time then present, in which were offered both gifts and sacrifices, that could not make him that did the service perfect, as pertaining to the conscience.
>
> – Hebrews 9:1, 6–9 –

The writer states that the Mosaic system was appropriate for "the time then present" (v. 9) only because Christ had not yet been revealed (v. 8). Later, he says,

> 5 Wherefore when he cometh into the world, he saith, Sacrifice and offering thou wouldest not, but a body hast thou prepared me:
> 6 In burnt offerings and *sacrifices* for sin thou hast had no pleasure.
> 7 Then said I, Lo, I come (in the volume of the book it is written of me,) to do thy will, O God.
> 8 Above when he said, Sacrifice and offering and burnt offerings and *offering* for sin thou wouldest not, neither hadst pleasure *therein;* which are offered by the law;
> 9 Then said he, Lo, I come to do thy will, O God. He taketh away the first, that he may establish the second.
>
> – Hebrews 10:5–9 –

Here, the writer not only describes the old covenant as incompatible with the new covenant, but also as something that God "taketh away" (v. 9). Elsewhere he elaborates:

> 8 For finding fault with them, he saith, Behold, the days come, saith the Lord, when I will make a new covenant with the house of Israel and with the house of Judah:
>
> 9 Not according to the covenant that I made with their fathers in the day when I took them by the hand to lead them out of the land of Egypt; because they continued not in my covenant, and I regarded them not, saith the Lord.
>
> 10 For this *is* the covenant that I will make with the house of Israel after those days, saith the Lord; I will put my laws into their mind, and write them in their hearts: and I will be to them a God, and they shall be to me a people:
>
> 11 And they shall not teach every man his neighbour, and every man his brother, saying, Know the Lord: for all shall know me, from the least to the greatest.
>
> 12 For I will be merciful to their unrighteousness, and their sins and their iniquities will I remember no more.
>
> 13 In that he saith, A new *covenant,* he hath made the first old. Now that which decayeth and waxeth old *is* ready to vanish away.
>
> – Hebrews 8:8–13 –

After introduction of the new covenant, the Mosaic covenant is now old and decaying and "ready to vanish" (v. 13). The writer clearly did not envision any future renewal of this covenant that God was putting aside. His statements that God would take it away and cause it to vanish must, in the absence of any qualification, stand as absolute. We conclude that the obsoleteness of the old covenant is a timeless principle which the Rapture will not negate.

3. On the day of Pentecost, Peter explicitly promised that the gift of the Holy Spirit would be granted to all those in future generations who confess the name of Christ.

> 38 Then Peter said unto them, Repent, and be baptized every one of you in the name of Jesus Christ for the remission of sins, and ye shall receive the gift of the Holy Ghost.
>
> 39 For the promise is unto you, and to your children, and to all that are afar off, *even* as many as the Lord our God shall call.
>
> – Acts 2:38–39 –

Scripture gives us no warrant to believe that the offer of the Spirit will someday be withdrawn. The phrase "gift of the Holy Ghost" (v. 38) refers to the new function that the Spirit began to perform at Pentecost. Previously, He had on occasion entered into men to influence or empower them, but now He began to baptize believers into the body of Christ.

> For by one Spirit are we all baptized into one body, whether *we be* Jews or Gentiles, whether *we be* bond or free; and have been all made to drink into one Spirit.
>
> – 1 Corinthians 12:13 –

All who become one flesh with Christ constitute His Bride, the church.

> 29 For no man ever yet hated his own flesh; but nourisheth and cher-
> isheth it, even as the Lord the church:
> 30 For we are members of his body, of his flesh, and of his bones.
> 31 For this cause shall a man leave his father and mother, and shall be
> joined unto his wife, and they two shall be one flesh.
> 32 This is a great mystery: but I speak concerning Christ and the church.
>
> - Ephesians 5:29–32 -

On the basis of Peter's declaration at Pentecost that "the promise is unto you, and to your children"—a promise conspicuously not excluding any future descendants however distant in the future—we infer that the Spirit's work of building the church will not cease at the Rapture. Those left behind who later believe will be added to the church also.

4. We know that many during the Tribulation will believe in Christ, for prophecy often speaks of them. Various texts mention "saints" living on the earth at that time (Dan. 7:25; Rev. 8:3–4; 13:7; 14:12). The error in denying that they will be equal in status to Christians today becomes obvious under the penetrating light of the following passages.

> 9 And when he had opened the fifth seal, I saw under the altar the
> souls of them that were slain for the word of God, and for the testi-
> mony which they held:
> 10 And they cried with a loud voice, saying, How long, O Lord, holy and
> true, dost thou not judge and avenge our blood on them that dwell on
> the earth?
> 11 And white robes were given unto every one of them; and it was said
> unto them, that they should rest yet for a little season, until their
> fellowservants also and their brethren, that should be killed as they
> *were,* should be fulfilled.
>
> - Revelation 6:9–11 -

> 9 After this I beheld, and, lo, a great multitude, which no man could
> number, of all nations, and kindreds, and people, and tongues, stood
> before the throne, and before the Lamb, clothed with white robes, and
> palms in their hands;
> 10 And cried with a loud voice, saying, Salvation to our God which sit-
> teth upon the throne, and unto the Lamb.
> . . . .
> 13 And one of the elders answered, saying unto me, What are these
> which are arrayed in white robes? and whence came they?
> 14 And I said unto him, Sir, thou knowest. And he said to me, These are
> they which came out of great tribulation, and have washed their
> robes, and made them white in the blood of the Lamb.
> 15 Therefore are they before the throne of God, and serve him day and
> night in his temple: and he that sitteth on the throne shall dwell
> among them.
>
> - Revelation 7:9–10, 13–15 -

It is evident that the multitude of martyrs during the early years of the Tribulation will be raised from the dead and taken to heaven. Yet no one is worthy of heaven unless he belongs to the body of Christ. That is the degree of perfection required of anyone who wishes to dwell in God's presence. Old Testament saints did not reach heaven until the risen Christ conducted them from their place of rest in Abraham's bosom to their place of joy forever (Luke 16:19–31; Hos. 6:1–3; Matt. 27:52–53; Heb. 12:1, 22–23).

5. Jesus said that during the first portion of the Tribulation, before the abomination of desolation is set up, "this gospel of the kingdom shall be preached in all the world" (Matt. 24:14). Then years later, after the Antichrist virtually silences the witness of all human believers, the gospel will still sound forth from the sky.

> 6 And I saw another angel fly in the midst of heaven, having the everlasting gospel to preach unto them that dwell on the earth, and to every nation, and kindred, and tongue, and people,
> 7 Saying with a loud voice, Fear God, and give glory to him; for the hour of his judgment is come: and worship him that made heaven, and earth, and the sea, and the fountains of waters.
>
> – Revelation 14:6–7 –

Here it is called "the everlasting gospel" lest anyone think that the passage is talking about a modified form introduced after the Church Age. No, it is the good news exactly defined by Peter when he addressed thousands on Pentecost (Acts 2:38–39 on p. 162). Central to his message was the promise of the Holy Spirit, whose work in each believer includes bringing him into full union with Christ. As we have said, to be joined with His body is the special privilege of all who belong to the church.

6. The claim that the world after the Rapture will be empty of Christians like us leans heavily on a single Pauline text.

> 6 And now ye know what withholdeth that he might be revealed in his time.
> 7 For the mystery of iniquity doth already work: only he who now letteth *will let*, until he be taken out of the way.
> 8 And then shall that Wicked be revealed, whom the Lord shall consume with the spirit of his mouth, and shall destroy with the brightness of his coming:
>
> – 2 Thessalonians 2:6–8 –

Virtually all dispensational teachers insist that "he who now letteth" (v. 7) is the Holy Spirit; also, that His being taken out of the way before the Antichrist is revealed (v. 8) means that He will be removed from this world at the beginning of the Tribulation, when the Rapture occurs. Since He is the One who baptizes new believers into the body of Christ, the exact point in history when He departs will therefore mark the time when the body of Christ will receive no further additions.

The vagueness of the passage in question makes interpretation difficult. It will be sufficient for our purposes to point out that even if the Holy Spirit leaves this world in the sense of ceasing His restraint of the evil one, He need not at the same time leave this world in the sense of ceasing His work in the hearts of believers. We have shown that there will be saints on the earth during the Tribulation. "Saint" means a "holy one," a "person consecrated to God."[3] To achieve this special standing requires a supernatural work of the Holy Spirit. Therefore, if He leaves the world altogether, mankind will no longer include saints. But if He does not leave altogether, He will still be able to bring new believers into union with the body of Christ.

After the Rapture, no one will be saved who previously rejected the gospel.

Often when I have heard a pastor proclaim that the Lord is coming soon to steal His children out of this world, he has warned unbelievers that they dare not put off a decision for Christ. Why? Because after the Rapture, it will be too late. No one who previously rejected the gospel will then be saved.

It is true that many unbelievers who hear sermons on the end times say to themselves, "This is nothing but nonsense. I'm certainly not going to join these strange fanatics who expect to suddenly disappear. If they do, well . . . maybe then I'll consider the gospel." It is therefore not surprising that many preachers today see pragmatic value in threatening all hearers with certain damnation if they do not get saved before the Rapture.

No doubt many of the unbelieving will in fact be quick to accept one of the devil's explanations for this miraculous event. But the teaching that certain doom hangs over the heads of them all fails two tests of credibility. The first is what Scripture actually says. The second is the true extent of divine mercy.

Bible teachers who think that scorners of truth before the Rapture will be hopeless cases afterward plead in their defense the following words of Paul.

1 Now we beseech you, brethren, by the coming of our Lord Jesus Christ, and *by* our gathering together unto him,
2 That ye be not soon shaken in mind, or be troubled, neither by spirit, nor by word, nor by letter as from us, as that the day of Christ is at hand.
3 Let no man deceive you by any means: for *that day shall not come*, except there come a falling away first, and that man of sin be revealed, the son of perdition;
4 Who opposeth and exalteth himself above all that is called God, or that is worshipped; so that he as God sitteth in the temple of God, shewing himself that he is God.
5 Remember ye not, that, when I was yet with you, I told you these things?
6 And now ye know what withholdeth that he might be revealed in his time.
7 For the mystery of iniquity doth already work: only he who now letteth *will let*, until he be taken out of the way.
8 And then shall that Wicked be revealed, whom the Lord shall consume with the spirit of his mouth, and shall destroy with the

brightness of his coming:

9 *Even him*, whose coming is after the working of Satan with all power
and signs and lying wonders,

10 And with all deceivableness of unrighteousness in them that perish;
because they received not the love of the truth, that they might be saved.

11 And for this cause God shall send them strong delusion, that they
should believe a lie:

12 That they all might be damned who believed not the truth, but had
pleasure in unrighteousness.

– 2 Thessalonians 2:1–12 –

The same Bible teachers argue that they who "received not the love of
the truth, that they might be saved" (v. 10) refers to all who heard
and rejected the gospel <u>before</u> the Tribulation; also, that as soon as
the church is raptured, the Antichrist will come (v. 9), and all these
unbelievers will persist in unbelief because they will fall prey to Satanic delusion (v. 11). Their final destiny will be damnation (v. 12).

Our reply is that Paul in verses 10 and 12 is talking about unbelievers <u>during</u> the Tribulation; specifically, those who resist God's
grace to the point of exhausting His patience. It is true that they will
have no further opportunity to repent. Although they live at a time
when many supernatural events might otherwise turn their hearts
toward God simply out of fear devoid of true repentance and faith,
Satan will also perform great wonders, holding in his camp all stub-
born rebels against the truth.

Paul provides enough information for us to determine exactly
where these unbelievers will appear on the timescale of events. The
immediate context of his references to them is not verses 1–2,
speaking of the Rapture, but the verses where the references appear;
that is, verses 8–11. These speak of the Antichrist coming onto the
world scene and, by means of a lie that feeds strong delusion, convincing the gullible masses that he is divine. A fuller account appears in Revelation 13.

1 And I stood upon the sand of the sea, and saw a beast rise up out of
the sea, having seven heads and ten horns, and upon his horns ten
crowns, and upon his heads the name of blasphemy.

2 And the beast which I saw was like unto a leopard, and his feet were
as *the feet* of a bear, and his mouth as the mouth of a lion: and the
dragon gave him his power, and his seat, and great authority.

3 And I saw one of his heads as it were wounded to death; and his
deadly wound was healed: and all the world wondered after the beast.

4 And they worshipped the dragon which gave power unto the beast:
and they worshipped the beast, saying, Who is like unto the beast?
who is able to make war with him?

5 And there was given unto him a mouth speaking great things and
blasphemies; and power was given unto him to continue forty *and*
two months.

6 And he opened his mouth in blasphemy against God, to blaspheme
his name, and his tabernacle, and them that dwell in heaven.

7 And it was given unto him to make war with the saints, and to overcome them: and power was given him over all kindreds, and tongues,
and nations.

8 And all that dwell upon the earth shall worship him, whose names
are not written in the book of life of the Lamb slain from the foundation of the world.

- Revelation 13:1–8 -

Based on this account, we conclude that the Antichrist's self-
promotion to deity will happen not at the outset of the Tribulation,
but at the outset of its last forty-two months (v. 5). The throwing
down of his gauntlet before the real God must be preceded by a com-
plex history of other events after the Rapture.

Here we cannot survey them in detail. One source giving more
information is my commentary on Daniel.[4] It will suffice to say that
after the Antichrist is assassinated during the early portion of the
Tribulation (Dan. 11:45 on p. 41), two witnesses, probably Moses and
Elijah, will descend to the earth and perform great wonders, which
will stir up spiritual revival everywhere, but especially among the
Jewish people (Rev. 11:3–6 on p. 28). After they prophesy 1260 days,
the soul of the Antichrist will return from the bottomless pit (Rev.
11:7 on p. 28), repossess his dead body (Rev. 13:3 above), and kill
the witnesses (Rev. 11:8–13 on p. 28). With the backing of the
dragon and the false prophet, the Antichrist will immediately take
control of world government (Rev. 13:1–2 above) and present himself
to the world as a god that all peoples must worship (Rev. 13:8 above).
To make his claim believable, he will boast of his return from the
dead (Rev. 13:3 above), and the false prophet will perform miracles in
his name (Rev. 13:11–14 on p. 35).

It is the Antichrist's reappearance on the world scene after his as-
sassination that Paul means when he speaks of his "coming . . . after
the working of Satan with all power and signs and lying wonders" (2
Thess. 2:9 above), and the lie that they will believe because of strong
delusion (2 Thess. 2:11 above) is the Antichrist's claim of deity supported by all manner of quasi-supernatural tricks such as the devil
can perform. The somber decree of damnation pronounced upon all
who refused to believe applies not to anyone before the Rapture, but to
the multitudes who refused to believe the gospel when it was
preached by the two witnesses. It is therefore lifting Paul's words out
of context if they are used to justify the teaching that rejecters of
gospel witness before the Rapture will be ineligible for salvation
afterward.

This teaching therefore fails the test of Scripture. It also fails the
test which considers the true extent of divine mercy. In fact, it so un-
derestimates the mercy of God that it is no less than an affront to His
character. We can easily imagine scenarios where people who have
rejected the gospel now will receive His special mercy after the saints
disappear. Take, for instance, a young person who, before the Rapture, was seriously wronged or even abused by a respected member
of the church, perhaps even by a pastor. For this young person, rejecting the gospel may have been primarily a statement of protest

against sin and corruption. Don't you think that after the Rapture, God might look with special mercy upon this young victim of hypocrisy? One illustration is enough to support my argument. We dare not set contrived limits on what God might do.

Satan's Explanations for the Rapture

Satan's strategy for minimizing any good effects the Rapture might have on the people left behind will, I think, involve three countermeasures, which he will probably introduce sequentially rather than all at once.

The first countermeasure will be denial. We have said that the number actually taken at the Rapture will be relatively small in relation to the world's population. Many will belong to small churches in inconspicuous places. It will not be as hard for the media to ignore the Rapture as you might think. For a while at least, it will not be difficult to suppress general knowledge of the Rapture in countries where the media are under tight state control, as in China, Russia, and Muslim nations. Even in America, the initial response of the media is likely to be silence, although word-of-mouth and local coverage might bring the event to national attention within a short time, perhaps only days. Eventually, the whole world will know about it. Yet any delay Satan achieves will serve his purposes, for in that time souls will die and go to hell.

The second countermeasure will be to fit the event as much as possible into the existing worldviews of those who hear about it. In the Christian world, for example, Satan's main tool will be the media, which will rush to the pope and other remaining church leaders and demand their interpretation of what happened. Most of these leaders left behind will scorn the possibility that fundamentalists were raptured and will suggest instead that if God removed them, the reason is that He had lost patience with their backward religion.

In the Muslim world, Satan will likely represent the Rapture as the ultimate jihad, waged by the direct intervention of Allah himself for the purpose of ridding the world of all fanatical Christians. As a result, Muslims will think that these Christians were simply zapped to death and delivered body and soul to eternal torment. Allah destroyed them because they were the greatest friends of the Jews and the greatest enemies of Islam.

Among Hindus and other followers of Eastern mysticism, Satan will take a different approach. Again, he will represent Christians as enemies of human progress, but he will claim that the force removing them was nature itself, or nature's oversoul, or nature's inherent vital force acting in revulsion at Christian contempt for the truth found in more enlightened religions and clearing the way for a more general understanding of truth. Much the same lie will be circulated in the Western world among adherents of religions basically Eastern in their outlook. Besides the traditional Eastern religions, these include theosophy, Wicca, the New Age movement, and all their bedfellows in the realm of the occult.

But what explanation will Satan offer people around the world who are secular and irreligious, who think that a scientific view of reality demands skepticism? The lie Satan will tailor for them will claim that Christians were removed because they were a threat. In this respect the lie will be similar to what he will tell everyone else in the world. But for these irreligious people he will add novel touches. A threat to what? Specifically, man's evolution. Removed by what? For people committed to the philosophy of materialism, Satan cannot invoke any spiritual force, so he will represent the force as extraterrestrial beings (ETs) of higher intelligence. In other words, space aliens. To make this lie plausible has been the ultimate goal of science fiction in the past century. By the device of fanciful stories, Satan has been so successful in laying the groundwork for this lie that the average man on the street actually believes that the universe is teeming with life forms at all stages of evolution. Why would ETs want to take Christians out of this world? Satan will probably say that the ETs who removed them are the same ones who planted life on the earth in the first place. In recent years, to counter the mounting evidence that the origin of life by chance is a wild impossibility, Satan has introduced the theory of Panspermia, which has been endorsed by some of the world's leading intellectuals, including Sir Fred Hoyle and Richard Dawkins. This theory proposes that life was sown on the earth by advanced ETs who viewed the earth as a cosmic laboratory for raising another strain of intelligent beings. After the Rapture, Satan will say that the same ETs are intervening to save the human race from the many perils that are threatening its continuing existence. Foremost in their plan of action to avert global catastrophe is to remove the adherents of a backward religion which is hindering mankind from taking the steps essential to its survival, such steps as uniting under a world government with totalitarian control over all aspects of justice, economy, and education. To make this explanation more plausible, Satan has been working hard especially during the last century to create sightings of UFOs, which in popular myth are widely interpreted as alien spaceships. In June, 2019, President Trump and three members of the U.S. Senate were briefed about several UFO sightings that the Navy viewed as strange enough to require the attention of government leaders.[5]

Satan's third countermeasure to the Rapture will be his last. When the Antichrist returns from the dead and assumes power over the whole world, he will demand worship as supreme deity. At that time, he will claim that he personally brought about the disappearance of Christians. He will say that by his own power he rid the world of this disgusting group of loyalists to a bigoted and benighted religion. He may admit that Christianity has a supernatural dimension. After all, the world will see the miracles done by the two witnesses (Rev. 11:3–6 on p. 28). Yet he will say that his power is greater, and he will cite as proof his success in stopping their work and killing them (Rev. 11:7–8 on p. 28). He will say that by the same power he removed the whole church of Jesus Christ years earlier.

Revival after the Tribulation Begins

We have already presented two passages in Revelation that foresee a mighty work of God after the Rapture (Rev. 6:9–11; 7:9–10, 13–15 on p. 163). Here is another passage, this one coming from Jesus' Olivet Discourse, which He presented shortly before His death.

> 7 For nation shall rise against nation, and kingdom against kingdom: and there shall be famines, and pestilences, and earthquakes, in divers places.
> 8 All these *are* the beginning of sorrows.
> 9 Then shall they deliver you up to be afflicted, and shall kill you: and ye shall be hated of all nations for my name's sake.
> 10 And then shall many be offended, and shall betray one another, and shall hate one another.
> 11 And many false prophets shall rise, and shall deceive many.
> 12 And because iniquity shall abound, the love of many shall wax cold.
> 13 But he that shall endure unto the end, the same shall be saved.
> 14 And this gospel of the kingdom shall be preached in all the world for a witness unto all nations; and then shall the end come.
>
> - Matthew 24:9–14 -

The disciples who had gathered around Jesus to hear instruction probably assumed that when He said "you" (v. 9), He was referring to them. But although His words applied to them in some measure because they too would undergo severe persecution, it would not be exactly the kind that Jesus described in this passage. He must therefore have been using "you" in a more general sense, referring to any group of disciples. We can determine which group He specifically intended only by looking at the whole discourse. What do we find? The disciples whose allegiance to Christ will make them targets of the world's hatred will be living "then" (v. 9). In context, "then" is at the "beginning of sorrows" (v. 8); in other words, at the beginning of the Tribulation. As Jesus gazed ahead to this faraway moment in the future, He foresaw many of His own disciples alive on the earth not long after the Rapture. The only way to explain their existence so soon after the earth has been emptied of all disciples is to suppose that a great revival will intervene.

A source of important insights as we reconstruct events following the Rapture is Christ's letter to the Laodiceans (Rev. 3:14–22 on p. 125). After severely rebuking them for a self-satisfied and world-centered religion that has wandered away from God's design for a true church, Christ says, "As many as I love, I rebuke and chasten: be zealous therefore, and repent. Behold, I stand at the door, and knock: if any man hear my voice, and open the door, I will come in to him, and will sup with him, and he with me" (Rev. 3:19–20). What chastening will they suffer? First, He will spit them out of His mouth (v. 16), a gesture picturing exclusion from His body. Christ meant that at the Rapture, most Laodiceans will not ascend to the gathering of saints in the sky. Yet for many in the majority left behind, this dramatic rejection will not lead to their damnation. Rather, being judged unworthy of the Rapture will be painful and humiliating. As an expression of Jesus' compassion, it will deflate their delusions and bring them to their senses. They will suddenly understand how estranged they were from the One they professed to love.

Spitting them out will not, however, be the end of their chastening. The Rapture will be followed immediately by the world's fierce persecution of any who decide to come forward with a testimony for Christ. Yet all those Laodiceans who truly want the eternal blessings awaiting God's children will meet the challenge. The opposition will only strengthen their resolve to do right. They will start by satisfying the requirements that Christ laid on them in His letter to their church. Recognizing their spiritual poverty, they will acquire from Christ the precious materials—especially faithfulness, purity, and wisdom—needed for spiritual enrichment (v. 18). They will repent of their past lukewarmness exhibited in a lifestyle of compromise (v. 19). They will open the door to Christ for true heart-centered fellowship with Him (v. 20). In brief, their exclusion from the Rapture will spur revival on a scale that perhaps has never been seen before. Multitudes who had only given lip service to Christ and other multitudes brought to Christ by the witness of repentant Laodiceans will gain public attention around the world. The response of the godless masses and their spiritually blind leaders will be cruel repression, to the extent of imprinting on the pages of church history another lengthy roster of martyrs. But the end result for all liberated from this evil world will be the joy of a perfect world.

Footnotes

[1] Berry, 727.

[2] J. Dwight Pentecost, *Things to Come: A Study in Biblical Eschatology* (Findlay, Ohio: Dunham Publishing Co., 1958), 226–234; Charles F. Baker, *A Dispensational Theology* (Grand Rapids, Mich.: Grace Publications, 1971), 565–569.

[3] Berry, 874; Arndt and Gingrich, 9.

[4] Rickard, *Daniel*, 178–187.

[5] Andrew Daniels, "Trump, Senators Have Been Briefed on UFO Sightings," Popular Mechanics, 6/20/19, Web (popularmechanics.com/military/research/a28119115/trump-senators-ufo-sighting/), 7/20/20.

Appendix

✛ The Seven Churches of Asia ✛

Christ's message to each church deals with its typical strengths and weaknesses. Yet when speaking to each of the last six churches, He addresses primarily its members on the eve of His return. His counsel to these churches relates especially to the forms they will assume in the Last Days.

Each letter has four parts: a salutation designed to remedy some deficiency in the Christology of that church, an acknowledgment of the service which that church has performed, an exhortation pointing out good things that should be shored up and bad things that should be eliminated, and a promise designed to satisfy the particular aspirations of that church. The exhortation has one or more of the following elements: criticism, warning, prediction, commendation, and assurance. When examined in detail, the contents of each letter demonstrate that we have correctly identified the intended recipient.

The Message to Each Church

Ephesus/New Testament Churches

Message Element	Message	Relevance to This Church
Salutation	Christ walks in the midst of the seven candlesticks.	This church thought of itself as encompassing the whole church. Christ informs Ephesus that as history unfolds, there will be other churches also.
Acknowledgment	He notices seven instances of work, patience, and discernment.	In its achievements, this church was superior to all the others. It excelled especially in its ability to distinguish truth from error.
Exhortation/ Criticism	They have lost their first love.	In the course of a few centuries, the remnant of New Testament churches lost their zeal for service and their devotion to Christ.

Warning	He may remove their candlestick.	Ephesus will not survive until Christ's return.
Commendation	They have rejected the Nicolaitanes.	The Nicolaitanes, which means "conquering of the people," perhaps represent those in the early church who wished to give leaders more power at the expense of local-church autonomy and individual soul liberty.
Promise	Overcomers will eat the tree of life in the midst of paradise.	The members of this church, so dedicated to work and separated living, denied themselves much pleasure. Christ reminds them that the hope of the faithful is to live forever in a place where pleasure abounds.

Smyrna/Persecuted Churches

Message Element	Message	Relevance to This Church
Salutation	Christ is the ever-living One who rose from the dead.	As those facing death, the members of this church need to understand that Christ has conquered death.
Acknowledgment	He notices their works, tribulation, poverty, and persecution by the synagogue of Satan.	The chief persecutor of true religion has always been false religion.
Exhortation/ Prediction	They will be cast into prison and will suffer tribulation ten days.	Although all true believers in Smyrna will be taken at the Rapture, the church will reappear when intense persecution breaks out anew during the Tribulation (Matt. 24:9–10).
Assurance	If they are faithful unto death, they will receive a crown of life.	They must understand that death is merely a bridge to an exalted life.

Promise	Overcomers will escape the second death.	One motive driving them to accept death as the penalty for faith is fear of the second death. Christ promises them that the second death will not touch them.

Pergamos/Pentecostal-type Churches

Message Element	Message	Relevance to This Church
Salutation	Christ bears the sharp two-edged sword.	This sword is the Word of God, which they have dishonored by giving greater authority to experience.
Acknowledgment	He notices their works, and their faithfulness under persecution.	This church has never shrunk from persecution. Under the Communists, for example, the Pentecostals maintained a good testimony for Christ.
Exhortation/ Criticism	They tolerate those who hold the doctrine of Balaam, the prophet who, in return for favors, drew Israel into gross sin, and they tolerate also the Nicolaitanes.	No church is more infested with crass profiteering, blatant immorality, and unashamed worldliness than modern Pergamos. Modern Pergamos has also been friendly to ecumenism, another movement that transfers more power to church hierarchies.
Warning	If they do not repent, He will catch them by surprise and fight against the unruly with the sword of His mouth.	When Christ returns, the leaders of this church will face judgment according to the strict measure of Scripture. The evildoers will be punished severely (Matt. 24:48–51).

Promise	Overcomers will receive the hidden manna and the stone with secret writing.	To answer the craving of this church for private revelation, God will share wonderful secrets with every overcomer.

Thyatira/Medieval Churches

Message Element	Message	Relevance to This Church
Salutation	Christ is a glorious Being with eyes of fire and feet of brass.	The true picture of Christ is a corrective to the idols that this church has condoned.
Acknowledgment	He notices six instances of works, charity, service, faith, patience, and works again, the last better than the first.	This church has produced many people who have devoted their lives to religious and charitable work. It has also founded countless charitable institutions. The works of this church have been more outstanding in modern times than before, as many Thyatirans in missions around the world have devoted themselves to selfless assistance of the poor and needy.
Exhortation/ Criticism	They have Jezebel in their midst.	Jezebel is the papal church. The papal church has promoted fornication by imposing celibacy on those who pursue a religious vocation. The sin of eating "things sacrificed unto idols" is a reference to the mass.
Warning	Because she has had opportunity to repent, He will bring great trouble upon her and upon her lovers, and He will kill her children.	The Tribulation will fall especially hard on Roman Catholic countries.

Assurance	Upon the rest in Thyatira, He will put no other burden than to hold fast what they have already.	So long as the rest in Thyatira stay clear of Rome, Christ in His mercy will overlook their many faults.
Promise	Overcomers will receive power over the nations. Also, they will receive the morning star.	The leaders of Thyatira have sought power and splendor. Christ offers Thyatira true power and true splendor.

Sardis/Reformation Churches

Message Element	Message	Relevance to This Church
Salutation	Christ has the seven spirits and the seven stars.	Sardis has a carnal pride in its superiority to the other churches, some in Sardis even priding themselves as absolutely right. Christ reminds them that He is not so parochial.
Acknowledgment	He notices their works, which are deficient. Their true condition does not match their good reputation.	Though once alive, this church is now almost dead. Indeed, little vital Christianity remains in northern Europe and other former strongholds of the Reformation church. This church has never been outstanding in works, because most of its people have centered their lives on family and business. By the time Christ returns, Sardis will retain little interest in charitable and evangelistic endeavors.
Exhortation/ Warning	They must remember their traditions, hold fast, and repent. If they do not watch, He will come upon them as a thief, when they are not expecting Him.	This church has stubbornly resisted new insights on prophecy, instead holding to false systems of interpretation. In consequence, Sardis is blind to signs of the times, and the coming of Christ will take it by surprise.

Commendation	A few names in Sardis are worthy to walk with Him in white.	Still today, some in Reformation circles strive for personal holiness and for personal devotion to Christ.
Promise	He will not reject overcomers. Rather, He will give them white raiment and confess them before the Father.	Many people in this church have never had much spiritual ambition beyond a desire to be known as good Christians. Christ promises overcomers the public standing they seek.

Philadelphia/Fundamentalist Churches

Message Element	*Message*	*Relevance to This Church*
Salutation	Christ is holy and true and holds the key of David. What He opens no one can shut, and what He shuts no one can open.	At some time in the lives of many Philadelphians, victimization by unholy liars in the church has brought them into peril of spiritual disillusionment. But Christ assures them that He is holy and true. Also, despite the many reverses this church will suffer, Christ exhorts them not to doubt His sovereignty.
Acknowledgment	He notices their works. Because they have kept His word and have not denied His name, He will set before them an open door.	Because this church has sought to obey the Scriptures and to honor Christ, He will take them alive into heaven.
Exhortation/ Prediction	The synagogue of Satan will worship at their feet.	When evil church leaders and other persecutors come to judgment, they will be forced to bow down in respect before those they have oppressed.
Commendation	They have kept the word of His patience.	This church has patiently waited for Christ's coming, maintaining its watchfulness even when other churches decided that His coming was not imminent.

Assurance	He will keep them from the hour of temptation.	As a result of being raptured, Philadelphia will escape the Tribulation.
Warning	They must hold fast what they have, lest any man take their crown.	The people of Philadelphia must be wary of attempts to draw them into compromises. By such compromises they would forfeit the special privileges that Christ offers them.
Promise	Overcomers will be pillars in the temple of God, so that they need "go no more out." Upon them will be inscribed the name of God, the name of the New Jerusalem, and Christ's new name.	Most of the people in Philadelphia have come there from other churches. They are weary of the sacrifice and maltreatment that, in their quest for vital Christianity, they have suffered by leaving decayed churches. Christ assures them that He will give them a permanent home.

Laodicea/Modern Evangelical Churches

Message Element	*Message*	*Relevance to This Church*
Salutation	Christ is the Amen, the faithful and true witness, and the beginning of God's creation.	This church has freely affirmed "Amen," has defended the authority of Scripture against liberalism, and has insisted that the world arose by creation and not evolution. But in maintaining these doctrines, Laodicea has tended to ignore the Person whom these doctrines adorn.
Acknowledgment	He notices their works, and His verdict is that they are lukewarm.	In the brief history of this church, little has been accomplished, since most of its people live largely self-indulgent lives.

Exhortation/ Criticism	They are self-deluded in thinking they have everything. In reality, they have nothing.	Outwardly this church is very successful. It has large congregations, sumptuous facilities, and extensive exposure in the media. Yet it teaches an easy-believism that gives security without salvation.
Warning	As many as He loves, He will rebuke and chasten.	Most of the people in this church will not take part in the Rapture. The shock of being left behind and the rigors of the Tribulation will bring the elect among them to a saving knowledge of Christ.
Assurance	Any who repent will enjoy fellowship with Christ.	After the Rapture, it will not be too late to accept Christ. Any in Laodicea who then repent will be saved.
Promise	Overcomers will sit with Him in His throne.	Though they may for a time suffer exclusion from Christ's presence, the overcomers will someday enjoy intimate fellowship with Christ, even sitting by His side upon His throne.